The *Wiley Financial Advisor* Series

Tax-Deferred Investing: Wealth-Building and Wealth-Transfer Strategies
Cory C. Grant and Andrew D. Westhem

*Getting Clients, Keeping Clients: The Essential Guide for Tomorrow's
    Financial Adviser*
Dan Richards

Managing Family Trusts: Taking Control of Inherited Wealth
Robert A. Rikoon and LarryWaschka

Advising the 60+ Investor: Tax and Financial Planning Strategies
Darlene Smith, Dale Pulliam, and Holland Toles

Tax-Smart Investing: Maximizing Your Client's Profits
Andrew Westhem and Stewart Weissman

TAX-DEFERRED INVESTING

Wealth-Building and Wealth-Transfer Strategies

Cory C. Grant
Andrew D. Westhem

A Marketplace Book

John Wiley & Sons, Inc.
New York • Chichester • Weinheim • Brisbane • Singapore • Toronto

Library of Congress Cataloging-in-Publication Data:

Grant, Cory C.
    Tax-deferred investing : wealth-building and wealth-transfer strategies / Cory C. Grant and Andrew Westhem
       p.   cm. — (Wiley financial advisor series)
    Includes index.
    ISBN 0-471-35733-2 (cloth : alk. paper)
    1. Investments—Taxation—United States. 2. Tax shelters—United States. 3. Tax planning—United States. I. Westhem, Andrew D., 1933– II. Title. III. Series.
HG4910.G752   2000
336.24'26—dc21   99-043401

Printed in the United States of America.

10 9 8 7 6 5 4 3 2 1

This book is dedicated to my wife Emily. Her consistent and unconditional love and caring has allowed me the time to develop a successful and enjoyable business practice. Her wonderful smile and zest for life provide me with phenomenal inspiration in every aspect of life.

C. C. G.

Acknowledgments

I would like to thank my business partners for helping me with this book as well as my staff, especially Renee Gallardo and Terry Smith who helped with the charts and projections. Thanks also to Brentmark Software for providing me with the software to provide illustrations for the book and to run my practice. And, of course, to my wife for her patience in living with me while the book was put together.

A special thanks to Don Korn for his editorial help and patience in working with me in making this book a reality. And finally, thanks to all of the volleyball players at 29th Street in Del Mar for helping me relieve stress and lead a balanced life.

C. C. G.

Contents

CONTENTS

Introduction

Not many years ago, "401(k) plans" and "rollover IRAs" were not houschold words. Today most employees at most companies have 401(k) accounts, and more than a few avidly watch their gradual buildup. On separation from service, often those ample 401(k) balances are rolled into individual retirement accounts (IRAs) for continued wealth building and eventual distribution. In fact, with sophisticated planning, the money in the tax-deferred retirement plans of many of your clients will grow to become their largest asset. Therefore, tax-deferred retirement plans represent both an opportunity and a trap for financial advisors. If you can help your clients to make the most of this tax-deferred buildup, you're well on your way to outstanding success in your own career. But if you fail to serve your clients well in this area, you're likely to be outpaced by other advisors.

When it comes to retirement plans, though, squeezing the juice from the orange can be sticky business. These plans are creations of the Internal Revenue Code so more than a few pitfalls must be avoided to remain in compliance. What's more, there are investment aspects to consider (over the course of decades, even slight differences in performance can have a huge impact on wealth accumulation) and, for those clients who are employers, liability concerns as well.

To help you deal with clients' retirement plans, the first six chapters of this book discuss the buildup stage. Assuming that you're working with clients who are employers as well as employees, we discuss plan selection, investment strategies, and asset allocation. Most clients will need to build up sizable amounts in tax-deferred plans to enjoy a comfortable retirement, and we explain how they can do so.

Then we discuss distribution strategies. When it comes time to take money from retirement plans, critical decisions must be made, including some that are irrevocable. That's where you can truly add value as an advisor. What's more, many clients will find that taking money from a retirement plan is a delicate balancing act. They'll want to take enough to support a comfortable lifestyle, but they won't want to pull out too much too soon and run out of money. Again, we show you how to provide ongoing services to your client base throughout their retirement years.

Other clients will accumulate so much in their tax-deferred plans that they won't spend down the total and neither will their surviving spouse. In fact, substantial amounts can be left to the next generation. In these circumstances, advanced planning can make a huge difference. Some retirement plans are taxed heavily while moving from one generation to the next, leaving little in the way of a bequest, while others are forced to pay out rapidly, curtailing tax-deferred growth. However, well-designed plans may enjoy many additional decades of tax shelter, enriching clients' children and even grandchildren.

Those heirs, by the way, may be your next generation of clients. Therefore, it's certainly in your best interest to keep as much cash flowing for as long as possible. That's the goal of our book: to show you how tax-deferred retirement plans can put clients on Millionaires' Row and keep them there, far into the future.

For Investors, the Best Is Yet to Come

Wealth Building with Tax-Deferred Plans

The history of the 20th century was grim in many respects—world wars, the Great Depression, the Cold War, runaway inflation, unprecedented taxation, mounting public debt. Greater disasters would be hard to imagine. And yet the century rewarded investors enormously. Suppose someone had invested $1 in Standard & Poor's Composite Index in January 1926. (That index tracked the share prices of 90 large U.S. corporations.) Further suppose that for the next 72 years that money had been kept in U.S. blue chip stocks, switching to the S&P 500 Index in 1957. All that time, dividends were reinvested in the same index of large-company stocks.

How would that $1 have grown by the start of 1998? To $10? To $100? According to Ibbotson Associates, a research firm in Chicago, a $1 investment would have compounded to $1,828.33!

To put it another way, if one of your clients had had an ancestor with the foresight to invest $100 in established stocks back in the heyday of Babe Ruth, and if other family members had had the discipline to let that money compound, that $100 would now be worth $182,833.

If the stock market rewarded investors so well in the turbulent 20th century, there's no reason to expect any less from the market in the 21st century.

High Signs

Indeed, some observers expect the coming years to be even better for investors. Harry S. Dent, a consultant and economic forecaster based in Moss Beach, California, forecasts the Dow Jones Industrial Average will hit 35,000 by 2008. In 1993, Dent published a book entitled *The Great Boom Ahead* (Hyperion), accurately predicting a coming surge in stocks. Therefore, his upbeat projections must be taken seriously.

Dent's optimism stems from demographics. For the average individual, savings accelerates from age 35 to age 68 while spending peaks around age 46.5. Thus, both patterns are moving up between ages 35 and 46.5. Money moves into stocks at that stage of life, when families have both high discretionary income and a relatively long time before retirement.

At the beginning of the 21st century, the famed baby boom generation is moving into that age cohort. The first boomers appeared in 1946, right after World War II, so they turn 54 in the year 2000, with their younger siblings right behind them. In 1987, there were about 20 million Americans in the 45–54 age bracket; that number is projected to peak at more than 40 million in 2008. That's when the most baby boomers move into their peak spending and investing years, so the stock market may bound from peak to peak.

The Millionaire at Home

If you advise clients to participate in the stock market, you welcome such bullish views. Dent is forecasting that the market will rise by about

16% per year. Even if you take a less aggressive stance and assume, say, a 12% annual return—the average over the last 65 years—your clients' money will double every six years.

Think about that for awhile. Suppose one of your clients is now 55, with a modest $200,000 saved for retirement, and you recommend that $200,000 be invested in stocks. If those stocks earn 12% for the next 6 years, that $200,000 will become $400,000. Assume another 12% return over the subsequent 6 years. That money will double again, to $800,000.

And that's just the money your client already has saved. Assuming that your client continues to save and invest, over the intervening 12 years, he or she will likely have more than $1 million by then. Perhaps well over $1 million. By age 67, when this client is ready to retire, he or she will be a millionaire.

Withdrawal Pains

Unfortunately, that's not quite the case. For most Americans today, the primary investment vehicle is a tax-deferred retirement plan. Such plans are marvelous for accumulation because taxes aren't paid while the account builds up. Earning 12% a year may double a portfolio's value in 6 years but there would be a huge shortfall if taxes had to be paid each year. The catch is that these retirement plans merely defer taxes rather than eliminate them. At some point, all the deferred tax must be paid.

Assume that a client withdraws money from a plan after retiring and that the client's effective tax bracket is then around 35%. (That includes state and local income tax as well as all the gimmicks buried in the Internal Revenue Code.) If that's the case, every dollar pulled out of the plan will be worth only 65 cents in spendable income. Thus, a "million-dollar retirement plan" is really worth only $650,000.

Of course, $650,000 is certainly nothing to sneer at. In fact, it may well be the key to a comfortable retirement for many clients. Essentially, your clients' retirement plans are valuable assets that need to be managed with care.

To help your clients in this crucial area, you need to know the tax rules affecting their plans. If you understand these rules and help clients implement some basic planning strategies, you can show them how to turn today's modest retirement accounts into long-term wealth-building machines that literally can pay out millions of dollars throughout the coming century.

The Taxman Cometh

Retirement plans are often described as great tax shelters. Contributions are made with pretax rather than after-tax dollars, always a great advantage. Then, assuming those contributions are invested well, the money in these accounts will build up over the years, free of current taxes.

To see the benefit of such tax deferral, consider the example of Vanguard's S&P 500 Index Fund, one of the most popular mutual funds on the market. According to press reports, someone who invested $1,000 in this fund at its creation, in 1976, and reinvested all distributions back into the fund would have had nearly $15,000 by the end of 1996. That's a 15:1 return over 20 years.

Because this fund is an index fund, designed to mimic the S&P 500, the fund manager does little trading and seldom realizes taxable gains, which have to be passed through to investors. In the lingo of financial pros, this fund is "tax-efficient": The tax bite on investors is relatively low.

Nevertheless, an investor paying the top tax rate each year would have less than $10,000, not the $15,000 reported in the magazines. Instead of 15:1, the investor would have earned 10:1 on her money. If a tax-efficient mutual fund causes investors to lose 36% of its pretax return, with a less tax-efficient mutual fund the loss to taxes can be much higher.

Switch Hits

The foregoing example assumes that the money is invested in a regular, taxable account. With an IRA, 401(k), or other tax-deferred plan, there's no annual tax bite each year, so clients really do get the 15:1 buildup that's reported in the press, not just 10:1. That's the advantage of investing in a tax-deferred plan.

What's more, in a tax-deferred plan, clients can switch funds. Suppose, in the previous example, you think Vanguard's S&P 500 Index Fund has had its day and you advise clients to switch to Vanguard Explorer (an aggressive small-company fund) or a fund sponsored by another company. In a taxable account, all of the accumulated gains would be immediately taxable. Within a retirement plan, though, your clients can switch at will and not owe a penny to the Internal Revenue Service (IRS).

Silent Partner

Tax-deferred retirement plans are a great deal for your clients, but they also can be a great deal for the IRS.

In the previous example, one of your clients invested $1,000 in 1976. If that money had been invested in a retirement plan, the $1,000 deduction would have cut the client's income tax by $350, assuming an effective tax rate of 35%.

Twenty years later, that $1,000 would have grown to $15,000 inside the plan, as we've seen. If your client withdraws that money now, all $15,000 will be taxable. At that same 35% effective tax rate, he'd owe $5,250 in tax.

So the tax collectors do pretty well, too: they pass up $350 today in return for $5,250 in the future. All the while your clients' money is building up for their own retirement, it's also growing for the IRS, for the state government, and perhaps for a local government.

Strategic Plans

How should you react to this undeniable fact of life? There are several strategies you might follow when advising clients about a tax-deferred retirement plan.

1. Grin and bear it. After all, the client in the previous example will still have nearly $10,000 after tax—10:1 on a $1,000 outlay. However, if you don't pay attention to the tax consequences, you're passing up a great opportunity to create wealth for your clients and their families.

2. Advise clients to take their money out of their retirement plans after their tax bracket drops. After clients retire or semiretire and their earned income shrinks, they may find themselves in a lower tax bracket than they were in during their working years. In 1998, for example, a married couple could have more than $42,000 in taxable income and still be in the 15% federal tax bracket.

Clients who are in that situation will receive an extra tax benefit from a tax-deferred retirement plan. Not only will they enjoy tax deferral, they'll gain from tax reduction: avoiding tax at 35%, for example, and paying it later at, say, 18%.

For those clients who'll need to tap most or all of their retirement plan while they're alive, this approach works very well. However, not everybody works until 62, spends the next 30 years on the beach, and pays income tax at minimal rates throughout retirement.

Many executives and professionals continue to work, full- or part-time, well beyond normal retirement age. In such cases, there may be little or no bracket reduction as your clients grow older. Even when they do retire altogether, they may have so much income from other sources (pensions, investments) that their tax brackets remain the same.

Therefore, some clients may not be able to count on tax bracket reduction to enhance the tax advantages of a retirement plan. What's more, tax rates may be higher in the future than they are today. Ever since the present federal income tax was introduced in 1913, rates have generally risen. They were as high as 70% as recently as 1981, only to be cut to a 33% maximum rate by 1986. Since then, two tax acts have raised the official top rate to 39.6% while some technicalities push the top rate well over 40%. Which way do you think tax rates will move in the years to come?

3. Advise your clients to accumulate money in a retirement plan and extend the tax deferral as long as possible. Many people find their needs modest after they retire. If a client's home mortgage has been paid off and there are no more college bills due, your client may be able to maintain a comfortable lifestyle without touching his or her retirement plan. The longer the money stays inside the plan, the less painful the tax bite will be.

Unfortunately, the tax code doesn't permit this to go on forever. Most people must start taking a certain amount of money out of their retirement plans after they reach age $70\frac{1}{2}$. If you know the rules, you can help your clients minimize distributions and maximize tax-deferred buildup. (See in Chapter 10).

4. Evaluate the benefits of converting a regular IRA to a Roth IRA. These retirement plans, first effective in 1998, allow investors to pay the deferred income tax sooner rather than later. Why would anyone do that? Because the subsequent buildup and withdrawals may be completely tax free, not just tax deferred. Many rules must be observed and conditions met, but a Roth IRA may be an excellent planning arrangement in some circumstances.

5. Show your clients how to minimize distributions during their lifetimes, leaving the maximum amount in the plan at their death. If clients are married, this may well be a good strategy. Chances are that clients will want to leave their plan to a surviving spouse, who may need the income in the future. The tax code generally permits individuals to leave a plan to a spouse, tax free; the survivor can then treat the retirement account as her own. ("Her own" is probably the correct phrase because about 11 out of 12 married women outlive their husbands.)

From Dream to Nightmare

Leaving a retirement plan to anyone other than one's spouse can be a tax disaster, though. The same problem will confront a surviving spouse at her death, assuming that considerable assets are left in the plan. In case you think that's unlikely, recall the previous example that showed how a $200,000 balance in a plan today could easily top $1 million in the foreseeable future.

Say, for example, that a retirement fund grows to $1 million by the time your client Joe Smith retires. If it continues to earn 12% per year, that's an increase of $120,000 per year. Even if Joe takes out $25,000, $50,000, even $75,000 per year for living expenses, his retirement fund will continue to grow. Of course, if Joe doesn't need to tap his retirement plan, it will grow even faster.

The bottom line is that large retirement plans grow to become larger retirement plans, even very large retirement plans, over the years. It's likely that Joe's plan could contain $1.5 million, $2 million, or more by the time it passes to the next generation.

What happens next depends a great deal on what you, as an advisor, tell your clients to do. Take the case of Mary Anderson, for example. She plans well so her $2 million IRA is left to her two children, who are then in their 60s, with a 25-year life expectancy. Therefore, that $2 million can be slowly withdrawn over 25 years. In that time period, continued tax-deferred buildup will produce many millions of dollars for Mary's children.

Janet Baker doesn't plan so well. She, too, dies with a $2 million estate but her estate contains no other assets that can be used to pay her estate tax bill. Therefore, her executor has to draw $1 million from her IRA, to meet estate tax.

That $1 million, however, becomes taxable income after it's withdrawn from her IRA. To meet that income tax obligation, another $400,000 has to be withdrawn from the IRA, which generates another income tax. And so on, until Janet's $2 million IRA is virtually stripped by the combination of estate and income tax.

What does Mary know that Janet doesn't? We reveal that later in this book. In the meantime, you need to keep in mind that the income tax obligation attached to a retirement plan doesn't die with the plan's owner or with a surviving spouse. Those taxes have to be paid someday, by someone. The secret is to pay it early (with a Roth IRA) or to pay it as late as possible, by implementing some basic planning techniques.

In essence, you want to show your clients how they can pay that income tax when it's best for them, not when it's best for the tax collectors.

SUMMARY

- Stocks were big winners throughout the 20th century and likely will reward investors in the 21st century.

- A relatively modest amount of money, invested in the stock market, can grow into a million-dollar portfolio in 10 or 15 years.

- For many investors, portfolio growth is achieved within a tax-deferred retirement plan.

- Because taxes are deferred, not forgiven, when money is withdrawn from a tax-deferred retirement plan, attention must be paid to the tax impact.

- Without sophisticated planning, a combination of estate taxes and income taxes can virtually strip a plan when it passes to the next generation.

- Savvy planning can turn a tax-deferred plan into a multigenerational, multimillion dollar wealth generator.

Choice Cuts

How Employers
Can Choose
among
Retirement Plans

For most financial advisors, a sizable portion of the client base consists of business owners or professionals. Such clients can sponsor a tax-deferred retirement plan for their employees, including themselves. Contributions made to these plans are deductible while earnings build, tax free, until withdrawal.

In many cases, your clients' own retirement accounts will receive the largest contribution and enjoy the greatest buildup, helping them to fund their own retirement. Suppose, for example, a client's business or professional practice contributes $30,000 per year to her own retirement account each year for 20 years, or a total of $600,000. Here's how much those contributions will be worth:

If the average investment return is	*The account will grow to*
8%	$1,482,750
10	$1,890,000
12	$2,421,000

Not only will your clients build up a sizable amount for themselves, such plans likely will help to attract and retain capable employees, thus adding value to their business or professional practice.

Simple Pleasures

When you're advising a client who wants to sponsor a retirement plan, there are several types of plans to choose among.

SIMPLE Plans

Created by tax legislation in 1996, SIMPLE (Savings Incentive Match Plan for Employees) plans are available only to companies with 100 or fewer employees. They can be structured either as IRAs (everyone goes his or her own way) or 401(k)s (participants pick from a menu of investment choices).

In truth, "SIMPLE 401(k)" is an oxymoron. If an employer's goal is to avoid paperwork, why go to the trouble of setting up a menu of choices for employees to choose among? SIMPLE IRAs may have their virtues, though. SIMPLE plans require little paperwork. There's no nondiscrimination testing, so your clients can maximize contributions to their own accounts regardless of how many of their employees elect to participate.

Unfortunately, contributions to your client's own SIMPLE account can't exceed $12,000 per year, including a 100% employer's match. (That's the 1998 maximum; it will increase gradually in future years.) Other retirement plans permit greater contributions. Moreover, in some cases SIMPLE plans can be expensive because employers are required to make contributions on behalf of their employees.

Altogether, then, you might consider recommending a SIMPLE plan for clients who are content with a relatively small contribution to their own accounts. This may be the case for clients with a business that tends to be short of cash so it can't afford to contribute any more than the SIMPLE limits.

Even Simpler

SEP Plans

Simplified Employee Pension (SEP) plans have been around longer than SIMPLEs and they continue to be popular. Again, SEP paperwork requirements are minimal: There are no IRS reports to file. Contributions may be as much as $24,000 per year, twice as much as SIMPLE plans permit.

Even at $24,000 per year, the maximum contribution isn't as great as it can be with some other plans. What's more, all the contributions come from the employer and it's not possible to skew contributions to the benefit of the business owner or professional.

For employers with only a few employees, SEPs may be ideal: They're inexpensive and hassle-free. As long as your clients can accept the $24,000 annual limit on the contribution to their own account, SEPs are worth considering.

Sharing the Load

Other types of retirement plans require more paperwork but the payoff may be greater.

401(k) Plans

Now that most large companies have 401(k)s, many small companies also offer them. Small employers often buy packaged plans from banks, insurers, brokers, and mutual fund families to reduce the administrative burden.

These plans have become popular in corporate America because employees fund most—even all—of their own retirement by deferring current income. Employers can match contributions but they don't have to do so. Combining a 401(k) with a profit-sharing plan (see following section), contributions to your client's own account may be as great as $30,000 per year. Because of complex nondiscrimination rules, however, highly paid executives may not even come close to the $30,000 limit. Thus, many employers offer matching contribution to encourage the rank-and-file to participate.

What's the bottom line? In some cases, 401(k) plans are suitable for employers who want to provide a retirement plan yet have employees pick up the tab. If your clients and other key executives run into restrictions, contributions can be increased with a companion profit-sharing or deferred compensation plan.

Sharing the Wealth

Profit-Sharing Plans

Profit-sharing plans may be the most popular retirement plans among small companies and professional practices. They provide flexibility as to how much or how little you contribute each year. By pairing a profit-sharing plan with a "money-purchase plan," your clients make a modest annual commitment but gain the ability to contribute up to $30,000 per year to their own accounts.

What's the downside? Straightforward profit-sharing plans may require substantial expenditures on behalf of rank-and-file employees. Such "vanilla" versions may be good for companies with a few, low-paid employees but most employers prefer to skew benefits to the key executives, including owner-executives.

Skewed Profit-Sharing Plans

By (1) integrating plan benefits with Social Security benefits and (2) contributing more on behalf of older employees (who have fewer years to build a nest egg), many small companies can tilt contributions toward key personnel.

Indeed, with a sophisticated plan, your clients might receive $30,000 annual contributions while most of their employees get small contributions, perhaps as little as 3% of pay. In some cases, over 90% of the company's contributions can go into the accounts of the owner-executives.

To get these benefits, though, your clients will have to hire specialists in plan design, which becomes expensive. They'll likely have to spend several thousand dollars in upfront costs plus a few thousand dollars each year for administration. Nevertheless, the extra benefits accruing to your clients and other principals may be worth the added cost. If you bring in an employee benefits specialist to work with your clients, those clients may find a skewed profit-sharing plan to be the best choice for their personal retirement plans.

Pension Payoff

Defined Benefit Plans

Profit-sharing and 401(k) plans are "defined contribution": X amount goes into each employee's account and whatever accumulates is that employee's retirement fund. In contrast, a "defined benefit plan" (a real pension plan) promises to pay employees certain amounts after they retire.

For business owners and professionals, a defined benefit plan may allow the employer to contribute (and deduct) amounts much larger than $30,000 per year to personal accounts. However, defined benefit plans are expensive to administer, they lock the company into fixed contributions even in bad years, and they may require high contributions for older but nonvital employees.

For clients who are in their 50s or 60s with a much younger crew of low-paid employees, a defined benefit plan may be worth the cost. However, defined benefit plans have fallen out of favor in recent years.

Late Show

Deferred Compensation Plan

As the name suggests, deferred compensation plans promise future compensation. When the compensation is received, the company gets a deduction and the recipient owes income tax. They're often offered as supplements to other plans, such as those previously described. Deferred compensation plans can be targeted for a select group of employees, usually key personnel. They're not subject to all the federal regulations that come with sponsoring a retirement plan.

The major drawback of such plans is that the contributions aren't deductible upfront. They don't merit tax-free buildup, either, but money may be set aside in permanent life insurance policies to provide tax-free buildup and access to the cash value. Although deferred compensation plans can add to a company's costs, they also may help to motivate essential managers, especially if contributions to other retirement plans don't reach the full $30,000 per year.

Agreeing to Disagree

Deciding which type of retirement plan to sponsor may be only half the battle, especially for clients who are in a business or professional practice that has more than one prime mover. The money contributed to the retirement plan must be invested, and that's where the trouble may come in.

For example, suppose your client is part owner of a company that has three principals, aged 40 to 55. They all have different views about investing so they can't agree to invest the money as one pool of funds. Instead, your client and his coprincipals all want to control their own retirement funds. If everyone can't agree on how to invest plan money, they may not sponsor a qualified plan. Then, all the benefits will be lost.

In this situation, the solution may be to set up a "self-directed plan with segregated accounts." Such plans provide each principal with complete investment flexibility.

With this approach, each of the company's principals can have his or her own account, using different brokers if desired. Also, if desired, one co-owner can invest solely in an S&P 500 index fund while another can invest her retirement money in penny stocks.

Cutting the Costs

This kind of flexibility will cost a small business or professional practice a little bit more, but the extra investment involved in setting up the plan correctly will pay dividends over the life of the plan. Until the late 1990s, self-directed plans were extremely expensive because they needed specially drafted legal documents and complex accounting procedures. Now, prototype self-directed plans offered by independent trust companies can be very cost-effective.

Thus, a small company can buy a run-of-the-mill prepackaged retirement plan from a bank or a brokerage firm for virtually nothing. As an advisor, you may be able to help clients locate an independent trust company that charges as little as $100–$250 to provide a prototype self-directed plan. Such a trust company also handles all of the annual accounting requirements for an additional $250–$500 per year.

Responsibility Bites

If your clients and their partners each have a personalized account for their own retirement plan investments, what happens to contributions for the benefit of the rank-and-file employees? They'll have separate accounts, too. In this case, the principals can't let their (presumably unsophisticated) employees sink or swim on their own. Instead, you can offer to meet with each employee at least once a year. At these meetings, you can advise the employees about investments, usually in mutual funds.

Many business owners and professionals believe that letting their employees make their own retirement plan investment decisions absolves them of fiduciary responsibility. That's not true. If workers choose high-cost, low-return investments, the employers could face lawsuits when employees' results turn out to be disappointing. That's why all parties benefit if you can direct employees to appropriate investment choices.

As an advisor, you might distribute investment literature. For example, each of the employees should be told that stocks have outperformed bonds, long term. Make sure that there are many investment choices available to the employees, not just mutual funds sponsored by one brokerage firm or insurance company. Keep records of all your efforts to educate participants and to provide investment alternatives. You can't force the employees to make good decisions but you can show that several good choices were available.

Looking Out for Number One

Sponsoring a tax-deferred qualified plan is not for every business owner or professional. There are administrative costs and fiduciary responsibilities to bear; contributions to employees' accounts may far outweigh contributions to their own account. Therefore, your clients may ultimately decide that sponsoring a plan isn't worthwhile.

If that's the case, how can your clients provide for their own retirement? They can take their earned income, pay tax, and invest what's left. Fortunately, there are some ways to invest while avoiding annual income tax.

Variable Annuities

When a client buys a variable annuity, the money that's invested can build up, tax deferred, until withdrawal. With a variable annuity the premium can be allocated among several investment choices, known as *subaccounts*, which typically include mutual fund look-alikes, managed by outstanding performers. Therefore, variable annuities are touted as vehicles for "investing in mutual funds without paying taxes."

However, variable annuities are not for everyone. If clients have little taxable investment income, they won't benefit much from investing in a variable annuity. Suppose, for example, Mary Roberts's portfolio consists largely of municipal bonds, growth stocks, and aggressive stock funds. She's a buy-and-hold investor, so the only taxable investment income she has each year comes from stock dividends and mutual fund distributions. Without much investment income to shelter, why should she invest in a variable annuity?

However, suppose Lynn Martin actively trades her stocks and mutual funds, switching several times a year to catch market swings. What's more, the funds in which Lynn invests frequently make substantial capital gains distributions. Therefore, Lynn reports a great deal of taxable investment income on her tax return each year; she can defer that taxable income by investing inside a variable annuity.

Even for clients with tax returns that show considerable investment income, you should suggest variable annuities with care. Investing in a variable annuity means paying a variety of extra fees, over and above those that clients pay to invest in mutual funds. Fees vary widely, depending on the contract. Even with the lowest-cost annuity, though, it takes time for the advantages of tax deferral to outweigh the expense. A variable annuity probably should be held for at least 10 years, in order to pay off—the longer the better. At a minimum, a variable annuity should be kept intact until an investor reaches age 59½ and is no longer subject to a 10% early withdrawal penalty.

Moreover, variable annuities work best for aggressive investors. If a client invests in a low-return bond subaccount, he may never come out ahead with a variable annuity. Variable annuity buyers need high returns to make the tax deferral meaningful, and that generally means investing in stocks, junk bonds, and other high-return subaccounts.

With those factors in mind, when does it make sense to count on variable annuities for retirement funding? They might work for clients who (1) pay a substantial amount of tax on investment income each year; (2) probably won't need to tap the contract for at least 10 years or until reaching age 59½, whichever comes later; (3) are able to keep most of their money invested in the stock market throughout the holding period; and (4) don't expect to be in one of the highest tax brackets in retirement.

What's more, your clients should intend to fully draw down the variable annuity in retirement. If the contract is held until death, all of the accumulated buildup will be subject to estate and income tax, leaving little for the heirs.

Suppose your clients don't meet this profile yet they don't want to sponsor a retirement plan for their employees. Among their other options is to invest in a "tax-managed" mutual fund, one that intentionally seeks to minimize taxes to investors by curbing turnover and realizing losses to offset gains. Yet another alternative is to buy and hold individual securities. This approach not only reduces the tax expense of unwanted (and generally reinvested) capital gains distributions, it keeps investors in control of their own portfolios.

Variable Life Insurance

Yet another possibility is investing via a variable life insurance policy. Compared with a variable annuity, variable life is more expensive and is more difficult to obtain—investors must pass a physical exam. However, for clients who are reasonably healthy, a variable life policy is usually far superior to a variable annuity because of the favorable tax treatment enjoyed by life insurance policies. Loans and withdrawals may be tax free; the death benefit—which must be somewhat larger than a policy's cash value based on IRC (70)(C)—is not subject to income tax. Studies have concluded that your clients and their beneficiaries might receive 35% more in net dollars from a variable life insurance policy than from a variable annuity, assuming the same investment results.

Suppose that Bill Robinson, age 50, pays a $10,000 life insurance premium every year for 15 years. Assuming that the investments earn 10% per year, which nets to approximately 8.5–9% after expenses, Bill's $150,000 investment might grow to $265,000. At that point, Bill could withdraw and borrow approximately $20,000 per year, tax free. As long as earnings hold up, he could do so indefinitely, pulling out $500,000 by age 90, and still leave a death benefit of approximately $300,000.

Win-Win

Your clients might prefer investing through variable life because many states protect life insurance policies from creditors. As long as there is some loved one in the picture, variable life can be a great "heads I win, tails my kids win" investment. The cash value can be tapped, tax free, if necessary, or a larger death benefit can go to the survivors if cash isn't needed.

Once again, variable life insurance isn't for everyone. Careful monitoring is necessary to avoid a disastrous policy lapse. In addition, investors run the risk that a future change in the law will dry up those juicy tax benefits.

Limited selection may also be a concern. Even the broadest variable life policies have a few dozen available subaccounts; most have just a handful. Outside of a variable life policy, investors have thousands of mutual funds to choose among in addition to individual securities.

Investing through permanent life insurance locks your clients in to making substantial premium payments for a number of years. If they change their minds after several payments, they'll probably have little in the way of cash value. What's more, an insurance policy bought with one or just a few payments is a "modified endowment contract," which doesn't qualify for tax-free withdrawals and loans.

The bottom line? Variable life probably makes sense for clients who hate paying taxes, have a long time horizon, and want to provide for loved ones.

SUMMARY

- Clients of financial advisors tend to be high-income individuals, including many business owners and professionals.

- Clients, particularly business owners and professionals, may want to sponsor a tax-deferred retirement plan so financial advisors should be familiar with the benefits and disadvantages of various types of plans.

- Although some plans require little paperwork, they may limit contributions to the principals' retirement accounts.

- Other plans offer larger contributions on the owners' behalf, perhaps with scant contributions for the rank-and-file, but they require more administrative expense.

- If your clients have partners or co-owners who can't agree on a common investment philosophy, they can set up a retirement plan with segregated accounts for each principal.

- Employers who do not want the expense and responsibility of sponsoring a retirement plan may prefer to fund their own retirement through variable annuities, variable life insurance, or tax-efficient mutual funds.

A Fortune from 401(k)s

How Employees Can
Maximize Returns

Your clients may think of the money they'll receive in retirement as a "pension," but that's no longer true in many cases. A pension, as explained in Chapter 2, is a "defined benefit" a retiree receives from a former employer. To provide employees with a pension, based on earnings and years of service, an employer must make a commitment to contribute regularly to a retirement plan.

However, in recent years many employers have sharply reduced or even eliminated their pension commitments. Instead, they've replaced them with 401(k) plans, named after a section of the tax code. (Nonprofit organizations offer similar 403(b) plans while government employees have thrift savings plans.)

Why have companies shifted from pensions to 401(k)s? Because 401(k)s are funded largely by employees, not by employers. If you're advising a client who's an employee with a 401(k) plan, the amount the client winds up with is her responsibility—and perhaps yours—but not the employer's. Therefore, it's crucial that such clients understand their 401(k)s and make decisions that will lead to the greatest accumulation inside the plan.

Basic Training

With a 401(k), employees are offered the opportunity to reduce the amount of money they take home from their job. Depending on the plan, they can defer a certain percentage of their salary. Officially, participants can elect to defer up to 20% of their wages, up to a maximum amount ($10,000 in 1999), which increases each year because it is indexed for inflation. In practice, most companies limit deferrals to 10–15% of earnings.

The amount clients choose to defer is received later, along with accumulated earnings. When they elect to trim their income, they also trim their income taxes. Suppose Pete Thomas's gross salary is $50,000 per year. If Pete elects to direct $4,000 into his 401(k) account, he'll owe tax only on a $46,000 income. (For purposes of Pete's future Social Security benefits, he is treated as if his earnings were $50,000.)

Next, Pete must decide how to invest his $4,000. His choices depend on the menu that's made available through his employer. Some companies, especially small ones, offer only a few options: perhaps a money market fund, a bond fund, and a stock fund. Huge corporations, however, may offer dozens—even hundreds—of choices. Most 401(k) plans fall somewhere in the middle.

The choices that clients make for their 401(k) plans needn't be all or nothing. If Pete Thomas has $4,000 to invest, for example, he might put $1,000 into each of four funds. Most 401(k) plans offer participants the chance to move money around, from one investment to another, although there may be some limits on the frequency of the switches.

Once participants make their investment choices, any earnings can stay in the account to compound, free of income tax. Employees don't owe tax until they withdraw their money, which may be when they've retired and are in a lower tax bracket. Generally, participants owe a 10% penalty tax on withdrawals before age 59½.

Therefore, the basic advantage of a 401(k) plan is tax deferral. Instead of paying tax at age 30, 40, or 50, your clients pay the tax at age 60, 70, or 80. Meanwhile, their money can accumulate to a greater degree, because the earnings aren't taxed each year. If they also benefit from tax bracket reduction (say, they defer tax from years when they're in a 28% bracket to years when they're in a 15% bracket), the advantage of investing through a 401(k) plan may be even greater.

Match Making

Those are the basic advantages, but the 401(k) story is a bit more complicated. These plans are subject to *nondiscrimination* rules, meaning that highly paid employees can maximize their contributions only if the rank-and-file participate to a certain degree. To encourage lower-paid employees to participate, most companies make "matching" contributions. (Again, the language can be somewhat misleading: A "match" might be a quarter on the dollar, not a full dollar-for-dollar contribution.)

Perhaps the most common arrangement is a 50% match, up to 6% of salary. Thus, if Art Williams earns $50,000 per year, the match is in effect for up to $3,000 worth of deferral ($3,000 is 6% of $50,000). Up to $3,000, Art's company will contribute 50 cents for every dollar that he elects to defer. In this case, Art should defer at least $3,000, earning a 50% match—$1,500. If he doesn't elect to contribute at least $3,000 to his 401(k), he's passing up free money.

Most plans permit Art to defer even more. Should he increase his deferral? Probably. Going from a 6% deferral ($3,000 per year) to an 8% deferral ($4,000) is a difference of less than $20 per week. Yes, Art might buy fewer lottery tickets or dine out less often, but the extra two points that he contributes to his 401(k) may make a huge difference over time, swelling his account and providing for a more comfortable retirement.

Too Much, Too Soon

In contrast to Art, with his $50,000 salary, Jennifer Davis, earning $120,000 per year, wants the maximum $10,000 salary deferral for her 401(k) account. However, Jennifer must be careful not to get there too rapidly because she might forfeit some matching contributions.

Based on a 50% match, up to 6% of pay, Jennifer should be able to receive a $3,600 match on a $10,000 contribution (50% times 6% times $120,000 equals $3,600). However, if she contributes $1,000 per month, the $10,000 maximum will be reached after 10 months and $3,000 worth of matching $300 contributions—a $600 shortfall.

Instead, Jennifer can contribute $833 per month, extending contributions throughout the year. If so, her employer will match $300 per month for 12 months, bringing the annual match to the expected $3,600.

Room at the Top

Tax code technicalities may affect highly compensated executives in other ways. In some companies, the top executives can only contribute a few thousand dollars per year to the 401(k) plan because of nondiscrimination rules. What's more, limiting executives' contributions also means limiting the company's matching contributions to their accounts.

How can such companies reward their key people? Often, with a nonqualified deferred compensation plan, funded for selected key employees. Although there's no initial tax deduction, the company benefits by having happy executives. Those executives know there is a larger retirement fund in their future.

The IRS approves deferred compensation plans, provided they're handled correctly. In one letter ruling, the agency showed how such a plan could be coordinated with a 401(k). The IRS explained that a highly compensated corporate manager entered into a salary reduction agreement in the calendar year preceding the year of the deferred compensation. This election specified that a percentage of compensation in the succeeding year would be deferred in a nonqualified plan.

As soon as practical after the close of the deferral year, the employer performs various tests on its 401(k) plan to determine, on a preliminary basis, the amount that can be contributed to the 401(k) plan. After conducting these tests, but no later than March 15 of the year following the 401(k)'s plan year, the lesser of the amount deferred under the nonqualified plan or the amount that could be contributed to the 401(k) is contributed to the 401(k).

Suppose, for example, that in 1998 William Mason agrees to a 6% deferral. In 1999, his predeferral compensation is $200,000, so the deferral is $12,000. However, nondiscrimination rules prohibit him from contributing more than $3,500 to his 401(k) account. Before March 15, 2000, $3,500 of the deferred compensation is contributed to William's 401(k) account. The other $8,500 can continue to be deferred under the nonqualified arrangement.

By following this procedure, two advantages are realized. One, by waiting until preliminary nondiscrimination tests are performed before making 401(k) contributions, the risk of excess 401(k) contributions can be minimized or eliminated. Such excess contributions must be distributed—and taxed currently—so this problem can be diminished. Second, by using dual plans, the total deferral can be set at an amount deemed desirable by employer and employee.

Many large companies have adopted this type of arrangement. Small companies may use it, too, providing that they have a 401(k) plan and some highly compensated employees who face restrictions in the amount they can contribute to this plan. Typically, the nonqualified deferred compensation plan is designed to mirror the 401(k), with similar investment choices.

Core Comfort

Once your clients determine how much they'll contribute to their 401(k) accounts, you can help them decide how to invest that money. Generally, they should favor the stock funds in the plan. Specifically, most 401(k) contributions should be directed into one or two funds (it doesn't pay to spread money around too many funds) that invest in a diversified mix of U.S. stocks. These funds should emphasize large, well-established companies: Those companies probably will be around for many years so that's where clients should have most of their retirement money.

Don't advise your clients to invest before reading the fund's prospectus. How long has it been in existence? How long has the current manager been in place? What returns have been posted for the past 5 years? The past 10 years? Make sure you're comfortable with the answers to all these questions before you recommend a fund.

When you propose particular funds, lean toward funds with low expense ratios, as revealed in the prospectus. You also should look for low turnover rates, which can lead to low transaction costs. Over time, such economies can increase investors' returns dramatically.

Once your clients have put money into the funds you have recommended, trust your own judgment. Clients should stay with the funds they've selected rather than switching funds frequently. You should monitor those funds and suggest making a change if necessary, such as if a new manager takes over, but the most successful investors are those who make decisions and stay with them over the long term.

Round Numbers

As a rule of thumb, large-company stock funds probably should account for about half of your clients' 401(k) accounts. Then they can fill in the rest from the other choices on the menu.

Relatively young clients—those under 40, perhaps—should have most if not all of their 401(k) money in investments likely to produce superior long-term returns. Such clients might round out their 401(k) holdings with small-company stock funds, international stock funds and bond funds, real estate funds, specialty stock funds, and junk-bond funds, assuming that their 401(k) plan has solid entries in these categories. (Clients who are in a plan with only a few options have little choice beyond putting their money into the selections that seem appealing.)

You might recommend a different investment strategy for clients who are in their late 50s or 60s, nearing retirement. Although they'll still want a large amount of stock funds in their 401(k) account, they may want to mix in some bond funds and perhaps an allocation to a "stable income account." This type of portfolio is less exposed to stock market risk and may make more sense for clients who are planning to start withdrawals soon.

Helping Hands

In addition to various mutual funds, some 401(k) plans offer accounts in which someone else takes over the investment responsibility. In "balanced portfolios," for example, participants choose specific asset allocations. If Wendy Baker decides she wants 70% in stocks and 30% in bonds, the portfolio manager takes the responsibility for keeping the balance at 70-30.

"Asset allocation accounts" are also available in some 401(k) plans. In these accounts, asset allocations are moved, based on the manager's judgment. The manager might allocate 80% to stocks one year, then cut back to 50% if the market looks pricey.

Should you recommend such accounts for your clients' 401(k) investing? Probably not—they're mainly for employees who have no interest in steering their own course to retirement. Assuming you want to help your clients remain in control of their own destinies, you should help them select their own funds for their 401(k) accounts.

Spreading the Wealth

Many 401(k)s offered by publicly held companies include employer stock on the menu. Generally, you should advise clients to put little or none of their 401(k) money into their employer's stock: They already have enough of their future tied up in their employer's fortunes.

In some plans, the employer will match employees' contributions with its stock rather than cash. Furthermore, 401(k) participants may be restricted from selling any of that stock before age 50, for example. If this is the case, you should advise clients to sell the stock as soon as they're permitted; they're better off without too much exposure to any one company's stock price.

Don't Borrow Trouble

Many 401(k) plans allow participants to borrow from their accounts. Clients can get a hassle-free loan and pay themselves back, with interest. In general, employees can borrow as much as half of their account value, up to $50,000.

Suppose Jim Benson has $80,000 in his 401(k) account. His daughter Jane has just been accepted at Dartmouth so Jim has a pressing need for cash. He likely can get a loan of up to $40,000 from his 401(k) plan with a minimal amount of paperwork.

In most companies, the loan repayments will come out of Jim's future paychecks, with interest rates set at about a point or two over the banks' prime lending rate. In 1999, interest rates on 401(k) loans were typically around 10%. Therefore, borrowing from a 401(k) plan looks like a good deal. Your clients get money that they need and their 401(k) accounts earn a reliable 10% on the money that's been loaned out.

There are some disadvantages, though. Money that's borrowed from a 401(k) is not sitting in a stock fund, earning 15%, 20%, or more per year. Investors may realize better returns over the long term by leaving money in their 401(k) account and borrowing from another source.

Although the money that's borrowed from a 401(k) is not subject to income tax—an obvious advantage—there are tax problems, too. Loan repayments are made with after-tax dollars. However, clients will pay tax again when they withdraw money from their account. Thus, 401(k) loans expose borrowers to double taxation. Moreover, if your client leaves the company, any outstanding 401(k) loan needs to be repaid immediately. If repayment is not made, the loan is treated as a distribution, subject to income tax and possibly a 10% penalty tax before age 59½.

What's the bottom line? You should advise clients to consider their 401(k) account as a lender of last resort. If they need money and bank loans aren't available, a 401(k) loan is better than a credit card loan with interest rates up to 21%.

SUMMARY

- Many clients who are employees participate in a 401(k) or similar plan in which they're responsible for making investment decisions.

- When advising clients about their 401(k)s, you should recommend that clients defer at least enough of their salary to receive the maximum matching contribution from the company.

- Diversified U.S. stock funds focusing on large companies should be the core of a 401(k) portfolio.

- Younger investors can fill out their 401(k) accounts with aggressive holdings while older participants may want to be more conservative, assuming a good selection is available.

- Clients should hold little company stock in their 401(k) plan to avoid overexposure to one single stock.

- Clients can borrow from their 401(k) accounts if there is a pressing need for cash and no other likely source of that cash.

From $2,000 to $2 Million (or More)

IRAs and Roth IRAs

Almost every year, it seems, the IRS adds a new type of IRA or changes the rules regarding existing IRAs. Helping your clients make the most of their IRA options may not be easy, but it's not astrophysics, either. If you know what's available, you can decide which IRAs will work for which clients and help them to dodge the traps that may snare the unwary. First, though, you must become familiar with the IRA lineup.

Rules for Regular IRAs

The basic IRA rules permit everyone who earns at least $2,000 to contribute up to $2,000 to an IRA each year. (Alimony counts as earned income for this purpose.) One-income married couples can have two IRAs, up to $2,000 apiece.

Although individuals can *contribute* $2,000 per year to an IRA, whether that contribution is *deductible* is a different matter. Depending on their circumstances, some, all, or none of their IRA contribution may be deductible. Here are the ground rules:

- If a single client is not an active participant in an employer-sponsored qualified plan, she can get a full deduction.

- For married couples, if neither participates in an employer's plan, both can take full deductions.

- If one spouse participates in an employer's plan but the other does not, the nonparticipant can get a full deduction if joint adjusted gross income (AGI) is $150,000 or less. Smaller deductions are permitted up to $160,000 in AGI.

Suppose Paul Morris is covered by his employer's plan but his wife Jan is in law school. In 1999, their AGI is $157,000. Paul can make a $2,000 nondeductible IRA contribution. Jan isn't covered by an employer plan so she can get a deduction. However, because their AGI is 70% through the "phaseout range" ($150,000–$160,000), her deduction is limited to 30% of $2,000, or $600. In addition to her deductible $600 contribution, Jan can make a nondeductible IRA contribution of up to $1,400, if she wishes.

- Even if clients are covered by an employer plan, they can deduct IRA contributions if their AGI is below a certain level. For full deductions in 1999, AGI must be below $31,000 (single filers) or $51,000 (on a joint return). Partial deductions are available up to $41,000 and $61,000, respectively.

These phaseout ranges will increase each year until 2005, when it's $50,000–$60,000 for single filers. For joint returns, the increase continues until 2007, when the phaseout range reaches $80,000–$100,000.

Once contributions (deductible or nondeductible) are made to an IRA, the accounts are self-directed. Clients can keep an IRA in a bank, stock fund, bond fund, or virtually any kind of investment. (Collectibles are excluded, though). They can move money among various investments and avoid income tax as long as the money stays inside the IRA.

This income tax avoidance pays off. Suppose, for example, Jane Smith contributes $2,000 per year to an IRA for 20 years and earns 8% each year. Jane's $40,000 in contributions would grow to more than $90,000, much more than she would have if she had invested that $40,000 in a taxable account that earned 8%.

That's the good news. Unfortunately, taking money out of an IRA can be a taxing experience. Assuming Jane funds that IRA strictly with deductible contributions, every penny that comes out will be taxed at her regular rate by the IRS and perhaps by her state and local tax collectors as well. She may get bumped into a higher tax bracket because of her taxable IRA income, she may have to pay more taxes on her Social Security benefits, and she may owe a 10% penalty tax if she takes money out before age 59½.

The bottom line is that Jane avoids tax on small amounts each year and winds up paying tax on larger amounts in later years. This may be a good deal depending on the length of the tax deferral and her tax bracket when the money comes out, but the deferred taxes definitely take a lot of the fun from an IRA.

What if some or all of her IRA contributions were nondeductible? Then some or all of her IRA withdrawals are not included in her taxable income. However, Jane needs to keep meticulous records, perhaps for decades, to support her claim of tax-free withdrawals: The paperwork burden may not be worth the effort of making nondeductible IRA contributions.

The Rewards of Roth IRAs

The 1997 tax law created a new type of IRA, named after Senator William Roth. Taxpayers can contribute up to $2,000 per year to a Roth IRA instead of (not in addition to) a regular IRA. Roth IRA contributions are not deductible, but, in certain circumstances, all of the earnings *and the withdrawals* can be tax free.

Just as in the previous example, Jane can invest $2,000 per year for 20 years and watch the money grow to more than $90,000, tax free. With a Roth IRA, though, Jane may be able to pull out all the money in the account and owe nothing to the IRS.

Jane might withdraw, say, $20,000 for living expenses one year and leave the other $70,000+ to continue to grow. This can go on and on— she can leave her Roth IRA to her spouse or her children—until the tax-free withdrawals have lasted for decades.

Jane has to meet some conditions to enjoy the benefits of tax-free withdrawals. First, she can't draw out the earnings from a Roth IRA until she reaches age $59\frac{1}{2}$. Second, if Jane starts her Roth IRA when she's older than $54\frac{1}{2}$, she must wait at least 5 years before withdrawing earnings. (Earnings of up to $10,000 may be withdrawn at any time to help with a first-time home purchase, tax free.)

In reality, Roth IRAs are even more advantageous. When Jane takes money out, she's considered to be taking out contributions first, then earnings, and withdrawals of contributions don't count as taxable income.

Suppose Jane starts her Roth IRA at age 35 and decides to retire after 20 years, at 55. She's not $59\frac{1}{2}$ so she doesn't qualify to withdraw *earnings* tax free. She can, however, withdraw up to $40,000—the amount she's contributed over the years—and owe no tax or penalties. Then, when she reaches age $59\frac{1}{2}$, she can withdraw the earnings, too, tax free.

The main problem with Roth IRAs is that they're not for everyone. To contribute the full $2,000 per year to a Roth IRA, a client's AGI can't exceed $95,000 on a single return, $150,000 on a joint return. Partial contributions are allowed up to $110,000 (single) or $160,000 (joint). Taxpayers with greater incomes are shut out of Roth IRAs.

- Bob Brown, a single filer, has a $94,000 AGI: He'll be able to contribute $2,000 to a Roth IRA.

- Joe Green and his wife Joan have an AGI of $154,000. They're 40% into the phaseout so they can contribute only 60% of the maximum—$1,200 apiece.

- Sam Black and his wife Sue have an AGI of $161,000, making them Roth-less.

The planning possibilities are numerous. Suppose, for example, you have a client who is at least $59\frac{1}{2}$ and still working. Assuming the client meets the AGI test, there is nothing to lose (except, perhaps, some administrative fees) by taking $2,000 that would otherwise sit in a taxable account and transferring it to a Roth IRA.

At the other end of the spectrum, consider a client whose teenage daughter earns $2,000 from a summer job. In most cases she could make a deductible $2,000 contribution to a regular IRA, but she probably shouldn't. Children with low incomes get only a small deduction or no deduction at all. Then, all the money that comes out of the IRA is taxed at ordinary income rates. With a Roth IRA, that money might build up for many years and never be taxed.

If a client has a business or profession, he could hire his youngster and deduct the $2,000 that goes to fund the Roth IRA. The $2,000 that was earned doesn't have to be the $2,000 that goes into the Roth IRA. The youngster could use the money for some other purpose and the parent could make a $2,000 gift, covered by the annual $10,000 gift tax exclusion, to fund the Roth IRA.

The only risk to such a strategy is that earnings as well as principal might have to be withdrawn before age $59\frac{1}{2}$, triggering a 10% penalty tax as well as income tax on the withdrawn earnings. But the time value of tax deferral might exceed the cost of the penalty; moreover, there are some exceptions to the rules on early withdrawals:

- No penalties will be imposed in case of death or permanent disability.

- Clients can avoid the penalty by taking "substantially equal" payments from an IRA based on life expectancy. Such payments must last at least 5 years and until age $59\frac{1}{2}$.

- Clients who are out of work for at least 12 consecutive weeks can take enough money from an IRA to keep health insurance in force, penalty free, and keep doing so until they're back to work for 60 days.

- Money used for higher education is not subject to the penalty.

- Withdrawals up to $10,000 used for a first-time home purchase are not subject to penalty.

With those rules, is there any reason for a qualified client *not* to establish a Roth IRA? Someone who is 70 years old and financially set for life might say, why bother? Otherwise, clients should contribute to a Roth IRA if they can.

A somewhat thornier question concerns the decision of whether to choose a Roth IRA or a deductible IRA, if a client is eligible for the deduction. That decision usually depends on the years from retirement and the expected tax bracket in retirement. The fewer years until retirement and the lower the anticipated tax bracket, the more desirable a deductible IRA.

There is a real benefit to deducting at 31% and eventually paying tax at 15%, for example, especially if the withdrawals will take place fairly soon. Nevertheless, most clients will be better off with the Roth IRA, which requires a tax payment up front in return for what could be many years of tax-free wealth building.

Roth IRAs work particularly well for young people just starting their careers at low salary levels and for your clients' children who earn some money with a part-time summer job. (Assuming a 9% annual return, $2,000 invested at age 16 will grow to $128,000 by age 64!)

There are a few situations, though, in which a deductible IRA beats a Roth IRA. According to T. Rowe Price, the mutual fund company, a deductible IRA is the better choice for taxpayers who are (1) approximately 44 or older; (2) expect their tax bracket to fall from 28% or higher while working to 15% in retirement; (3) set up a separate account to invest the tax savings from their deductible contribution; *and* (4) hold investments that earn approximately 9–10% per year. Other clients who don't fit into that mold will likely do better in a Roth IRA.

Cashing in on Roth IRA Conversions

There's another aspect to the Roth IRA: Clients may be able to convert a regular IRA to a Roth IRA. They'll have to pay the deferred income tax but, after converting, if they hold on to a Roth IRA at least 5 years, until age 59½, they'll owe no tax on the withdrawals.

Again, take the example of Jane Smith, who has built up a fund of $90,000 in an IRA, all from deductible contributions. If she converts to a Roth IRA, that will mean recognizing $90,000 in taxable income. That extra $90,000 may push Jane into a higher tax bracket while the increase in AGI may have adverse consequences elsewhere on her tax return. Counting state and local income tax, Jane may owe approximately 40% in tax on the conversion, an extra $36,000 on her $90,000 IRA. In return, after she has held onto her Roth IRA for 5 years, until age 59½, that $90,000 plus any future earnings will all be tax free.

Roth IRA conversions are permitted only in years when the account owner's AGI is under $100,000, on a single or joint return. (The income realized from the conversion itself doesn't count toward this limit.)

Some clients must take required minimum distributions from regular IRAs if they're 70½ or older, and those distributions count toward the $100,000 limit. A 1998 tax law provides relief, but not until 2005. Until then, clients are risking a disallowance of a Roth IRA conversion if they disregard income from a required IRA distribution. Fortunately, they can rescind the conversion after the fact if they go over the $100,000 mark.

Many clients will be so far above the threshold, though, that a Roth IRA rollover may not be possible until retirement and perhaps not even then. For clients who are relatively young, it may be worth taking some steps to keep their AGI at or under $100,000 and thus qualify for a rollover. Clients might take a few months off from work. They might take early retirement or semiretirement. There's no reason they can't go back to work full-time the next year.

Another possibility is for a client to enter into a deferred compensation agreement with his employer—even with his own closely held corporation. For a deferred compensation agreement, the client should enter into a salary reduction agreement in the calendar year preceding the year of the deferred compensation, specifying that a portion of his compensation (perhaps the annual bonus) in the succeeding year will be deferred in a nonqualified plan. The deferred compensation agreement should be written and formally adopted by a resolution of the corporation's board.

Deferred compensation arrangements for 2001 should be in place by year-end 2000. If clients wait until 2001 to make the arrangement, the IRS may assert there was "constructive receipt" of all the compensation and include the deferred amount in the client's taxable 2001 income.

Moreover, clients who change jobs may get retirement plan distributions that they can roll into an IRA. Assuming their AGIs are below $100,000, the money can then be rolled into Roth IRAs.

Yet another possibility exists for professionals and business owners who sponsor retirement plans. Such people might terminate the retirement plan and roll over their account balance into an IRA. Then they can complete their rollover to a Roth IRA. Such maneuvers may be worthwhile for young professionals or for those in semiretirement, with modest AGIs.

Clients who terminate retirement plans for IRA rollovers might install a new plan and continue to make contributions. For the sake of appearances, it might make sense to wait awhile or to install a different type of plan.

Ideally, clients who convert IRAs to Roth IRAs will be able to pay the extra tax from other sources, leaving their Roth IRA intact to keep accumulating. If so, a Roth IRA rollover is almost always a good choice. Clients who need to pay the tax out of their Roth IRAs are essentially accelerating the tax they would have had to pay if they had kept the money in a regular IRA. If they die soon after, they may be worse off with a Roth IRA rollover. At some point, though, the lines likely will cross and the Roth IRA will be a better choice.

If your clients have an IRA and their income is under $100,000, should they convert to a Roth IRA? The more years they have for a buildup. The higher their retirement tax bracket and the higher the likelihood the IRA will be left to heirs, the more they'll have to gain from a Roth IRA conversion.

Rolling Up Big Numbers with Rollover IRAs

Although IRA contributions are limited to $2,000 per year, many clients have hundreds of thousands—even millions—of dollars in their IRAs. These amounts result not from a $2,000-per-year buildup but from rolling over a large sum from an employer-sponsored retirement plan into an IRA.

When employees leave a job where they've been covered by an employer-sponsored retirement plan, they probably will be given the balance in their account, whether they are retiring or continuing to work. At that time, they can roll over that distribution—which could be from a profit-sharing plan, a 401(k) plan, or other plan—into an IRA. Such a rollover, which must be done within 60 days, preserves the tax deferral so no taxes are owed.

Generally, a rollover IRA is in the form of cash, so you'll be responsible for helping clients decide how to invest their funds. Savvy advisors look at a client's total holdings, including IRA and non-IRA money, to come up with a comprehensive asset allocation plan.

There's a nasty surprise in store for some people who roll over an IRA from an employer's retirement plan. Employers are required to withhold 20% for taxes and employees must settle up with the IRS when their next tax return is due. However, the 20% that's withheld is subject to income tax and possible early withdrawal penalties unless clients make up the difference in the account. For example, if Dan Baker has a $100,000 rollover and his employer withholds 20%, Dan will have to add $20,000 to keep his IRA intact and maintain this tax deferral.

To avoid this problem, Dan should set up an IRA account and ask his employer for a "trustee to trustee" rollover. The money goes directly from Dan's employer's plan to Dan's rollover IRA; he never touches a penny of it. In that case, no money needs to be withheld and Dan saves himself from a huge tax headache.

Rolling to Roth IRAs

IRA rollovers can provide clients with IRAs worth six and even seven figures. After such rollovers, Roth IRA conversions are permitted and may well be desirable. Roth IRA conversions may work even for older clients, including those with large IRA balances. In some cases, clients in their late 60s with IRAs over $1 million may be suitable for such conversions.

Of course, such clients must have income under $100,000 in order to convert, as per the tax law. In addition, these conditions should be present:

- The tax on the conversion is payable from sources other than the converted IRA.

- Neither spouse is likely to need the money in the IRA during their lifetime. Thus, the IRA will pass to the next generation.

- Life insurance, held in an irrevocable trust, will be available to pay the estate tax when the Roth IRA passes to the next generation.

Suppose Jerry Jackson retired and rolled $800,000 from his company's profit-sharing plan into an IRA. By now, his IRA has grown to $1.2 million. In retirement, his AGI is about $80,000.

If Jerry converts his IRA to a Roth IRA, all $1.2 million becomes taxable. Assuming an effective 40% tax rate, Jerry will have to find $480,000 to pay the tax. If that's possible, a Roth IRA conversion is usually a good choice. With a Roth IRA conversion, a 69-year-old taxpayer might increase wealth by about 50%, compared with a do-nothing stance.

Simplify Life with SEPs and SIMPLE IRAs

Employers who want to keep things uncomplicated might set up a Simplified Employee Pension (SEP) plan rather than a more elaborate plan. Clients who are self-employed also can have a SEP. These plans are sometimes called SEP-IRAs because they are covered by many of the rules that govern IRAs.

The big difference: Clients can contribute much more to a SEP-IRA than they can to a SEP. An employer can contribute up to 15% of a participating employee's salary (in 1999, a $160,000 cap on eligible compensation limits SEP contributions to $24,000 per year). The math is a little bit different for self-employed people but the bottom line is that they can contribute up to 13.04% of their self-employment income. Thus, SEP-IRA contributions can be much more than the regular $2,000 IRA limit, and SEP-IRA contributions are deductible.

With a SEP, every covered employee has his or her own account and takes responsibility for investing that money. SEP-IRAs are flexible, so employers can cut the contribution in any given year. As you'd expect, the paperwork is easy to handle. If a company contributes to a SEP-IRA it must contribute the same percentage of pay for all eligible employees, generally those who have worked for at least 3 years.

The 1996 tax law created SIMPLE IRAs (along with SIMPLE 401(k)s), which are available to the self-employed and to companies with up to 100 employees. With a SIMPLE IRA, employees can contribute (and deduct) up to $6,000 per year by reducing their compensation, as long as they earn at least that much.

If a SIMPLE IRA is sponsored by a client's company, that client and any family members who work there may make pretax contributions up to $6,000 to their own accounts, regardless of whether any other employees elect to make contributions. The company must match any employee contributions, up to 2% or 3% of pay.

Thus, even if most employees defer little or none of their earnings, the owner and selected others can contribute the maximum. SIMPLE IRAs may work for companies that have few employees, if those employees are not likely to elect to reduce their current earnings for SIMPLE contributions. The smaller the amount of employee deferrals, the smaller the company's match has to be.

Learning about Education IRAs

Although IRA stands for Individual Retirement Account, this version can't be used for retirement. Instead, contributions must be made on behalf of children 18 and under while the payouts must be made for college expenses.

As long as the money comes out of an education IRA for higher education costs, no taxes are due. However, contributions are nondeductible and they can't exceed $500 per student beneficiary per year. Contributions on behalf of a particular student can't be made in the same year that student receives contributions for a prepaid tuition plan, which are available in many states.

The income limits are the same as they are for Roth IRAs: To make the maximum $500 annual contribution, clients must have AGI below $95,000 on a single return or $150,000, filing jointly. Smaller contributions can be made up to $110,000 and $160,000 in AGI, respectively.

The income limits are not really meaningful because *anyone* can contribute to an education IRA. Suppose, for example, that your client Al and Betty Jones earn $175,000 per year so they're over the limit. Laura Jones, Al's mother, is a retiree whose income is under the limit so she's allowed to contribute $500 per year to her grandchildren's education IRAs.

Thus, IRAs can be wealth builders for your clients and their families, starting long before retirement and continuing long afterward. As we'll see in Chapter 14, IRAs can continue to defer tax and create wealth for future generations.

SUMMARY

- IRAs are not limited to $2,000 annual contributions.

- Six- and seven-figure sums can build up in IRAs that hold rollover accounts from employer-sponsored retirement plans.

- Roth IRAs offer tax-free withdrawals as well as tax-free accumulation but they may not be available to upper-income clients.

- Clients may be able to convert regular IRAs to Roth IRAs if their income does not exceed $100,000.

- The long-term benefits of Roth IRA conversions may be so great that clients may want to plan to hold down their incomes for a given year in order to qualify.

- Financial advisors need to be familiar with other types of IRAs, such as SEP-IRAs and SIMPLE IRAs, in order to advise clients who are self-employed or business owners.

CHAPTER

5

Cans and Can'ts

Plan Loans, Prohibited
Transactions

Inevitably, one of your clients will need a loan from time to time. They made need funds to pay for tuition or for home improvements. Clients can borrow from a bank but that means going through the qualification process and then paying interest to a third party.

For some clients, borrowing from their retirement plan may be a better option. There are no credit checks or lengthy applications to fill out; the plan trustee (who might be the client, in the case of a business owner or professional) makes the decision. What's more, the loan interest goes back into the client's retirement account rather than to a third-party lender.

Thus, there are advantages to borrowing from a retirement plan. Participants need to be careful, though, especially those who are principals in the company sponsoring the plan. Some plan sponsors have gotten into trouble by treating a retirement plan as their own personal bank account. If they don't follow the rules, their entire plan can be disqualified and then they face an enormous tax bill.

Loan Arrangements

In a typical qualified plan, participants owe income tax whenever they take money from the plan and they owe a 10% penalty tax if they're under age 59½. Some plans, though, permit borrowing; if so, participants can get at their money, tax free, and avoid a penalty tax, provided they follow all the rules:

- There must be specific authorization in the plan documents for loans to be made. Therefore, a client's ability to borrow from a qualified plan is up to the plan sponsor, which might be the client's own business or professional practice.

- Loans are allowed only if the sponsor has a written document in its retirement plan, spelling out the identity of the person or persons authorized to make loans and the loan application procedures.

- The criteria for approving or denying loan applications and the limits on the amounts that may be borrowed must be formalized.

- The rules relating to plan loans should include the events constituting default and the steps to be taken in case of default.

- Plan loans must be made available to all participants and beneficiaries on a reasonably equivalent basis. That doesn't mean everyone automatically gets a loan; because the plan must be prudently administered, it must act as a commercial lender would, focusing on each applicant's creditworthiness.

- Loans must be adequately secured, typically by the participant's vested account balance.

- Loans must bear a reasonable rate of interest, similar to commercial lending rates. In practice, retirement plans generally charge anywhere from the prime rate to two points over prime. If the banks' prime lending rate is 8%, for example, interest rates in the range of 8.5–10% likely will be considered reasonable.

- Plan loans must be repaid within 5 years, on a regular amortization schedule, with payments made at least quarterly. "Balloon payments" aren't permitted, meaning that a loan can't be interest-only until the maturity date. Loans issued for excessive time periods are deemed to be distributions—they're considered taxable income to the borrower.

Suppose, for example, that Jack Davis's company permits him to borrow $20,000 from his 401(k) account. Six years later, that loan is still outstanding and no interest has been paid. To the IRS, this looks like a distribution that's subject to income tax and perhaps a 10% penalty, if Jack was younger than 59½ when he received the money.

A Fast $50,000

If all the necessary paperwork is in place, retirement plan participants usually can borrow as much as 100% of their plan balance, up to $10,000. If their plan balance is over $20,000, a plan loan can be as much as half of the vested benefits, up to a maximum of $50,000. Therefore, many clients can borrow up to $50,000.

Excess loans are considered taxable distributions. There are rules in place that prevent someone from borrowing $50,000, repaying that amount, and borrowing another $50,000 right away. Thus, clients should work with a tax adviser to avoid excess loans.

If a plan loan is secured by a personal residence and the proceeds are used to purchase the house, the term may exceed 5 years. In some circumstances, the interest on a plan loan secured by a home can be tax deductible, although interest on retirement plan loans generally is not deductible.

Moreover, not all clients will be able to borrow from their tax-deferred retirement plans because plan loans cannot be extended to "owner-employees," unless an exemption is obtained from the Department of Labor. For the purpose of this rule, clients are considered owner-employees (1) if they're self-employed; (2) if their business is a partnership and they have a stake that's over 10%; or (3) if their business is an S corporation and they have a stake that's over 5%. Thus, business owners and professionals are most likely to be able to borrow if they're treated as employees of a C corporation rather than an S corporation. No matter what the client's business structure, borrowing from an IRA or Keogh plan isn't allowed.

An owner-employee who borrows improperly may run into a penalty that's 5% of the applicable interest charges. This penalty is applied to the borrower, not to the plan. What's more, this penalty is assessed for each year until the transaction is corrected (the loan is repaid). If the transaction is not fully corrected by the time a tax deficiency notice is mailed by the IRS, a 100% penalty may be assessed.

Opportunity Costs

Therefore, clients must be extremely careful when they borrow from a qualified plan. Assuming that they are entitled to borrow from their plan and they intend to play by the rules, should they do so? The thought of effectively borrowing from yourself and paying yourself back can be enticing. A $30,000 auto loan might trigger interest payments of about $20,000 over 5 years. If a client borrows from a plan to buy a car, that $20,000 goes to the client's retirement fund, not to a bank or finance company.

But borrowing from a retirement plan has drawbacks, too. Anyone who defaults on a plan loan will have taxable income from the distribution. Such a default may be triggered whenever the borrower misses an installment payment. The entire outstanding loan balance may become taxable income at that time, so borrowers must be extremely careful.

Clients who borrow from a qualified plan should arrange to have loan repayments withheld from their paychecks. Similarly, if a client parts with his employer and no longer participates in the plan, he must repay the loan or take the unpaid balance as taxable income. Another disadvantage of plan loans: The retirement plan will be a lien holder on the client's personal residence, if the loan is secured by the house.

Perhaps most important, the client's retirement plan will earn a relatively low rate if it loans money to the client. Long-term, the client's account probably will earn more by investing in stocks. When a client borrows from a plan, assets are liquidated and the proceeds are loaned to the client, so the loan becomes the retirement plan's investment rather than stocks, bonds, or mutual funds. Thus, borrowing today may lead to a leaner retirement tomorrow.

Borrowing from a retirement plan may pose additional dangers. If there's no payroll deduction in place, borrowers may not take repayment as seriously as they would with a bank loan. Even well-intentioned borrowers may go astray. A client might lose a job and be unable to repay the outstanding plan loan. If so, he'll wind up owing income taxes and the 10% penalty tax.

Plus Signs

Nevertheless, there may be times when borrowing from a plan makes sense. If a client has an important short-term cash need and the proper authorization is in place, a loan from a qualified plan can be a valuable convenience, especially if no other credit lines are available. (Often, clients are better off borrowing on a home equity line of credit, where the interest probably is deductible.)

Take the example of Larry Franklin, who intended to send his son Ken to a public university and who expected financial aid to be available. As it turned out, Ken chose a private college while Larry's income and net worth had grown to the point where the family didn't qualify for aid. Larry needed a great deal of money so he borrowed from his retirement plan.

In Larry's retirement plan, borrowing was limited to two outstanding loans. Thus, instead of borrowing each year, Larry borrowed two years' worth of expenses the first year and a similar amount two years later.

Borrowing from a qualified plan for increased consumption is not likely to help clients in the long term—no one should borrow $150 to buy a television set. However, borrowing may be justified for an investment, a capital improvement, or to take the place of a loan that otherwise would have to come from a third party.

Better Than Bonds

It's true that a plan loan likely will not offer the return of a stock market investment, long term, but not every retirement account is fully invested in stocks. Some clients put a portion of their 401(k) money into bond funds or stable income accounts such as guaranteed income contracts (GICs). In these circumstances, the clients might be better off borrowing some money and repaying the plan with interest, assuring a 9% or a 10% return on that portion of their accounts.

Thus, a retirement plan loan may be considered a proxy for a bond fund or bond-type investment. Because such loans are limited to 5 years, they're the equivalent of short-term bonds and they might be appropriate in specific situations.

Say a client has some 401(k) money invested in a GIC or short-term bond fund yielding 5% or 6% while also paying 9% or 10% on a non-deductible college loan. This client would be better off borrowing from his retirement account rather than from a bank. As long as he has to borrow anyway, why not direct the interest payments to his retirement account while locking in greater earnings on the fixed-income portion of his retirement plan?

What are some other situations in which a retirement plan loan can work? People who have poor credit might use such loans. For example, Ann Brown couldn't get any credit after she went through a divorce so she used a plan loan to help buy a house. In addition, wiping out or avoiding credit card debt is a valid use for a retirement plan loan, if the borrower avoids running up new credit card balances in the future.

Leery Lenders

If a client's business or professional practice sponsors a qualified plan, should you recommend that it include a loan provision, even if the client might never borrow money personally? Many plan sponsors don't allow loans or limit them severely. There's an administrative burden to making sure loan applications are accepted or rejected fairly as well as a procedure that must be followed for collecting loans in default or loans from former employees who have left the plan.

Administering plan loans can be a chore but it may be worthwhile, especially for clients who sponsor 401(k) plans that rely on voluntary contributions. For low or moderately paid employees, the thought of putting their money away for many years can be intimidating. If they think they'll be able to borrow from the plan, in case the money is needed, they'll be more willing to participate.

Such participation not only helps employees build a retirement fund, it may enable client-sponsors to increase their own contributions under federal regulations governing retirement plans. Moreover, loan costs should be minimal—typically, under $100—and they may be passed on to the borrower.

The basic guideline for offering plan loans as a sponsor is the same as borrowing as a participant. Employers have to follow the rules scrupulously or pay stiff penalties. Otherwise, employers and employees alike are just borrowing trouble.

In the Penalty Box

The requirements covering plan loans are not the only complex rules relating to retirement plans. Indeed, the IRS and the Department of Labor have established extensive regulations as to what plan sponsors can do with the plan money. Some sponsors forget that money in a retirement plan is not "their money" any longer—they may not realize that they're not allowed to use that money for personal or business purposes.

Clients who break the rules will owe nondeductible penalties, which can become incredibly steep. The tax code spells out specific prohibited transactions in its provisions on retirement plans. When plan sponsors fill out IRS Form 5500 each year, as required, they're specifically asked about prohibited transactions.

As mentioned, entering into a prohibited transaction incurs a 5% penalty; if that error is not corrected in a relatively short time, an additional penalty may be assessed for 100% of the amount of the transaction.

In addition, federal law enables the Department of Labor to assess a minimum 20% civil penalty against any plan fiduciary or any other person involved in a fiduciary breach, although that penalty is reduced to the extent of IRS penalties assessed.

Penalties for prohibited transactions may be imposed regardless of whether the violation was inadvertent or entered into in good faith. The penalties apply even if the plan makes money from the prohibited transactions and even if an individual was acting on the advice of an attorney or accountant.

Disqualifying Tests

With penalties potentially so severe, you should know how to avoid them. Prohibited transactions are those between retirement plans and "disqualified persons." The latter term refers to:

- The employer of any plan participant.
- Individuals who control 50% or more of the enterprise, directly or indirectly.
- Plan fiduciaries, including investment advisors.
- Plan service providers, including lawyers, accountants, and actuaries.
- Unions whose members are plan participants.
- Officers, directors, 10%+ shareholders, or highly compensated employees of corporations that are disqualified parties.
- Any spouse, ancestor, lineal descendant, or spouse of a lineal descendant of a disqualified person.

Thus, most clients who sponsor qualified plans are disqualified persons.

Suppose one of your clients, a business owner, sells property to his company's retirement plan, expecting that the property will appreciate. That's a prohibited transaction, regardless of the intent or the result.

Similarly, if a client exchanges property for assets already in the plan, such a transactions is prohibited, regardless of whether the property is fairly valued. In fact, even if a client sells property to a qualified plan at a bargain price, it would be a prohibited transaction.

Say a client has just purchased a new house. He can't sell his present house on the open market and he needs cash so he sells the house, valued at $400,000, to his qualified plan for $300,000. Eventually, he hopes, the plan will sell the house and keep any profit.

However, this is a prohibited transaction. The client would owe a $15,000 penalty (5% of $300,000). What's more, a 90-day "correction period" ends 90 days after the IRS mails out a deficiency notice. If the plan cannot undo the transaction within that 90 days, it will owe a $300,000 penalty.

Another common error occurs when a retirement plan buys stock of the sponsoring corporation. To do so, there has to be a special provision in the plan documents. Most prototype plans, which are widely used by small employers, do not include permission for the plan to buy company stock.

The bottom line is that self-dealing should be avoided by qualified plans. As a fiduciary, a business owner or professional is compelled to invest with the plan's best interests in mind—and he can't do that when buying from or selling to himself. Especially if a client serves as trustee to a plan, his first loyalty must be to the trust rather than to his own pocket.

Out-of-Bounds

What other types of transactions are prohibited? Loans or extensions of credit between a plan and a disqualified person are not allowed and neither is the furnishing of goods, services, or facilities between these parties. In essence, clients can't use plan assets or income for their own benefit. Even if they make a plan contribution one week and need cash the next, they can't just pull the money out.

There are some circumstances in which plan sponsors can borrow from a pension or profit-sharing plan, as explained previously, but the

IRS has been known to take a hard look at this area. For example, in two letter rulings, the IRS disapproved loans to a partnership in which a plan trustee was a 39% partner and loans to clients of a law firm sponsoring a plan. In both cases, it made no difference whether the loans were properly drawn up or repaid. The IRS closely scrutinizes any nontraditional use of plan assets.

A 1993 Supreme Court decision further tightened the rules on prohibited transactions. Now, anyone who contributes real estate or equipment to a plan, instead of cash, risks running into prohibited transaction penalties.

The tax code clearly states that "encumbered" (mortgaged) property cannot be contributed to a retirement plan by a disqualified person. However, in 1983 and 1984, Keystone Consolidated Industries contributed unencumbered property to defined benefit plans. The IRS called these contributions prohibited transactions but the tax court and a federal appeals court held for Keystone. The Supreme Court, though, took the side of the IRS. The Court ruled that mandatory contributions of property are considered a prohibited transaction, referring to the fact that these plans had minimum funding obligations. Thus, giving property to defined benefit plans likely will be prohibited. Giving property that's not mortgaged to a profit-sharing plan in which contributions are voluntary may be valid but the rules are tricky here, so clients may want to avoid such transactions.

Sour Notes

Contributing accounts receivable can get plan sponsors into trouble, too. One self-employed real estate broker gave $114,000 worth (at face value) of third-party promissory notes to his one-person defined benefit plan. The tax court upheld his deduction but an appeals court reversed it, saying that such contributions are potentially abusive.

Leasing is a potential problem area that's often overlooked. Leasing property between a disqualified person and a qualified plan is prohibited. Moreover, the consequences of such transactions are especially severe because of the manner in which the amount involved is computed for leases. The penalty is in effect for each year of the lease.

Suppose, for example, a client wanted to acquire new computer equipment for her small business. Instead of borrowing the money or leasing the equipment directly, she has her retirement plan buy the equipment and lease it to the business. Now, the business gets to use the equipment and the plan gets a stream of future revenues.

Unfortunately, such transactions are prohibited. If there's a 5-year lease, with payments of $10,000 per year, there would be a prohibited transaction of $50,000 the first year. On the first day of the next tax year, there would be a $40,000 prohibited transaction. And so on. Thus, leasing property from a retirement plan can be disastrous.

Naturally, you should advise clients to be meticulous. The more of a paper trail they leave, the greater their chances of demonstrating that they've acted prudently, in case of a dispute. All plans are required to have a written statement of objectives, spelling out specific goals. If loans are made to key employees, there should be a record of the terms of those loans, placing them in the framework of the plan's overall objectives (for example, an 8% annual return).

What if you discover that a client already has entered into a prohibited transaction? You should advise him to undo such transactions as rapidly as possible to avoid spilling over into another tax year. Generally, that means reversing the prohibited transaction. For example, if a client has sold real estate to a qualified plan, the sale must be rescinded and the property's full value must be returned to the plan. If a plan sells the property for less than it paid, the disqualified person is required to make sure the plan is in no worse financial position than it would have been in otherwise.

Because of all the possible complications, clients are better off giving cash to a retirement plan and letting the money stay there, invested in high-quality stocks and bonds. In addition to the prohibited transaction rules mentioned previously, clients who sponsor qualified plans have a fiduciary responsibility to invest prudently, on behalf of participants. If they don't invest prudently, they're vulnerable to employee lawsuits as well as penalties from the IRS and the Department of Labor.

If you recommend that clients contribute cash and invest plan money sensibly, you may help your clients dodge all the pitfalls, provide for their workers, and wind up with a healthy balance in their own retirement accounts.

SUMMARY

- Clients may like the idea of borrowing from a retirement plan, tax free, and paying themselves back, with interest.

- Generally, such loans are not recommended because they may stunt the growth of a client's retirement funds.

- Nevertheless, plan loans may be appropriate for clients who have a genuine need for ready cash and who otherwise would borrow from a third party.

- Owner-employees may not be able to borrow from their retirement plans.

- Certain plans, including IRAs and Keoghs, do not permit loans.

- In addition, owner-employees are generally prohibited from entering into transactions with their retirement plans, a prohibition that extends to relatives as well.

- Because of all the regulations, clients who sponsor retirement plans should contribute cash rather than property, in most circumstances.

Putting the Pieces Together

Savvy Asset Allocation Strategies

Stocks, bonds, and cash equivalents are the basic building blocks for constructing sound portfolios for clients. Most financial advisors counsel clients to blend these asset classes to create a smooth path to long-term wealth building. Indeed, you may well go beyond stocks-bonds-cash to recommend specific allocations for, say, large-cap stocks or foreign bonds.

However, there's often one more piece to the asset allocation puzzle. If a client has substantial funds to invest inside a tax-deferred retirement account as well as outside such a plan, what goes where? Do the large-cap stocks belong in the IRA? The foreign bonds in a personal, taxable account?

As might be expected, the answers depend largely on the client's circumstances. For example, consider Joe Adams. Everything he has to invest is held inside his company's retirement plan so no taxes are due, no matter where he invests or how often he trades.

Joe needs to have a complete portfolio inside his retirement plan. Because stocks have consistently outperformed bonds, Joe might hold about 75% of his retirement plan in stocks and stock funds with the other 25% in bonds. What's more, a good portion of those stock market holdings should be outside the United States, for the following reasons:

- Not all of the best companies are inside the United States. If Joe limits himself to American companies, he might be overlooking some outstanding investments.

- Investing outside the United States may increase returns, if foreign stocks perform well.

- Regardless of performance, risk will be reduced because foreign markets aren't correlated with the U.S. market. They move out of sync, smoothing out year-to-year returns for Joe's overall portfolio.

Based on historical evidence, Joe can minimize his risk by investing about 25% of his portfolio in foreign stocks. Of that 25%, he wants 5% in emerging markets, where long-term growth may be exceptional.

Know Where to Hold 'Em

Penny Bell's situation is the same, yet different. Again, she wants a portfolio that's 75% stocks, 25% bonds. Of her 75% in stocks, she wants the same split among domestic, international, and emerging markets stocks. Thus, her desired portfolio is the same as Joe's: roughly 50% in domestic stocks, 20% in international stocks, 5% in emerging markets stocks, and 25% in bonds. Penny has to put half of her holdings inside a retirement plan and half outside of her plan. What goes where?

To start with, Penny probably will do best to hold her 25% international allocation outside of her plan. This will keep her from losing a tax break.

Whether Penny invests through individual foreign stocks or foreign mutual funds, dividends she receives may be reduced by withholding of foreign taxes. For example, if Penny receives $600 in foreign dividends in 1999, $90 (15%) might be withheld by the host countries. She'll receive one or more Forms 1099-DIV, showing the foreign taxes withheld. Then, Penny will have the option of deducting that $90 as an itemized tax paid or claiming a $90 credit for foreign taxes. (Claiming the credit usually works out better.)

However, if Penny invests through her company's qualified retirement plan, she won't receive a Form 1099 and won't be able to deduct foreign taxes or claim a credit. Therefore, the foreign taxes investors pay are a dead loss inside a retirement plan. (The same holds true for foreign investments inside IRAs.) For that reason, Penny decides to hold her foreign stocks, which make up 25% of her total portfolio, in her personal, taxable account.

What about the other 75% of her portfolio? Penny still has to invest 50% in domestic stocks and 25% in bonds. Where do they go?

One approach is to fill out her taxable account with tax-exempt bonds. With $1 million altogether, Penny holds $500,000 outside of her plan, including $250,000 in foreign stocks. The other $250,000 (25% of her portfolio) could be in munis. Then, $500,000 (50%) could be held in domestic stocks, inside the plan.

That's the standard strategy, but that may not be a good plan, taxwise, for two reasons. First, the retirement plan tax shelter may be wasted on domestic stocks and stock funds. Penny is a buy-and-hold investor, not a trader. She emphasizes low-dividend stocks and stock funds, aiming for growth rather than current income. Therefore, her stock market portfolio doesn't generate much in the way of income tax each year.

Suppose her $500,000 in domestic stocks generates $10,000 (2%) in investment income each year. Holding the stocks inside a plan saves her only $4,000 per year, assuming a 40% tax bracket, a meager amount on a $500,000 holding.

Second, she may lose the advantage of long-term gains by holding stocks inside a plan. In the future, Penny plans to sell the (hopefully appreciated) stocks to help provide retirement income. Because she has emphasized growth in her stocks, rather than dividends, she expects to be rewarded with substantial gains over a 10-year holding period or longer.

If those stocks are held outside of a retirement plan, those gains would largely be long term, eligible for favorable tax treatment (depending on the tax laws in effect at the time the gains are realized). Under present law, the federal income tax on long-term gains is capped at 20%.

However, when long-term gains are realized inside a retirement plan, the proceeds are taxed as ordinary income when they're withdrawn. The tax rates will depend on the tax laws then in effect and Penny's income in retirement. Assuming today's laws are still in effect, Penny could be converting a 20% tax bill into a 31%, a 36%, or even a 39.6% tax bill by holding stocks inside a retirement plan.

Moreover, the same two reasons strengthen the case for holding foreign stocks outside of a retirement plan, in addition to the foreign-tax offset issue mentioned previously.

So how might Penny structure a tax-wise portfolio? Perhaps like this:

Inside plan		*Outside plan*	
Bonds	25%	Foreign Stocks	25%
Domestic Stocks	25%	Domestic Stocks	25%

The bonds held inside the plan should be taxable, perhaps a mix of Treasuries, corporates, and mortgage-backed securities (for example, Ginnie Maes). Also, the domestic stocks and stock funds held inside the plan could be those that generate the highest dividends.

If Penny wants to include utility stocks, oils, banks, real estate investment trusts (REITs), and other high-yielding stocks in her portfolio, this is the place they should go. Generally, larger companies are more likely to pay substantial dividends.

Altogether, the stocks and bonds inside the plan might pay an average of 5% from interest and dividends. That's $25,000 per year on $500,000: At a 40% tax rate, the shelter is worth $10,000 per year—much more shelter than the $4,000 annual tax savings she'd enjoy by holding all her domestic stocks inside the plan.

Outside the plan, along with foreign stocks, can go the domestic stocks and stock funds that pay low or no dividends. Therefore, the annual tax bill likely will be scant. (The foreign tax credit reduces the tax bill, too.) When the time comes to sell holdings and use the proceeds for retirement income, any profits probably will be favorably taxed as long-term capital gains.

If there is no need to sell the securities in the taxable account until Penny's death, she can leave them to her spouse or to their children. The survivors will inherit with a step-up in basis to market value. Thus, they can sell the shares after Penny's death and owe no tax at all on the prior appreciation.

By contrast, anything that comes out of the retirement plan is fully subject to income tax, after as well as before Penny's death. That's yet another reason to hold assets that are likely to appreciate outside of a qualified plan or an IRA.

The Inside Story

Not every client's asset will fit so neatly into an inside-outside formulation. To help you deal with the gray areas, here are some guidelines. They're especially suitable for those clients who (1) have a regular, taxable account and a tax-deferred retirement account and (2) do most of their investing in mutual funds.

Clients who invest in municipal bond funds should never hold them in a tax-deferred account. They'll convert tax-exempt interest to taxable interest when they pull money out of the plan.

Cash reserves should be kept in a money market fund (perhaps a tax-exempt money market fund) outside of the plan. Doing so increases access to these funds without paying taxes or penalties. Many of your clients will prefer tax-exempt money market funds because a top-bracket investor will do better earning, say, 3% in a tax-exempt money fund than 5% in a taxable fund. Again, tax-exempt funds (including tax-exempt money market funds) don't belong in a tax-deferred retirement plan.

Taxable bond funds, including junk bond funds, belong inside the plan. The plan provides shelter for the high level of income these funds generate.

Among stock funds, clients should put the most tax-efficient funds outside the plan. For example, Schwab 1000 Fund tracks the Schwab 1000 Index of the largest public companies. From its inception in 1991 through 1998, the fund paid out 1–2% per year in income dividends and never distributed any capital gains. (Turnover is virtually nil at this buy-and-hold fund.) Holding this fund inside a retirement plan would be a mistake because the plan's tax shelter would be wasted. Indeed, many index funds are good choices for your taxable accounts.

In general, "growth-oriented" funds are more tax-efficient than "value-oriented" funds while "small-company" funds are more tax-efficient than "large-company" funds. Thus, clients will probably want to hold small-company growth funds in a taxable account. Moreover, small-company growth funds tend to be volatile. If they lose ground, clients can sell them and use the tax losses to offset gains elsewhere, which they can't do with funds held in a retirement plan.

The least tax-efficient funds belong inside retirement plans. American Century Value Fund, for example, is a solid fund, returning almost 18% per year (pretax) for the 5 years through 1998. However, the fund frequently makes sizable capital gains distributions so a top-bracket investor would have netted only 12.5% aftertax: 30% of the pretax return would have been lost. Such funds are better off held in a tax-deferred retirement plan.

An increasing number of funds are designed specifically to trim investors' taxes. They offset gains with losses or they sell high-basis shares when reducing a position in a given company.

Beyond funds that are intentionally tax-efficient, funds that trade their stocks infrequently tend to be more tax-efficient. For example, MFS Massachusetts Investors Growth Stock Fund "outperformed" IDS New Dimensions Fund, over the 10 years through 1998, 21.25% to 19.90% in annual total return. Aftertax, though, the IDS fund has actually done better, 17.98% to 16.95%. For one reason, the tax-efficient IDS New Dimensions Fund has had turnover rates from 32% to 38% in recent years while MFS Massachusetts Investors Growth Stock Fund has posted turnover rates of 93% and 107%. (A fund with a 100% turnover rate holds each investment for an average of one year before selling it.)

The higher a fund's turnover rate and the greater its annual capital gains distribution, the better the fit inside a tax-deferred plan. Inside the plan, those distributions can be sheltered. In the foregoing example, the IDS fund would fit well outside of a tax-deferred plan while the MFS fund probably belongs inside a plan.

Moreover, high-dividend stock funds (utility funds, real estate funds) belong inside a retirement plan, where the distributions can be sheltered.

Many clients do most of their tax-deferred investing through a 401(k) or similar plan. Although the situation is changing, many 401(k)s offer only a few options The client may have to direct 401(k) money into the best of those options, and that choice may determine which assets go inside and which go outside. For example, if a client chooses a large-company fund for a 401(k) because it's the superior choice among the funds offered, a small-cap may have to be bought outside the plan, with after-tax dollars.

More Than Mutual Funds

The following inside-out strategies may apply to clients whose holdings go beyond mutual funds:

- Clients who mix individual securities and mutual funds should hold the mutual funds inside their retirement plan, where capital gains distributions can be sheltered. Stock funds tend to generate higher yearly tax obligations than individual stocks. Most stock funds trade their portfolios and they're required to distribute net trading gains, which are taxable to investors. Individual stocks, however, may be bought and held, so the only taxable income is dividends—inconsequential for many growth stocks.

- Clients who buy and sell stocks frequently should hold those stocks in a retirement plan where any trading gains can be sheltered. Similarly, clients whose money is professionally managed may want to put those holdings most likely to be actively traded inside a tax-deferred retirement plan.

- If clients intend to give away assets to family members to reduce their taxable estate, they're better off giving away unappreciated assets, such as bonds and bond fund shares, so those securities should be held on the outside. Appreciated securities held outside a retirement plan can be used for tax-efficient charitable donations.

- Variable annuities (sometimes called tax-deferred wrappers for mutual funds) belong on the outside. These investments allow investors to choose among "subaccounts" (which resemble mutual funds) and defer the income tax until money is withdrawn. Thus, there is no reason to hold a tax-deferred annuity inside a tax-deferred retirement account. The same reasoning applies to fixed annuities. However, in certain situations deferred annuities with enhanced principal guarantees can be included inside a tax-deferred account. (This might be the case if the client is not sophisticated and values the guaranteed return.)

- If clients are likely to need bond interest for living expenses in retirement, those bonds should be held outside of a plan for easier access. Clients can spend the interest income without having to pay tax on retirement plan distributions.

- Collectibles, such as artwork and antiques, should be held outside of a plan. Such items pose valuation problems and are prohibited from some types of plans, such as IRAs.

SUMMARY

- The following types of securities should be held *inside* a tax-deferred retirement plan:
    - Taxable bonds and bond funds, including junk bonds
    - High-dividend stocks, including REITs
    - Stock funds, for clients who hold a mix of stock funds and individual stocks
    - Tax-inefficient stock funds, which might include small-cap funds and growth funds
    - High-turnover stock funds
    - Stocks in an actively traded account
    - Professionally managed money
- The following types of securities should be held *outside* a tax-deferred retirement plan:
    - Cash equivalents, including money market funds
    - Municipal bonds and municipal bond funds
    - Foreign stocks and stock funds
    - Individual stock, for clients who hold a mix of stock funds and individual stocks
    - Tax-efficient stock funds, including index funds and low-turnover funds
    - Bond fund shares meant to be used for lifetime gifts to family members.
    - Appreciable assets meant to be used for charitable gifts
    - Appreciable assets meant to be bequeathed to heirs
    - Variable and fixed deferred annuities, although some annuities with strong guarantees may be held inside plans.

CHAPTER 7

Taking Over

IRA Rollovers, Roth IRA Conversions, and Other Shrewd Strategies

In the previous chapters we described ways to help clients accumulate a sizable amount in a tax-deferred retirement account. Retirement accounts, naturally, are meant to support a comfortable retirement. The next chapters tell you how to help clients get from here to there: the best ways to cash in those retirement accounts.

After clients retire (or when they change jobs), they'll have to decide what to do with the money in their retirement plan. Here are the options:

Take a lump-sum withdrawal. Many plans offer participants the chance to receive their balance all at once. If they choose this option they'll receive their money but they'll immediately owe income tax on that money, plus a 10% penalty tax if they're not yet 59½.

In some circumstances, though, clients can use income averaging to reduce the tax bite:

- Ten-year averaging is available to clients who were born before 1936.

- Five-year averaging is available to clients who are at least 59½ years old, but can't be used after 1999.

Either way, clients recognize taxable income in the year they receive the money. However, they pay tax at lower rates.

The way the math works, averaging is truly effective only for distributions under $100,000. Therefore, some clients might want to put a small retirement plan balance into their pocket, assuming they qualify for 5- or 10-year averaging. Otherwise, the only reason for clients to cash in a retirement plan is to fill an important need for ready cash. They might want to pay off debts, for example, or make a down payment on a retirement home.

Take an annuity. Some plans offer to convert participants' account balances into an income stream after retirement. Annuitants usually receive such payments each month for their lifetime and perhaps for a spouse's lifetime as well. In most cases, annuity payments are taxable. The major advantage to receiving an annuity is security. Clients know that retirement income will never stop.

However, some employers pay relatively low annuities to their retirees. If receiving an annuity appeals to some of your clients, they may be better off rolling the plan balance into an IRA, as explained later in this section. Then they can use the money in the IRA to buy the most attractive annuity, after shopping among insurance companies.

Generally, annuities don't appeal to sophisticated clients, who'll regret the lack of access to principal and the absence of inflation protection. Recently, some companies have begun to offer better deals on annuities—access to principal and variable annuitization schedules that can provide an inflation hedge—and these contracts often are superior to fixed-payout annuities.

Transfer to a new plan. Clients who are changing jobs may be able to roll the money from their old employer's plan to their new employer's plan. Such a rollover maintains the tax deferral.

Inside the new employer's plan, the account will enjoy more protection from creditors, compared to a rollover IRA. In many cases, courts have been reluctant to attach balances in employer-sponsored plans such as 401(k)s to satisfy creditors' claims. IRAs enjoy some protection, depending on state law, but as a group they don't enjoy the protection of employer-sponsored plans.

Another benefit may result from a transfer to a new employer's plan. If cash is needed, participants may be able to borrow a certain amount, tax free, with little hassle; again, an IRA does not offer this feature. However, neither you nor your clients have control of their money if they roll a retirement plan balance into a new employer's plan. In most cases there are restrictions on the access your clients will have to this money.

Therefore, the attractiveness of this option depends on specific circumstances. If your client's new employer has an outstanding plan, consider such a transfer.

Roll over to an IRA. For most clients, this choice is the best. After the rollover, you can advise your clients and help them invest virtually any way that seems desirable while the tax deferral is maintained.

Partial IRA rollovers provide the same advantages. Suppose, for example, Ken Green retires with $400,000 in his plan and he needs $100,000 to clean up credit card debt and to make a down payment on a vacation home. Ken could roll over $250,000 to an IRA while taking the remaining $150,000 in cash. On that $150,000, assuming a 33% effective tax rate, he'd wind up with $100,000, enough for his cash needs.

Although an IRA rollover or a partial rollover may well be the best choice, you shouldn't advise your clients to execute a rollover without making them aware of these disadvantages:

- In some states, IRAs don't enjoy the same creditor protection as an employer-sponsored plan.

- Borrowing from an IRA is not permitted.

- Money that has been rolled into an IRA is not eligible for 5- or 10-year averaging.

Convert to a Roth IRA. After rolling over a plan balance into an IRA, clients can convert that IRA to a Roth IRA. For more on Roth IRA conversions, see the subsequent section, "Rolling to a Roth."

Planning Pointers

Married clients probably will need their spouse's written acceptance of the choice that's elected. Without such consent, a rollover may be invalidated and the entire amount might become taxable income, especially in community property states, which treat retirement plan assets acquired during a marriage as belonging equally to both spouses.

Whenever clients execute any type of rollover, they shouldn't take personal possession of their funds. Instead, they should ask for a direct (trustee-to-trustee) rollover to an IRA or a new employer's plan.

Unless there's a direct rollover, the former employer will be forced to withhold 20%. Then the client must make up the difference from other funds or else owe income tax (and perhaps a 10% penalty) on the amount that was withheld.

Taking Stock of Company Stock

When you're advising clients about IRA rollovers, you may need to be selective about the assets involved. Many employees of publicly held corporations hold company stock in their tax-deferred plans, including 401(k)s. Thanks to a booming stock market, that stock may be highly appreciated.

If such clients sell those shares and withdraw the cash, they'll owe tax at ordinary income rates, up to 39.6%. The tax break for long-term capital gains will be lost. Moreover, the same tax advantage will be lost if those clients roll their retirement plan account into an IRA and eventually pull out cash. Instead, your clients can pull the actual shares out of the company-sponsored plan. If they do, they'll owe tax only on imputed compensation—the price of the stock when contributions were made. The appreciation won't be taxed until the shares are sold and capital gains rates (probably 20%) will apply.

Suppose, for example, Margie Miller's retirement account includes 2,000 shares of her employer's stock, now selling for $40 per share. The company's basis in those shares (the price when contributions were made) is $12 per share. If Margie pulls those 2,000 shares from her plan, she'll recognize $24,000 worth of ordinary income (2,000 shares times $12). However, the appreciation from $12 to $40—and any subsequent appreciation—will be taxed as a capital gain.

Mission: Control

What can be done with the $80,000 worth of shares Margie now holds, in this example?

She can hold on.   No further tax will be due as long as she retains the shares.

She can sell some or all of the shares.   Margie's basis, in this example, is $12 per share. If she eventually sells the shares for $60 apiece, her $48-per-share gain likely will be taxed at a bargain 20% rate.

She can use the shares to fund a charitable remainder trust or charitable gift annuity.   Employer stock withdrawn from a retirement plan can be used in these planned giving strategies. Indeed, the IRS has supported such a strategy in a private ruling. (For details, see Chapter 17.) Giving these shares to charity will permit Margie and her husband to receive a lifetime income, based on the full appreciated value of the shares, as well as a partial income tax deduction and the chance to benefit a favored cause, which eventually will receive a contribution. With a remainder trust, some of the income they receive will be taxed at capital gains rates. (This strategy works even better for high-net-worth individuals, where the difference between ordinary income and capital gains taxes can be significant [see Appendix B].)

Withdrawing employer stock from a retirement plan offers tax advantages but there are risks, too. Clients who hold on to their shares may be severely exposed to future declines in that one stock. This risk can be reduced by selling or donating the shares.

Another way to reduce the risk of concentration is to mix a withdrawal with a rollover. For example, instead of withdrawing all 2,000 shares, Margie might withdraw 1,200 shares, pay the tax, and hold on. The remaining 800 shares can remain in her plan, which she'll roll to an IRA. After the rollover, she won't qualify for the tax break just described, so she might as well sell those 800 shares of employer stock and reinvest in other issues.

Rolling to a Roth

After your clients roll over the money in their retirement plan to an IRA, they have yet another option to consider: converting that IRA (or part of it) to a Roth IRA. Most employer-sponsored plans, such as 401(k)s, don't permit "in-service" rollovers. Thus, clients probably will have to leave their company, by changing jobs or retiring, in order to roll their plan balance into a traditional IRA. Then, conversion to a Roth IRA may take place any year in which income doesn't exceed $100,000. In fact, some planning may be desirable to keep income below $100,000 so that a conversion may take place.

Converting a regular IRA to a Roth IRA triggers all the deferred income tax. Subsequently, clients can enjoy both tax-free buildup and tax-free withdrawals, as long as they keep all earnings in the Roth IRA for five years *and* until age 59½. There are no required withdrawals from a Roth IRA so clients can maintain the tax-free buildup throughout their lifetime, if desired.

Even before age 59½ or the 5-year mark, principal can be withdrawn, free of income tax. However, withdrawals of that principal may be subject to the 10% penalty tax before age 59½. Suppose, for example, that Linda Farrell converts a $100,000 regular IRA to a Roth IRA when she's 50 years old, paying the required income tax. Subsequently, the first $100,000 she withdraws from her Roth IRA are considered a nontaxable return of principal, but those same withdrawals before she reaches 59½ are subject to the 10% penalty tax.

Fortunately, the normal exceptions to the early withdrawal penalty for IRAs apply to converted Roth IRAs. These include:

- Death
- Disability
- Substantially equal periodic payments received over the IRA owner's life expectancy

- Certain expenses related to first-time home purchases
- Higher education outlays

In general, a Roth IRA conversion probably makes sense for clients who expect to let the money grow for at least 10 years before any withdrawals. Such conversions work best for clients who can pay the upfront tax with non-IRA money, keeping the Roth IRA intact.

Advisors need to be diligent about Roth IRAs. For example, you should warn clients about making an improper Roth IRA conversion. Such conversions are not allowed if income is over $100,000 that year, on a single or joint return, and that amount includes required minimum distributions from a traditional IRA for clients who are $70\frac{1}{2}$ or older. A 1998 tax law provides relief, but not until 2005.

As an example, say Mike Nelson turned $70\frac{1}{2}$ in June 1999. At the end of 1998, his IRA balance was $1 million. Based on his life expectancy and that of his spouse, his first required minimum distribution is $45,454. Mike decides to make that withdrawal in April 2000, as permitted by law.

Aside from that required withdrawal, Mike's AGI in 1999 is $70,000. Thus, he's eligible for a Roth IRA conversion—if he can exclude the required minimum IRA distribution. Apparently, however, the IRS will assert that the $45,454 must be added to Mike's 1999 AGI, putting him over the $100,000 limit for Roth IRA conversions that year.

Under legislation passed in 1998, required minimum distributions won't be accelerated in this manner, but this doesn't take effect until 2005. Until then, clients risk a disallowance of a Roth IRA conversion if they disregard income from a required IRA distribution.

Some tax pros think the IRS is off base on this issue. Nevertheless, you and your clients are risking a tax disaster by converting to a Roth IRA in the foregoing circumstances. Income should be monitored carefully if clients are considering a Roth IRA conversion.

Once a traditional IRA has been converted to a Roth IRA, there are no required minimum distributions. Thus, if the money is not needed by the client, the Roth IRA can be left to the spouse and then to their children, for decades of tax-free cash flow. Therefore, converting to a Roth often makes sense for wealthy clients. However, those clients will have estate tax concerns, so it's vital to advise them to have liquid funds available for estate tax, just as is the case with a regular IRA. This liquidity enables the Roth IRA to remain intact and extends the tax-free wealth building for subsequent generations. (For more on Roth IRAs, see Chapter 4.)

Good Timing

On the positive side, if income goes over the $100,000 mark, a Roth IRA conversion can be rescinded, right up until the time of filing the relevant tax return, including extensions. Suppose, for example, that Bob Harris converts a regular IRA to a Roth IRA in 1999. Due to unforeseen circumstances, he winds up 1999 with more than $100,000 in income, making him ineligible for the conversion. When he files his 1999 tax return in 2000, he can treat the Roth IRA conversion as if it never happened, provided he transfers the money back to his regular IRA before the filing date (including extensions).

Roth IRA conversions may be more appealing in years that the stock market has fallen. That is, if an IRA was worth $500,000 in January but only $400,000 in December, a year-end conversion would cost "only" $160,000, rather than $200,000, assuming a 40% rate.

What if a client converted this IRA in January? The tax bill is determined by the value of the IRA as of the date of the conversion. Thus, it makes sense to rescind the transaction, take the Roth IRA back to a traditional IRA, then reconvert with the IRA balance at $400,000. However, such reconversions can be done only once in 1999. Beginning in the year 2000, reconversions can't take place in the same tax year: Clients who "recharacterize" a Roth IRA back to a traditional IRA must wait until the next tax year or 30 days, whichever comes later.

Thus, if Bob Harris converts his IRA to a Roth IRA in January 2000, then goes back to a traditional IRA on December 31 because the value of his IRA has fallen, he must wait at least until February 2001 to reconvert and hope that the market doesn't take off in the meantime.

What if Bob converts an IRA to a Roth IRA and dies before he can reverse the transaction? Can the executor recharacterize the transaction, if that's desirable? The answer is not clear. Or what if he becomes incapacitated? If Bob has executed a power of attorney, his agent can act on his behalf.

Roth to the Rescue

In some circumstances, Roth IRAs may be used to correct prior planning mistakes. Take the case of Sue Collins, who named her estate rather than her son Dan as her IRA beneficiary. Generally, this would be a mistake.

Why? Because once people reach age 70$\frac{1}{2}$, they're required to withdraw money from IRAs. If a person is named as beneficiary the money can be withdrawn over a joint life expectancy, that slows down the pace of required withdrawals and provides more years of tax-deferred compounding. If the IRA owner's estate is the beneficiary, a single life expectancy is used so money must be withdrawn more rapidly.

Minimum withdrawals must begin by April 1 of the year after the IRA owner reaches age 70$\frac{1}{2}$ (although there's an exception for employees who continue to work.) If Sue dies before that date, with her estate named as the beneficiary, all the IRA money must be withdrawn—and income tax paid—within 5 years.

If Sue dies after that date, the entire IRA must be liquidated by December 31 of the year after her death. However, if Sue had named Dan as beneficiary, he probably would be able to spread IRA withdrawals over his entire life expectancy, building wealth through tax-free compounding.

Fortunately, if Sue has not reached the required beginning date, she can change her beneficiary and name Dan instead of her estate. If Sue has already begun to take required distributions, changing beneficiaries won't prolong the payout schedule. However, as long as Sue's income is not over $100,000, she can convert her IRA to a Roth IRA and get a fresh start, naming Dan as beneficiary.

After a conversion, Sue will owe income tax on all the deferred earnings but Roth IRAs have no required distributions. Five years after the conversion (assuming Sue is older than 59$\frac{1}{2}$ by then), she'll be able to take any amount from her Roth IRA, free of income tax. Or she can just leave her Roth IRA intact for Dan.

As Sue's Roth IRA beneficiary, Dan can elect to take distributions over his life expectancy. As long as Dan withdraws the money on that schedule, no income tax or penalties are owed.

However, even though an inherited Roth IRA may avoid income tax, it will be included in Sue's taxable estate when she dies. Depending on the size of her overall estate, estate tax may be due.

At that point, having liquid assets to pay the estate tax will pay off handsomely for Sue's heirs.

SUMMARY

- Among all the strategies available to clients when they retire or change jobs, rolling over a retirement plan balance to an IRA is often the best choice.

- Clients who are executing rollovers should specify a trustee-to-trustee transfer in order to avoid a 20% withholding requirement.

- Clients with company stock in a retirement plan may enjoy a substantial tax benefit by withdrawing those shares from the plan prior to rolling to an IRA.

- After a rollover to a traditional IRA, clients can convert some or all of the account to a Roth IRA, providing their income is not greater than $100,000 for the year.

- It's better to convert an IRA to a Roth IRA during or after a market correction because the account will be worth less and a small amount of tax will be due.

- Roth IRA conversions can be rescinded, bringing the money to a traditional IRA, but there are limits to subsequent reconversions.

- Roth IRA conversions may have significant estate planning benefits, because no distributions are required during the owner's lifetime.

Early Birds

Avoiding Withdrawal Penalties

etirement plans are designed to provide clients with money to live on after they stop working. But when will that be? According to Social Security, "normal" retirement age is 65, although that threshold is scheduled to increase to age 67. What's more, reduced Social Security retirement benefits are available at age 62. To make things even more complicated, the tax code sets an "unofficial" retirement age at 59½. If your clients withdraw money before that age, they'll owe a 10% penalty tax in addition to regular income tax.

For many clients, the age 59½ threshold won't be a problem. Others, however, will want to retire even earlier and pull money out of their plan. Still others will need the money before age 59½ for various purposes, such as paying off debts, buying a house, or putting children through college.

Fortunately, not every retirement plan withdrawal before age 59½ triggers a 10% penalty. Here are the exceptions:

- No penalties are imposed in case of death or permanent disability.

- The 10% penalty is also waived in the case of money withdrawn up to the amount of deductible medical expenses. Suppose George Parker has adjusted gross income (AGI) of $60,000 in 1999 and medical expenses of $10,000. Deductible medical expenses start at 7.5% of AGI, or $4,500 in George's case. Thus, he would be $5,500 over the threshold, so he could withdraw $5,500 from his retirement plan, penalty free.

George's AGI	$60,000
George's medical expenses	10,000
Threshold for deducting medical expenses (7.5% times $60,000)	(4,500)
Deductible amount ($10,000 minus $4,500)	5,500
Penalty-free retirement plan withdrawal	5,500

- Clients also can avoid the 10% penalty by taking "substantially equal" payments from a retirement plan, based on life expectancy. Such payments must last at least 5 years and until age 59½.

For Employees Only

The foregoing exceptions apply to IRAs as well as employer-sponsored plans. Clients who want to withdraw money prematurely from a company plan have some other options:

- They can annuitize the account, taking money out with a lifelong series of payments. However, annuity payouts tend to be low and there may not be any escalation to keep up with inflation. If a client annuitizes and dies before reaching life expectancy, principal is lost.

- The tax code provides penalty-free access to plan money as early as age 55 in case of "separation from service." This provision can help people who get laid off as well as those who retire early.

- No penalty is due if payments are required under a Qualified Domestic Relations Order (QDRO), which might result from a divorce negotiation.

The IRA Side

Some safe harbors nullify the penalty only for pre-59½ withdrawals from IRAs:

- Clients who are out of work for at least 12 consecutive weeks can take enough money from an IRA to keep health insurance in force, penalty free, and keep doing so until they're back to work for 60 days.
- Money used for higher education is not subject to the penalty. These expenses, which may include those related to graduate level courses, must be incurred on behalf of a client, spouse, child, or grandchild.
- Clients also may take penalty-free withdrawals up to $10,000 for a first-time home purchase. A qualified first-time home buyer is someone who has had no ownership interest in a residence during the previous two years.

What about Roth IRAs? If a client converts to a Roth IRA, withdrawals of the principal are subject to the 10% penalty tax until age 59½.

Suppose, for example, Kate Walsh converts a $100,000 IRA to a Roth IRA when she's 50 years old, paying the required income tax. Subsequently, the first $100,000 she withdraws from her Roth IRA is considered a nontaxable return of principal. However, withdrawals of that principal before she reaches 59½ are subject to the 10% penalty tax.

Otherwise, the 10% early withdrawal penalty applies only to the earnings inside a Roth IRA. Moreover, the normal exceptions to the early withdrawal penalty for IRAs apply to Roth IRAs, too. These include death, disability, substantially equal periodic payments received over a life expectancy, certain expenses related to first-time home purchases, and higher education outlays.

SEPP Solutions

The 10% penalty for premature distributions can affect planning. Generally, this penalty makes employer-sponsored retirement plans poor college funding vehicles. In some plans, getting money out before retirement is difficult—the participant may have to petition the administrator for distributions. Beyond that, your client will owe ordinary income tax on all withdrawals and a 10% penalty tax on withdrawals before age 59½.

Consider also the example of Jim Thomas, who was "downsized" at age 53, after building up a substantial amount in his 401(k) account. In his situation, Jim would have to leave his money in his ex-employer's 401(k) plan and receive permission to take withdrawals, in order to use that escape hatch. Even so, he would have to wait for two years, until age 55.

Jim would prefer to roll the money into his own IRA and use the money, as needed, until he finds a new job or reaches 62 and can begin collecting Social Security benefits. If he can tap his IRA without paying the 10% penalty, more can stay in his tax-sheltered plan for future retirement needs.

Jim can have all of the above—flexibility, access to his money, avoidance of the 10% penalty—by taking out Substantially Equal Periodic Payments (SEPPs) over his life expectancy. SEPPs can be started at any age but they must be taken at least annually for five years or until age 59½, whichever comes later.

Clients who decide to take early withdrawals from retirement plans using SEPPs can follow either of two broad strategies:

1. They can take out as much as possible, without penalty, because they need the money for living expenses.
2. They can take out as little as possible to provide some needed income now while keeping as much as possible in the plan to maximize tax-deferred buildup.

Making the Most of SEPPs

Clients who prefer to withdraw the maximum amount can calculate their SEPPs by using the amortization method. In essence, amortization entitles individuals to project retirement plan earnings throughout their lifetime, using a "reasonable" interest rate. This increases the pool of money from which they can take SEPPs.

In some cases, clients may be able to use mortality tables from an insurance company or a trade group that shows relatively short life expectancies. The shorter the life expectancy, the more money they can take out each year.

A client with a $200,000 IRA and a 33-year life expectancy would be able to take out about $6,000 per year, penalty free, on a straight-line annuity basis. However, by using the amortization method, that client might be able to take out $18,000 per year and still avoid the 10% penalty. With this method, withdrawals are the same each year, fixed when SEPPs begin.

Obviously, projected earnings are crucial to this calculation. The higher the estimate, the larger the amount that can be expected to build up in the client's account and the larger the permitted penalty-free withdrawal. IRS statements indicate that 80–120% of the federal long-term interest rate published monthly is safe to use. However, an even higher projection might pass IRS examination, if it can be justified.

For example, suppose the IRS' monthly long-term interest rate is 6% at the time of this projection. A client desiring to use this method would be entitled to use a 7.2% earnings projection (120% of 6%), according to the IRS.

However, your client might point to his experience over the past 10 years, during which time he has earned 12% per year in his retirement plan. Using a 12% rate for these projections would boost penalty-free withdrawals. There is no guarantee that the IRS will approve a 12% projection, but your client would have a reasonable ground for using it, in this situation.

Less Now, More Later

Clients who want to take less rather than more from a retirement plan before age 59½, penalty free, can use a straight life expectancy method, withdrawing money without an earnings projection. For married clients, a joint life expectancy can be used, which reduces the periodic payments further.

For clients who have built up a sizable amount in a retirement plan, the required SEPPs are relatively large, especially as they grow older and their life expectancy shrinks. With $1 million in an IRA and a 25-year life expectancy, for example, a client would need to withdraw (and pay tax on) $40,000, even if he only needed a $10,000 withdrawal for living expenses.

In such situations, clients with IRAs can make their SEPPs even smaller by splitting their IRAs, which are not aggregated, for purposes of this penalty. A $1 million IRA might be divided into four $250,000 IRAs: With a 25-year life expectancy, $10,000 could be taken from one, penalty free, while the other three IRAs remain intact.

The bottom line: By varying the size of their IRAs, your clients probably can generate annual withdrawals of virtually any amount they choose. A client with a 25-year life expectancy who wants to withdraw $6,000 per year, for example, could break off a $150,000 IRA and take SEPPs from that IRA, leaving the rest of his IRA to compound on a tax-deferred basis.

The 5-Year Hitch

SEPPs don't have to last forever. Individuals must keep up the periodic payments for 5 years or until age 59½, whichever comes later. A client who starts SEPPs at age 50 would have to keep them up until age 59½; one who starts at 58 would have to use SEPPs until age 63. SEPPs are reported on Form 5329, filed each year with the federal tax return.

After the SEPPs end, the money left in a client's IRA or IRAs can be left intact, for tax-deferred buildup, or they can be tapped as needed without any exposure to penalties. Moreover, money left in an IRA will some day be passed on to loved ones, if the account is not exhausted during the owner's lifetime or that of a surviving spouse.

What if clients don't follow through on their SEPPs? They face retroactive penalties, plus interest. Even so, that may be worthwhile.

Suppose Paula Nixon starts taking SEPPs at age 52 and gets a great job offer at 55, after taking $36,000 out of her IRA. A $3,600 penalty

(10% of $36,000) plus interest would be due, but the rest of her retirement fund can stabilize and grow now that she's working again.

Retroactive penalties also apply if withdrawals are increased beyond the SEPP limits. However, if separate IRAs have been created, a new series of SEPPs can be launched from an as-yet untouched IRA.

You and your clients can use SEPPs by working with a knowledgeable actuary to figure out the required payout. Another option is to buy an annuity from an insurance company: Some specialize in SEPP contracts for early withdrawals from deferred annuities as well as from IRAs and employer-sponsored plans. The insurer determines and distributes the appropriate amount of the SEPPs. Some insurers promise to pay any tax penalties if their calculations result in payments that don't meet IRS guidelines.

Thanks to SEPPs, you can include your clients' retirement accounts in their overall financial planning. Suppose you're advising a client who needs $500,000 to start a new business. That amount might be borrowed and the annual SEPPs might be used to service the debt while the client puts the loan proceeds to work in the business. Clients also might want to tap their retirement plan money prematurely to pay college bills or to support aging parents. Being able to access retirement plan money without a penalty may help those clients reduce withdrawals so that they can keep more money in the plan, enjoying greater tax-deferred growth.

Generally, you shouldn't encourage clients to use SEPPs—it's better to keep as much money in their retirement plans as long as possible, to maximize tax-free compounding. However, this provision can come in handy if you have clients who retire early and need extra cash flow.

For example, Harriet Morris was unhappy at work, she was having some health problems, and she wanted to spend some time with her young grandchildren. So she quit her job. At that point, Harriet was an unemployed grandmother who needed money for living expenses. The only asset that she could use was her IRA, in which she had accumulated about $200,000. She determined she could get by if she pulled out $2,000 per month, or $24,000 per year. This would leave the rest of her IRA to keep growing.

Harriet was only 51 years old at the time so she would owe a 10% penalty tax—$2,400 per year—on her IRA distributions. Fortunately, she was able to use the SEPP exception for 8½ years, until she reached age 59½, and thus avoid the penalty.

Word to the Wise

This chapter has focused on distributions before age 59½ and how to avoid the 10% penalty tax. Many advisors assume that clients who reach age 59½ can take retirement plan distributions without any problems other than paying income tax. Indeed, advisors may tell clients to take distributions after they reach that age.

However, such withdrawals may be illegal unless they're permitted by the plan's language. Some plans, for example, restrict distributions until retirement. This may affect a client's ability to take "in-service" distributions. Thus, you should read the plan documents carefully and perhaps advise clients to change the plan's language, if possible.

SUMMARY

- Clients generally will owe a 10% penalty tax for retirement plan withdrawals before age 59½ but there are some exceptions.

- Money can be withdrawn from an employer-sponsored plan (not an IRA) as early as age 55, penalty free, if clients retire or are laid off.

- Clients can gain access to money in any type of plan before age 59½ by withdrawing Substantially Equal Periodic Payments (SEPPs).

- SEPPs must be taken until age 59½ or for 5 years, whichever comes later.

- Depending on a client's situation, SEPPs can be maximized or minimized and penalties avoided.

- Even after age 59½, a client's ability to take distributions from an employer-sponsored plan depends on the plan language.

Stocking Up

Investment Strategies
for Today's Retirees

When it comes to retirement, getting there is only half the battle. For advisors, the other half is seeing that clients have enough financial resources for a retirement that could last 40 years. Often, the key to a long, successful retirement is the prudent use of money inside a tax-deferred retirement plan.

How should plan assets be invested after retirement? One factor that needs to be determined is the level of spending a client will maintain in retirement. Some clients have read articles indicating that they'll spend 60–80% of their preretirement income in retirement. Thus, it may come as a big surprise when they find out that they're actually spending 100%. Although it's true that once clients retire, they won't be spending as much on business suits, they probably don't all intend to cut down on their lifestyle after retirement. They may want to travel right after they retire, for example, and one trip to Australia more than makes up for a lot of suits.

As retirees age, spending may be maintained or even increased to provide protection from the environment. For example, a client might want to fly first class because long trips in coach have become uncomfortable. If clients want to move into a retirement community, they'll want to be sure it's an outstanding community with all the amenities, and such communities are expensive.

Fourscore and Ten

To calculate how a client's retirement plan will be allocated, some estimate of life expectancy is needed. The standard tables assume that people will die in their late 70s, but that's an average. Half the people will live longer. Advisors may want to assume that clients will live at least to age 90, and in some cases project them living until 95 or 100.

Projected rates of investment return also must be factored into the withdrawal plan. Naturally, over a 30- or a 40-year retirement, a small change in projected returns can make an enormous difference in outcomes. To play it safe, advisors may want to avoid projecting more than a 10% total return; many professionals use projections around 8% for a retiree's portfolio.

Even if a relatively conservative 8% rate of return is projected, clients may be tempted to think they can spend 8% of their retirement fund each year. After all, such spending will be replenished by new portfolio growth. But spending 8% of a retirement fund may turn out to be risky if financial markets fall sharply. That is, a client with $500,000 in an IRA may spend $40,000 (8%) one year, only to discover the IRA is worth $400,000, after a market correction. If that client spends $40,000 again, that would be 10% of the portfolio in one year. Therefore, a more conservative approach may enable clients to maintain their standards of living even if there is a market reversal.

Of course, not every client will need to take out 5%, 6%, or 8% from his or her retirement plan. Many clients will wait until age 70½ and then take minimum distributions, which might be 4% or less, depending on the age of the designated beneficiary. With a large IRA, say $2 million, a 4% required withdrawal (based on a joint life expectancy of 25 years) would be $80,000, or about $48,000 after income tax. Assuming other income is available, this $48,000 might be given away, to hold down future estate taxes.

For clients who will need IRA money in retirement, what level of spending makes sense? A number of articles have pointed to a 4% or 5% spending rate as a safe approach. That is, if a client wants to spend $50,000 per year in retirement, in excess of what might be received from Social Security and any pensions, then a fund of 20–25 times that amount ($1 million to $1.25 million) will be necessary, to permit that level of spending with a 4–5% drawdown.

Too Much, Too Soon

To see the potential risks of withdrawing too much from a retirement plan, suppose Tom Davis retires at age 65 with $1 million in his plan, which he rolls into an IRA. He and his wife expect to receive $16,000 in Social Security benefits and $6,000 from other sources of income, for a total of $22,000. Therefore, they decide to take $53,000 from Tom's IRA, to bring their gross income up to $75,000, which they consider necessary for a comfortable lifestyle.

This couple may run into trouble. Suppose they start with that $53,000 withdrawal and increase it each year by the rate of inflation. Further assume they hold a portfolio of 63% stocks and 37% bonds. If they had followed this strategy beginning in 1972, they would have run out of money after 23 years. If they had started their strategy in 1966, they would have run out of money in 18 years. Based on the past performance of the financial markets, there's approximately a 45% chance that this couple will run out of IRA money in a 30-year retirement.

These results may seem strange. Since 1966, stocks have returned about 11% per year while bonds have returned more than 8%. A portfolio that's 63% in stocks and 37% in bonds would have returned nearly

10% per year, compounded. If that were true, how would clients run out of money by withdrawing 5.3% of their IRA?

Several reasons explain this seeming paradox. Remember, 5.3% is the first year's withdrawal, followed by increases to keep up with inflation. If inflation shoots up, as it did from the late 1960s to the early 1980s, IRA withdrawals will have to grow rapidly to maintain a standard of living. Tom Davis, for example, would go from a $53,000 withdrawal to a $106,000 withdrawal in 12 years, if inflation runs at a 6% rate (which was the case from 1978 through 1989).

At the same time, markets—especially stock markets—are volatile. They don't go up a steady 11% per year. In 1973–1974, stocks fell by about 50%. If such a disaster recurs, Tom would have a $500,000 IRA, not a $1 million IRA, and he'd be committed to taking out $53,000, $55,000, $60,000 per year, and so on, in order to maintain his living standard. Even if the market rebounds, it may not grow fast enough to keep the IRA from future disintegration.

Balancing Act

After such a sobering look at history, clients might want to invest retirement plan money with caution. Their retirement plans might hold from 50% to 75% in stocks, at age 65, depending on their risk tolerance. The more risk they can assume, the more stocks they should own. As they get older, they might switch 1% of their portfolio from stocks to bonds each year. Thus, an aggressive investor who starts out at 75% in stocks at age 65 would have a 50-50 portfolio by age 90.

With that kind of a portfolio, clients might take out about 4% of their retirement plan money the first year. Thereafter, they can increase withdrawals to keep pace with inflation and have a 100% probability that their money will last 30 years, based on historical data. To follow this strategy, Tom Davis should withdraw $40,000 from his IRA the first year, rather than $53,000, to be sure the money will last for 30 years.

The younger a client is at retirement, the longer the expected retirement. Therefore, the first-year withdrawal should be lower. A client retiring at age 55, for example, might keep first-year withdrawals to around 3.5% of the IRA balance, in order to feel secure.

Of course, there are no hard-and-fast rules for retirement plan withdrawals. Some clients might want to take out larger amounts in their early retirement years, when they're still healthy enough to enjoy traveling, and limit later cost-of-living adjustments. The key point, though, is that retirement plan withdrawals need to be considered carefully. Clients can't withdraw 10% per year because they expect their portfolio to grow by 10% a year. Markets don't go straight up: A lower withdrawal rate provides insurance against downturns.

Not every advisor agrees that first-year withdrawals should be limited to 4% of retirement funds. Some insist that clients can start out with 5%, even 6% distributions, and still not run out of money. As clients grow older, life expectancy lessens and there's less risk that they'll spend all their retirement funds.

As a practical matter, many clients tend to spend freely during their working years. When they retire, it's hard for them to hold spending down to 3.5% or 4% of their retirement plan. However, if they want to maintain their spending, they should realize they run the risk of going through all their retirement funds.

Although most clients appreciate the need for safety, many are willing to bear some risk once the matter is explained to them. They generally are willing to increase their spending to 5–6% per year, acknowledging that they may have to cut their spending in case of a market drop. With a higher spending rate, clients need save only 17–20 times the amount they hope their portfolio will generate: If $50,000 is the annual spending goal, then they can retire once they've saved $850,000–$1 million. That is, if a client has $1 million in a retirement plan, he might withdraw $50,000 (5%) the first year. If inflation is 3% that year, he can increase withdrawals to $51,500 in Year Two. And so on.

Assume that a normal allocation for a young retiree is 65% in stocks or stock funds and 35% in bonds or bond funds. Such a portfolio might generate 3% per year in interest and dividends. Thus, clients can spend that 3% and make up the shortfall by selling securities to raise cash.

Clients probably should sell stocks or stock funds to bridge the gap. Chances are that these securities will appreciate over time so selling some shares will help keep a portfolio in balance. Ideally, clients will be able to sell shares for which they have small profits or even losses, for the best tax consequences.

Drops in the Bucket

After clients take early retirement, financial advice is probably more important than before, because earned income has diminished or disappeared. You should meet regularly with retired clients, discussing the flow of money and determining where cash will come from. If stocks or stock funds held inside their retirement plan need to be sold to raise cash, you may have to help clients with those decisions.

To advise retired clients, you should monitor their outflows. One strategy is to use a "cash bucket" approach, in which 12–18 months of spending is kept in a cash reserve such as a money market fund, within the retirement fund. Spending money is withdrawn from the cash bucket and poured into a checking account. Each quarter you can meet with retirees and decide how to replenish the cash reserve. Often, that's a matter of rebalancing the portfolio to get back to the client's original allocation.

Another cash bucket technique is to keep at least 2 years of cash needs in a bank account or money market fund for easy access. Suppose a client needs $3,000 per month in retirement and receives $1,600 per month from Social Security and a pension. The cash bucket should hold at least 24 months times $1,400—$33,600—which can be drawn down at $1,400 per month.

The rest of the money can be kept in stocks and bonds. Once a year, replenish the cash bucket by selling shares of those companies or those funds that have performed the best. This plan enables clients to reinvest dividends and interest while they keep their stock market portfolio in balance. They'll always have a cash cushion so they won't be driven by emotions into buying high and selling low.

Yearning for Yield

Even though stocks belong in retirement plans after retirement, many retirees also will want to include investments that generate high current income. Therefore, advisors should be familiar with income-oriented investments that go beyond treasuries or money market funds, especially in the low-yield environment that marks the turn of the 21st century. Such investments may be appropriate retirement plan holdings because the interest won't be currently taxable.

For example, Wall Street firms such as Donaldson Lufkin Jenrette and Goldman Sachs offer finite-life closed-end trusts under names like TRENDS and ACES. They're designed to trade for 3 to 5 years, after which they terminate. During the trust term, the funds' holdings might consist of one stock (or an option on one stock market index) and stripped U.S. treasuries. Reader's Digest Trust, for example, trades on the New York Stock Exchange.

The stripped treasuries are staggered so they mature quarterly, at which time the trusts pay "dividends" to investors. Typically, the trusts are structured to pay at an annual rate of 6–7% per year. When the trust terminates, investors are entitled to cash or shares, at the issuer's option, with a limit on the upside potential. Investors might get 83% of the market price of the trust's stock, for example, or they might get the dollar equivalent of the Nikkei 225, up to a cap of 20,000. Therefore, investors lock in a substantial yield but give up some investment opportunity and have a sizable exposure to the performance of one stock or one index.

Yield-oriented retirees have other choices for their retirement plans. Convertible funds, for example, offer dividends as high as 5%, as of this writing, as well as stock market participation because of the conversion feature. (The bonds may be converted into the issuer's common stock.) Closed-end convertible funds may offer higher yields: Some were paying 8–10% in 1999.

How can closed-end convertible funds offer such high yields? Trading at a discount to net asset value (NAV) may help. Moreover, many of these funds buy low-rated bonds or use leverage. That is, some funds issue preferred shares, betting that they will receive more income from the securities they buy than they will pay out in preferred stock dividends, thus boosting the yield. Such strategies are certainly chancy but investors must take some risks if they want a 10% or even an 8% yield in this environment.

Risk Adjustment, More or Less

Less risky but still high-yielding options include closed-end term trusts that hold mortgage-backed securities and corporate bonds. Again, these trusts mature on a preset date, when all the proceeds are distributed to investors. Most term trusts sell at a discount to NAV. Counting current distributions and redemption at par, term trusts maturing in about 5 years have been priced to generate 7–8% to maturity, excellent returns for short-term, high-quality bonds, without stock market risk.

Higher yields are available on other types of securities, such as junk bonds and emerging markets bonds. Closed-end junk bond funds were yielding 10–12% in 1999 but many of the best choices were selling at premiums: Clients might be better off buying funds that trade at slight discounts and yield around 10%. Closed-end emerging markets funds were yielding up to 20% but those with the best reputations were priced to yield around 12%.

Of course, many clients will be leery of investing retirement plan money in any type of junk bonds or emerging markets securities. However, one type of bond fund is designed to reduce risk and may be worth considering: multisector funds.

Such funds hold U.S. government, junk, and foreign government bonds. (Some multisector funds include other types of bonds such as municipals and asset-backed securities.) In theory, multisector bond funds provide investors with an all-in-one fixed-income portfolio to reduce volatility.

What's more, investing in a multisector bond fund can boost returns for investors who otherwise would have focused on U.S. treasuries. Over time, the high current yields offered by junk bonds and foreign bonds likely will help to provide higher returns than those from treasuries.

Safety Belt

With a multisector fund, investors get to enjoy those expected higher returns, to a significant degree. At the same time, holding several types of bonds that move out of sync with each other may actually diminish overall volatility, thus reducing risk—some sectors will zig while others zag. In the summer of 1998, for example, strength in U.S. treasuries offset weakness in junk and foreign bonds. Therefore, multisector funds may work for moderate or aggressive investors who are willing to accept some volatility in return for hefty yields.

According to Morningstar, the multisector category has held up fairly well: The average fund in this category returned 16.8%, 10.4%, and 8.8%, in 1995, 1996, and 1997, respectively, and even managed to register a 1.4% gain in 1998. The average yield in 1999 was 7.5%, lower than junk funds but a couple of hundred basis points higher than investment-grade bond funds were returning.

Again, there may be greater opportunities on the closed-end side. Several closed-end multisector funds have long histories of paying 8–12% yields, large amounts of U.S. treasuries in their portfolios, and solid performance records. In 1999, such funds were selling at discounts to NAV, offering yields more than 9%.

Many closed-end funds trade at a discount to NAV simply because there's no broker pushing to sell them, after the initial offering. With a lot of research and a little patience, you may find plump yields for your clients among closed ends.

If you have clients who want income but prize appreciation potential, too, you might consider real estate funds, most of which load up on high-yielding real estate investment trusts (REITs), which were beaten down in late 1997 and all of 1998. As a result, REIT dividends are way up, with some funds yielding 7.5% in 1999. Real estate funds have the potential for appreciation, too: The average fund in this category returned over 20% in four of the eight years from 1991 through 1998.

High-net-worth clients (those with $5 million or more in liquid assets) can afford to absorb some volatility so they're probably better off with a portfolio that's 100% invested in equities. When minimum withdrawals are required, they can sell stocks in their portfolio. Outside of a retirement plan, they can raise cash by selling appreciated securities: They're better off paying capital gains taxes at 20% or the alternative minimum tax (AMT) at 26–28% than they are with ordinary investment income, taxed up to 39.6%.

Patience Pays Off

What's the bottom line on retirees' investment strategies? Many professionals shy away from the traditional retirees-shift-into-bonds approach. Instead, these advisors might tell clients that they'll have to keep a portfolio allocation of 60% in stocks and 40% in bonds if they want to be able to spend 5–6% of their portfolio each year. If they hold more bonds, they probably won't get returns high enough to support that kind of spending. Some financial advisors still recommend a bond-heavy portfolio to retirees but, over the long term, stocks are likely to far outperform bonds.

A long retirement means a greater need for stocks in a client's retirement plan. If their time horizon is 10 years or more, they're probably better off with more than 50% of their retirement plan invested in equities. According to Ibbotson Associates, Chicago, investors who bought in at the worst possible time (the beginning of 1973) would have had a respectable 6.7% annual return from large-company stocks after 10 years and a double-digit return after 14 years. In small-company stocks. the annual return would have been nearly 20% after a 10-year holding period.

Some advisors report that many retirees are more than willing to keep 50%, 60%, or more of their retirement funds in stocks. They don't want to hold bonds at all, in some cases. They're too fond of stocks, after what the market has done recently. For these clients, you may have to explain that bonds bring stability and lower volatility to a portfolio, so some of their money should be in bonds.

Nevertheless, clients who wish to spend 6% of their portfolio in retirement should have a 75–25% asset allocation, equities to fixed income, and they'd better be prepared to spend less if the market falls as it did in 1973–1974. If they want a more conservative asset allocation, say 40% in equities and 60% in stocks, they should draw less than 6% of their portfolio each year.

Taxes are important to this kind of planning, too. That is, you have to adjust for taxes, perhaps by doing your planning on an after-tax basis. For example, it doesn't make sense to project pulling $50,000 out of an IRA if a client needs $50,000 to spend: After income taxes, the client might be left with only $30,000 or $35,000 to spend. Instead, a client might need to withdraw $75,000 in order to have $50,000 to spend.

Of course, a retiree who spends $50,000 in 1999 won't spend $50,000 per year throughout the next century. Some inflation factor needs to be assumed so spending patterns can be projected. For the past two decades, inflation has averaged around 4%. Nevertheless, there's a chance that inflation could go higher some time in the future, as it did in the 1970s.

With a 4% inflation rate, spending will almost double in 15 years and triple in 30 years. Is it realistic to assume that a 55-year-old retiree who spends $50,000 will need to spend $150,000 when he's 85? It's possible, especially if major health care or custodial care costs are incurred. The key is to start out with a realistic number, an amount that's sufficient to support a comfortable lifestyle yet reasonable in light of the client's resources.

One approach is to have clients "practice" retirement. After a number for retirement spending is agreed upon, the clients try it out for a month or two, to see how they like living on that number. If it doesn't work, further adjustments must be made; in some cases, retirement must be deferred until a greater amount is accumulated.

SUMMARY

- The traditional retirees' portfolio, with an emphasis on fixed income, may not serve clients well during a long retirement.

- Clients should continue to hold sizable amounts of equities in their retirement plans, even after retirement, because equities are likely to outperform bonds.

- The more equities in a client's retirement plan, the greater the amount of money that can be withdrawn for retirement living expenses.

- Even with a 75% allocation to equities, clients should not withdraw more than 6% from their retirement plan in the first year, and they should proceed with caution thereafter.

- Equities may have to be sold to withdraw money from a retirement plan, so a plan should be in place for cashing in stocks and stock funds.

- Retirement plans should hold some fixed-income vehicles, too, perhaps including some unfamiliar securities that pay above-average yields.

- Clients with more than $5 million in liquid assets likely can do without fixed-income vehicles and devote their entire portfolio to more volatile but more rewarding equities.

Tough Choices

Beneficiary Selection and Required Minimum Withdrawals

Most retirees roll their retirement plan accounts into IRAs, for investment control and continued tax deferral. From that point, though, retirees tend to be divided into two groups: those who need their IRAs for living expenses and those who don't.

Retirees who need to spend IRA money generally are concerned with the balancing act described in Chapter 9. They want to withdraw enough to live on yet not so much that they run out of money. For such retirees, the primary questions are how to invest inside the IRA and how fast to pull money out, as we explained. Beneficiary selection typically is straightforward—they name a spouse, their children, or some other loved one.

Wealthier retirees, though, may need little or none of the money in their IRAs for a comfortable lifestyle. Often, their goal is to maintain the tax deferral as long as possible, maximizing the amount that can build up in the IRA. For such retirees, the choice of beneficiaries can be critical.

Considering the importance of IRA beneficiary selection, your clients may not get much help for their IRA custodians—the banks, brokerage firms, and mutual fund companies that hold the accounts. Often, the beneficiary designation forms provided are so cramped that the IRA owner barely has room to put down the names of a spouse and children, and they have no room to explain a more sophisticated plan. (See Chapter 18 for more on IRA custodians.)

Even though beneficiary designation decisions are vital, they're frequently made with very little thought. For some people, a large IRA is their most carelessly handled asset. Suppose, for example, the IRA owner has minor children—what happens if the IRA owner and spouse are killed in a common disaster? If you, as a financial advisor, can help your clients address such issues, you are truly providing a value-added service. Unfortunately, many advisors neglect to learn about this vital subject.

Planning Pointers

On the subject of IRA beneficiary designations, here are some of the ways you can help clients:

Make certain your clients name contingent beneficiaries. Chances are, a client will have named a spouse as IRA beneficiary, but he may not have named a backup. Then, if your client and his spouse die in a common disaster, with no contingent beneficiary, the IRA must be distributed in a short time period. If a contingent beneficiary has been named, that person probably will be able to take withdrawals over his or her life expectancy, extending the tax deferral.

Remind clients that they needn't name their spouses as IRA beneficiaries if other assets are available to provide for a comfortable lifestyle. Instead, such clients might want to name children or grandchildren (or a trust for them) as IRA beneficiaries. If the spouse will need, say, half of the IRA to live on, the IRA can be split in two and descendants can be named as beneficiaries of the second account. In some states the spouse's consent is necessary if someone else is named as IRA beneficiary.

Advise clients that they can have as many IRAs as they want. Each child may be the beneficiary of a separate account, for example, while a charity is the beneficiary of yet another IRA. With this arrangement, younger children and grandchildren can maximize tax deferral if they each inherit their own IRA. If clients name more than one beneficiary for one IRA, distributions must be made over the *oldest* beneficiary's life expectancy, accelerating the tax payments.

Don't let your clients name a minor as IRA beneficiary or contingent beneficiary. If a minor is an outright beneficiary, a court will get involved in administering the money. Instead, an IRA can be left to a minor via a custodial account. Even better, clients can name a trust as IRA beneficiary and name the minor as trust beneficiary. Be sure to work with a knowledgeable attorney because only certain trusts can qualify.

Discourage clients from filling out the IRA custodian's beneficiary form. Many custodians (usually banks, brokerage firms, or mutual fund companies) have inadequate forms. There's no room to list all the beneficiaries and contingent beneficiaries clients would like to name. That is, most forms don't permit an IRA owner to name a contingent beneficiary in case a named beneficiary dies.

Some forms ask how rapidly the IRA is to be paid out to the beneficiary. If your client checks the wrong box, the account will be depleted in a relatively short time and the full advantages of an IRA stretch-out will be lost.

Fortunately, some professionals have customized forms that can be sent in to the IRA custodian by certified or registered mail, spelling out in detail how the IRA should be passed along. Have your client send in two copies along with a note asking to have one acknowledged and returned.

Trusted Solutions

Although most clients designate individuals as IRA beneficiaries, a trust may be a better choice because it can provide security to the beneficiaries. Under rules issued by the IRS in 1997, a revocable trust can be named a designated IRA beneficiary, as long as the trust becomes irrevocable at the IRA owner's death. Previously, only an irrevocable trust could be named an IRA beneficiary, if posthumous tax deferral was a goal.

Generally, if a trust is named as an IRA beneficiary, withdrawals from an IRA are accelerated during the IRA owner's lifetime and after death. However, tax deferral may be gained if certain conditions are met. Under the old rules, those conditions included having a trust that was irrevocable, providing a copy of the trust document to the plan administrator, and restricting the trust beneficiaries to individuals rather than charities, estates, or corporations.

Now, revocable as well as irrevocable trusts may be designated IRA beneficiaries. Testamentary trusts (those created in a will) are not explicitly covered in these rules. The IRS, however, has indicated that the new rules are intended to also apply to testamentary trusts. Thus, if a client already has an estate plan, based on a revocable trust or a will, the IRA can be handled under the existing plan without a need for a new, irrevocable trust.

The new rules made some further changes regarding trusts as IRA beneficiaries. Trust beneficiaries still have to be individuals. However, it's now sufficient to certify certain facts about the trust and provide a list of beneficiaries, rather than provide a copy of the trust document.

Under the old rules, an IRA owner could designate an unfunded irrevocable trust as a beneficiary. If necessary, the owner could tear it up and name a new unfunded irrevocable trust. The new rules permitting revocable trusts make things a bit simpler.

Beyond revocable trusts, being able to merely certify a trust's eligibility may or may not be an advantage. Not having to submit a copy of the trust to the plan can be dangerous: Some people may submit the required certification but never create the actual trust. If they keep procrastinating, the trust won't be in place at the time of death.

In many cases, high-net-worth clients won't have liquid assets to fund a *credit shelter* trust, designed to take advantage of the unified gift and estate tax credit. By the year 2006, up to $1 million can be left to such a trust, tax free.

One strategy is to have the IRA owner name the spouse as IRA beneficiary and a credit shelter trust as contingent beneficiary. At the IRA owner's death, the spouse can disclaim a portion of the IRA, which can go to the credit shelter trust. As long as the spouse is not a trust beneficiary and the children are beneficiaries, the IRA distributions can be spread over a longer time period. Thus, this strategy provides both estate and income tax advantages.

Considering all of these factors, what are some of the implications of the new rules? Many people already have revocable trusts, sometimes known as "living" trusts, which have become popular vehicles for probate avoidance and incapacity planning. This ruling allows IRA owners to use the revocable trusts they already have in place.

Before this ruling, some IRA owners faced a dilemma. They might have wanted to name a trust rather than an individual (or individuals) as IRA beneficiary. Suppose, for example, that Ben Williams has three children, including one who tends to be a heavy spender. A trust would be an ideal IRA beneficiary because the trustee could control distributions. However, under the old rules Ben would have had to create a separate irrevocable trust just for the IRA.

Now, Ben's revocable trust can serve as the IRA beneficiary. As is typically the case, Ben is trustee and beneficiary of the revocable trust, keeping control of trust assets. In case of any change in circumstances, the trust can be altered or revoked.

If you are going to advise using a trust as IRA beneficiary, you might suggest separate trusts, one per beneficiary. Then the younger heirs can take advantage of their longer life expectancy and extend the tax deferral.

Step in the Right Direction

These rules are likely to lead to greater use of trusts as IRA beneficiaries, which may be a positive step in many cases. Revocable trusts are likely to become popular choices because clients can change their minds, if necessary, reacting to the passage of time.

Clients who already have revocable trusts in place can name those trusts as IRA beneficiaries. But what is preferable for clients who are starting to create an estate plan, yet want to name a trust as IRA beneficiary?

If they are in a situation where they're making lifetime gifts to reduce their taxable estate, irrevocable trusts may be appropriate. Gifts to such trusts may be considered complete gifts. Otherwise, clients probably should consider using a revocable trust because such trusts offer more flexibility.

In addition, some clients feel more comfortable using revocable trusts because they still control the trust assets. In the past, when such clients had to use irrevocable trusts as IRA beneficiaries—which meant putting the assets truly out of reach—they might have stalled or declined to act altogether.

Overall, these rules create more incentive to use trusts as IRA beneficiaries. Indeed, trusts may appeal to some clients whose IRAs are relatively modest. Under the old rules, they may have decided that it was not worthwhile paying to create a new, irrevocable trust, so an IRA might have been left outright when a trust made more sense. Now, they can use their existing estate planning documents—revocable trusts or wills. So all their assets can be included in their plan and, if desired, a trust can be used as an IRA beneficiary.

The new rules don't specifically address the question of existing but illegal trusts—designating a revocable trust as an IRA beneficiary has been a fairly common error. Apparently, these new rules are meant to be retroactive, which will make those trusts permissible, but that's not spelled out by the IRS. However, the IRS hasn't said that existing, revocable trusts *won't* be permitted. Thus, you may want to examine clients' existing documents and consult with an attorney who keeps up with this area.

If clients want to name minors as IRA beneficiaries, you might advise them to create a trust rather than rely on a custodial account. Custodial accounts—set up under the Uniform Gifts to Minors Act—must be turned over to the youngster upon coming of age, at 18 in many states. You can keep control much longer with a trust, assuming a reliable trustee will restrict distributions to the required minimum and thus extend tax deferral.

Double Duty

Once minimum distributions from an IRA must begin, they can be taken over a joint life expectancy—those of the IRA owner and the trust beneficiary. (If the beneficiary is younger but not the IRA owner's spouse, life expectancy is calculated with no more than a 10-year spread between the two, until the IRA owner's death.) In case of multiple trust beneficiaries, the oldest one's life expectancy is used, subject to this 10-year rule.

After the IRA owner dies, a successor trustee will be named for what is now an irrevocable trust, and that trustee will manage IRA withdrawals as well as trust distributions to beneficiaries. Once the IRA owner dies, the 10-year rule no longer applies, so the trustee may be able to stretch out distributions—extend tax deferral—for additional decades. This typically is the best plan for clients who don't need all their IRA funds for their own retirement.

The same stretch-out is possible without using a trust: Dad can leave his IRA to Mom, who leaves the balance to their kids, who can take minimum distributions. So when does naming a trust as IRA beneficiary make sense?

Some clients will want to use an IRA to fund a credit shelter trust. That is, assets left to the trust will use up the decedent's unified gift and estate tax credit, which is $650,000 for 1999. Typically, the decedent's children are the beneficiaries of a credit shelter trust (sometimes known as a *family trust* or *B trust*) while the surviving spouse is entitled to the trust's income and perhaps access to principal in case of need.

In other situations, IRA owners might want to use a QTIP trust as beneficiary. QTIP (Qualified Terminable Interest Property) trusts are designed to qualify for the marital deduction, deferring estate tax until the surviving spouse's death, but delivering the remaining assets to beneficiaries named by the first spouse to die. Existing QTIP trusts may be designated IRA beneficiaries in some cases; in other situations, some modifications to the trust language may be necessary.

Roth Relay

The question of beneficiary selection is not limited to regular IRAs. Clients who convert their IRAs to Roth IRAs must designate a beneficiary. Again, one option is to name a trust, naming the client's children or grandchildren as the trust beneficiaries.

After the initial tax payment, upon the conversion, no other income tax will ever be due, assuming the client meets the 5-year, age-59½ holding period rules. There are no required distributions from a Roth IRA so that money can keep building up until death. After the client's death, money can trickle from the Roth IRA, deferring the payout and maintaining the tax-free buildup.

Suppose, for example, Kate Johnson converts $200,000 to a Roth IRA and names as the beneficiary a trust set up for her infant granddaughter Linda. At Kate's death, when Linda is 12, the trust has grown to $250,000—even though money has been pulled out to pay the income tax on the conversion.

At that point, Linda has a life expectancy of 69 years. Under the minimum distribution rules, the trustee must withdraw at least 1/69 of the trust balance the first year: 1.45%. On a $250,000 Roth IRA, only $3,623 needs to be withdrawn and distributed to the trust—and there's no income tax on distributions from the Roth IRA. The rest of the $250,000 can grow tax free, inside the Roth IRA.

The trustee has to decide what to do with that money: invest in stocks, bonds, or other options. If that $3,623 is invested in growth stocks yielding 1%, only $36 will be earned and the tax bill will be about $5.

The next year, when Linda is 13, 1/68 of the Roth IRA (1.47%) must be moved to the trust and invested. Each year the fraction grows a bit. Nevertheless, tax-free growth continues in the Roth IRA and the trust fund can build as well.

Over Linda's lifetime the Roth IRA can grow to incredible amounts—all free of income tax. According to the terms of the trust, set by Kate,

Linda can become the trustee and invade the trust principal once she reaches a certain age.

Do your clients need a Roth IRA for the foregoing strategy? Not necessarily. A regular IRA can do the same thing, without forcing your client to pay the income tax upfront. However, with a regular IRA, clients have to start taking taxable distributions after age $70\frac{1}{2}$.

Moreover, with a regular IRA, payouts to the trust after your client's death are taxable. Long term, the heirs will receive more after tax with a Roth IRA. The younger the trust beneficiary, the greater the benefit from long-term compounding.

There is a catch (with either a Roth or a regular IRA) if someone sets up the trust with several beneficiaries. Distributions must be based on the life expectancy of the oldest trust beneficiary. If there's a significant spread, the younger ones will benefit by splitting the IRA and setting up separate trusts for each beneficiary.

Helping Hands

Such sophisticated planning assumes that the IRA custodian will cooperate, but that's not always the case. How can you find a helpful, competent IRA custodian for your client?

Look for a separate retirement planning department. Specialists are needed to keep up with all the rules. Small institutions that try to make do with general counsel may not have enough know-how.

Interview the custodian's retirement planning specialists. If significant amounts are involved, it's worthwhile to get together with representatives of the institution before making any commitments. Ask if they know how to handle the title of an inherited IRA, for example, and if they'll let your client's beneficiary name a beneficiary.

Don't expect your client's broker to know about these matters; insist on meeting with an in-house expert. If you get a blank stare when you raise some of these issues, start looking for another custodian.

Keep copies of all correspondence regarding IRA distributions. Have a professional adviser keep these documents so they can be produced if and when a dispute arises. With so many mergers among financial institutions, beneficiary forms may be mislaid. Make sure you or your clients have acknowledged copies and the heirs know where they are.

Exit Strategies

In addition to choosing IRA beneficiaries, clients eventually must decide how to handle withdrawals. The tax code requires certain minimum distributions from IRAs and other tax-deferred plans, once taxpayers are in their 70s. Such decisions are irrevocable, so they must be made carefully. However, the rules governing these decisions are complicated, with plenty of room for error. As an advisor, you have the opportunity to provide your clients with invaluable services in this area.

To illustrate this wealth-building process, consider the case of Art Adams, who retired and rolled over his account in an employer-sponsored plan to an IRA. After his IRA rollover, he named his wife Betty as the beneficiary of the account, which then amounted to $1 million. Art had enough income from other sources, even after retirement, that he did not have to tap his IRA. Thanks to the strong stock market and some wise investing, Art's IRA kept growing, reaching $2 million by the time Art reached age 70.

At that point, though, Art had to make some decisions—irrevocable decisions. He wanted to withdraw as little as possible from the IRA each year, maintaining the tax deferral. However, federal tax law requires minimum distributions each year, with a 50% penalty on any shortfall. Generally, money is subject to income tax when it is withdrawn from an IRA or another form of tax-deferred retirement plan.

The required beginning date (RBD) for minimum distributions is April 1 of the year after the year an IRA owner reaches age $70\frac{1}{2}$. Art was born June 30, 1928, so he reached $70\frac{1}{2}$ on December 30, 1998. Thus, his RBD is April 1, 1999. (As you can see, this is the RBD for everyone born in the first half of 1928. People born in the second half of 1928 have April 1, 2000, as an RBD. If Art had been born one day later, he would have had an extra year of uninterrupted tax deferral.)

In the Balance

How much does Art need to take out by his RBD of April 1, 1999? That depends on two factors:

1. The balance in his IRA as of December 31, 1997. After making his first required withdrawal on April 1, his next required withdrawal date is December 31, 1999, based on his IRA balance as of December 31, 1998. Each subsequent December 31, he has to make a withdrawal, based on his IRA balance the previous December 31.

Required withdrawal date	*Based on IRA balance as of*
April 1, 1999	December 31, 1997
December 31, 1999	December 31, 1998
December 31, 2000	December 31, 1999

And so on. To make things even more complicated, suppose Art had $2 million in his IRA as of December 31, 1998. By April 1, 1999, he withdraws $95,000. For purposes of his December 31, 1999, withdrawal, he can treat his December 31, 1998, IRA balance as $1,905,000: $2 million minus the $95,000 withdrawal.

2. Life expectancy. As a simplified example, suppose Art, age 70, has $2 million in his IRA and a 16-year life expectancy. He would have to withdraw 1/16 of his IRA balance (6.25%), or $125,000. He'd owe income tax on a $125,000 withdrawal and have $1,875,000 in the IRA to keep compounding. (This is a required minimum withdrawal: If Art needs more money, he can withdraw more and pay more income tax. If he only withdraws $100,000, for example, he'll owe a 50% penalty on the $25,000 shortfall.)

In practice, most people name a beneficiary and use a joint life expectancy, which is longer than a single life expectancy, thus permitting a slower pace of withdrawals. If Betty is 69 when Art is 70, their joint life expectancy will be 21.1 years. Thus, they have to withdraw only 1/21.1 of their IRA, or 4.74%. With Art's $2 million IRA, that's a

$94,800 taxable withdrawal—instead of $125,000—and leaves more than $1.9 million in the IRA to continue tax-deferred compounding.

Youth Movement

With that thought in mind, Art considered naming his daughter Cheryl, who's 45, as beneficiary. Their joint life expectancy is 38.3 years, which would permit an even slower withdrawal. He discarded that idea because it wouldn't be fair to his wife Betty or his son Doug. But if Art were widowed or divorced, could he name a child or children as IRA beneficiaries and stretch out distributions?

There are instances in which it makes sense to name children or even grandchildren as IRA beneficiaries. However, whenever a nonspouse is named as IRA beneficiary, the joint life expectancy is calculated as if the age spread is no greater than 10 years. Again, spousal consent may be necessary if a nonspouse is named as the beneficiary.

For a client who's 70, for example, it makes no difference if he names a 60-year-old sister, a 40-year-old son, or a 10-year-old grandson as IRA beneficiary. Life expectancy is calculated as if the client is 70 and the beneficiary is 60. After the IRA owner's death, though, the beneficiary can take minimum annual withdrawals over his or her actual life expectancy, prolonging the tax-deferred accumulation. An 11-year-old, for example, might have a 70-year life expectancy so only 1/70 (1.43%) would have to be withdrawn the first year, leaving the rest to compound, tax free.

Thus, if Art names his daughter Cheryl as IRA beneficiary, their joint life expectancy is the same as if Cheryl were 60 years old: 26.2 years. The same is true if Art names his 10-year-old grandson Eric as beneficiary—withdrawals are calculated with a 26.2-year joint life expectancy.

There are a couple of quirks to keep in mind about these rules. For one, the 10-year rule applies only to nonspouses. If Art, age 70, were married to a 45-year-old, he could name his wife as IRA beneficiary and take withdrawals based on their actual 38.3-year life expectancy.

Another point to remember is that the 10-year rule expires after Art's death. If Cheryl is the beneficiary, she can use her own life expectancy to reduce continuing required distributions. In fact, as we'll explain later in Chapter 14, that's the basis for a vital wealth-building strategy.

Calculating Choices

Regardless of whom Art names as beneficiary, he has to make an irrevocable decision regarding how the life joint expectancy will change each year. One method he can use is the *recalculation* method, which is favored by most banks, brokers, mutual funds, and other financial institutions holding IRA assets.

As the name suggests, this method calls for joint life expectancy to be recalculated each year. Every year, the IRA owner and the beneficiary get older so life expectancy lessens.

Art's Age	Betty's Age	Joint Life Expectancy (years)	Required Minimum Distribution (%)
70	69	21.1	4.74
71	70	20.2	4.95
72	71	19.4	5.15
73	72	18.5	5.41
74	73	17.7	5.65

And so on. As you can see, each year Art and Betty are required to withdraw a higher percentage of their IRA assets. By the time they're 85 and 84, for example, their joint life expectancy will be down to 9.9 years and they'll have to withdraw more than 10% of their IRA balance that year.

With this recalculation method, Art and Betty will never run out of life expectancy. By the time they're 90 and 89, for example, they'll still have a 7.3-year joint life expectancy. They can withdraw only 13.7% of their IRA and leave 86.3% to compound. They'll never strip their IRA down to nothing.

Unfortunately, not every couple will both live into their 90s. Art, who's male and older, probably will predecease Betty. If that's the case,

Betty can claim the IRA as her own and name new beneficiaries. In those "normal" circumstances, the recalculation method works fine.

But what happens if Betty predeceases Art, after the RBD? Art is prohibited from naming a new beneficiary, for the purpose of extending the joint life expectancy. Thus, he must continue to recalculate, using his single-life life expectancy, and withdraw money rapidly from the IRA. He'd have to withdraw at least 8% at age 75, 10% at age 79, 14.5% at 85, 20% at 90, and so on. And, after Art's death, the children must distribute the entire IRA by December 31 the year after his death.

Therefore, if a married couple chooses the recalculation method and the IRA beneficiary dies first, the family loses the chance for truly long-term tax deferral.

That Certain Feeling

So what is the alternative? The *term certain* method, also known as the *reduce by one* method. Here, you start out with the same joint life expectancy: 21.1 years for Art and Betty. Then the joint life expectancy is reduced by one year every year. In our example, it will become 20.1 years, 19.1 years, and so on.

Compared with the recalculation method, term certain requires slightly faster withdrawals. At ages 74 and 73, as we saw previously, Art and Betty must withdraw at least 5.65% of their IRA balance, using the recalculation method. With term certain, at that age they would have a 17.1-year joint life expectancy and would need to withdraw at least 5.85% of their IRA. Ten years later, at 84 and 83, they'd need to withdraw 14.1% of their IRA with term certain, only 9.3% with the recalculation method. In addition, with term certain they'll completely strip out their IRA in 21.1 years, assuming they both live that long.

The advantage of term certain, though, is that it protects against the chance of the beneficiary dying first. If Art dies first, Betty (as a surviving spouse) can take the inherited IRA as her own and name a new beneficiary—the same as under the recalculation method.

However, if Betty dies first, Art will have locked in that 21.1-year withdrawal schedule. At age 80, for example, he'll have to withdraw about 10% of his IRA, versus 20% under recalculation, if he's the survivor. And, if Art dies before the 21.1 years are up, their children Cheryl and Doug can continue the schedule. Thus, if Betty dies in Year One and Art dies in Year Two, their heirs will have another 19.1 years of tax deferral.

Even for single clients, the term certain method may be preferred because it's easier to remember. After the client's death, the children can take distributions over a long life expectancy. The recalculation method might provide slightly more tax deferral but the differences between the numbers involved are minuscule for relatively young beneficiaries, generally a fraction of a year's worth of life expectancy.

For couples, some experts recommend a hybrid approach: recalculate Art's life but use term certain for Betty. Thus, if Betty dies first, minimum distributions won't be accelerated. Meanwhile, using the recalculation method for Art permits a longer stretch-out period and reduces minimum distributions, as long as Art is alive.

Unfortunately, many IRA custodians are not aware of this strategy. They're not set up to let IRA owners and beneficiaries use the hybrid method. If this strategy appeals to a client, find out if the IRA custodian permits it. If the custodian isn't up to speed, your client can switch the account before minimum distributions must begin.

Super Stretch

If you're able to stretch out IRA distributions, the payout can be exciting. As we've indicated, Art and Betty Adams were able to build up a $2 million IRA by their RBD. They were required to withdraw at least 4.74% by the first deadline: $94,800.

Therefore, if their IRA earned more than 4.74% that year, the balance would continue to grow, despite the withdrawals. Long term, a well-managed mix of stocks, bonds, and mutual funds should earn 8%, 10%, or more per year, enabling their IRA to keep growing for quite a while.

Assume conservatively that their IRA earns 8% per year, they choose the term certain method, and neither dies prematurely. Art and Betty can take minimum withdrawals for 10 years, until they're 80 and 79, and their IRA will continue to grow. They'll take out more money each year, too, as their IRA balance increases and their withdrawal percentage also gets larger.

As mentioned, if Betty dies first they'll have locked in a total of 21.1 years of IRA deferral. Over that time period, Art's $2 million IRA will provide the family with about $5 million, after tax, assuming 8% investment returns and a 35% income tax rate.

In most cases, though, Art will die first, Betty will take the IRA as her own, and she will name the children as her beneficiaries. Then she can stretch out IRA distributions over a joint life expectancy, using the 10-year rule outlined previously. If she's 80, for example, she and Cheryl (her older child) would have a 17.6-year life expectancy so only 5.68% of the IRA needs to be withdrawn that year.

After Betty's death, the children can continue the withdrawal schedule using their own life expectancy, which could be 20 or 30 years or more. Assuming that Betty dies at 89 when Cheryl is 65, her life expectancy will be about 20 years and she'll have to withdraw only 5% from the IRA. Again, as long as the IRA earns more than 5%, it will keep growing despite the required distributions.

Tax deferral of that magnitude truly can be amazing. If required distributions stretch over 40 years, Art's $2 million IRA can generate more than $5 million, after taxes, to his family. If Betty names Cheryl's daughter Dawn (Betty's granddaughter), who is 35 in 2000, and a 10.5% growth rate is attained, the after-tax distributions would top $16 million. Stretch the IRA over 50 years by naming Cheryl's younger daughter Erica and the after-tax proceeds can exceed $30 million!

Again, a few technical points should be kept in mind. If Betty names both her daughter Cheryl and her (Betty's) son Doug as IRA beneficiaries, after her death the children must use the life expectancy of Cheryl, the older beneficiary, when calculating required withdrawals.

A better strategy would be for Betty to split the IRA she inherits from Art into two IRAs. Cheryl could be named beneficiary of one IRA and Doug for the other. Then, after Betty's death, each child will control one IRA and take distributions over his or her life expectancy. This is especially important if there are large differences between the ages of the children.

Split the Difference

When clients begin minimum withdrawals, they must add up all the money in all of their IRAs, as of December 31st each year. Then they take out the required amount the next year. The required withdrawals can come from one or more of those IRAs, just as long as the total meets the minimum amount.

A client might split an IRA into two IRAs: one with the spouse named as beneficiary and one for a child or grandchild. (Individuals can have any number of IRAs, naming a different descendant as beneficiary of each one, if desired.) Suppose the required withdrawal from both IRAs is $20,000 in the year 2000. Your client can withdraw all $20,000 from the spousal IRA and leave the other to grow. In the year 2000, he can follow a similar strategy. And so on. By the time he dies, a substantial amount may be left to the children or grandchildren, through the nonspousal IRA or IRAs, and that money can be withdrawn over decades while the tax deferral continues.

What other types of situations are advisors likely to encounter? You might see someone such as Paul Collins, who has named his estate rather than his son Rick as IRA beneficiary.

As mentioned, clients who name a person as IRA beneficiary can withdraw money over a joint life expectancy; that slows down the pace of required withdrawals and provides more years of tax-deferred compounding. Because Paul's estate is the beneficiary, he's using a single life expectancy so money must be withdrawn more rapidly.

If Paul dies before the required beginning date (RBD), with his estate named as the beneficiary, all the IRA money must be withdrawn—and income tax paid—within 5 years. If he dies after the RBD, IRA withdrawals must be made by December 31 of the year after the year of Paul's death.

Fortunately, it may not be too late to correct Paul's mistake. If he has not reached the RBD, he can change his IRA beneficiary designation and name Rick instead of his estate.

What if Paul already has begun to take required distributions? As long as his adjusted gross income is not over $100,000, he can convert his IRA to a Roth IRA and get a fresh start, naming Rick as beneficiary.

A Roth IRA conversion means that Paul will owe income tax on all the deferred earnings. The good news, though, is that Roth IRAs have no required distributions. Five years after the conversion (assuming Paul is older than 59½ by then), he'll be able to take any amount from his Roth IRA, free of income tax. Or he can just leave the Roth IRA intact for Rick. In the latter case, Rick will have to take distributions after Paul's death but those distributions can be taken gradually, based on Rick's life expectancy.

SUMMARY

- Clients often make simple decisions when they designate IRA beneficiaries but sophisticated strategies might produce better results.

- Many IRA custodians have inadequate forms or faulty systems for handling IRA beneficiary designations so clients should shop around before choosing a bank, broker, or mutual fund company.

- Under relatively new IRS rules, revocable as well as irrevocable trusts can be named as IRA beneficiaries, which may facilitate planning.

- After clients reach age 70½, they must begin minimum distributions from tax-deferred retirement plans and select a method for taking those distributions. Clients should always choose a joint life expectancy even if they are single.

- With careful planning, clients who do not need to draw down their IRAs in retirement can provide decades of tax-deferred or tax-free wealth building for their descendants.

- IRAs may be split into two or more accounts and distributions may be taken from some IRAs but not from others, in order to achieve financial planning goals.

Real Shelter

Using Low-Income Housing to Offset Taxes on Distributions

Many clients won't need the money from their retirement plans, but after age 70½, they must start taking minimum distributions from tax-deferred plans. (Roth IRAs are a notable exception.) A client with a $1 million IRA, for example, might have to withdraw $40,000 or $50,000 per year and pay income tax at top marginal rates.

Fortunately, there is a technique that can keep such clients' retirement plans from being devoured by Uncle Sam. They can invest in certain affordable housing or low-income housing ventures and receive tax credits to offset the income tax on plan withdrawals. These tax credits can soak up the tax on as much as $25,000 worth of income per year.

Thanks to these tax credits, clients can effectively withdraw $25,000 per year from their retirement plans (more in some cases), tax free. This tax free cash can be given to a trust and allowed to build up, with little or no tax bite. If necessary, the money in the trust eventually can be used to pay estate tax, permitting the client's retirement plan to remain intact for extended tax deferral.

Where Credit Is Due

The tax credit for investments in affordable housing was created by the 1986 tax act to encourage private investors to build or rehab housing units for low-income residents. Although some tax breaks are off-limits to upper-income taxpayers, these credits are available to even your wealthiest clients. When clients invest in an affordable housing program, they can expect a 20% profit just from the tax savings. A $5,000 outlay likely would save $6,000, for example. If your clients merely break even on the real estate, they'll wind up with a double-digit after-tax return.

The tax credit pays off for 10 years. (Often, the period can stretch to 11 or 12 years because it may take some time for capital to be invested.) Tax credits are prefunded, attached to a property for the full time period. Congress can't change the rules in the middle of the game and rescind the tax benefits. Clients who invest $5,000 will probably get a tax credit of around $600 (12%) per year, until the credits reach $6,000. If they're $1,000 ahead, just from the tax savings, that's a $1,000 after-tax profit.

Later, the property might be refinanced or the real estate may be sold to a nonprofit group. Alternatively, a new group of investors might buy the property for the tax credits. In some manner, clients are likely to get a further benefit, probably at least a return of their investment, at the end of the deal. On a $5,000 investment, they'd wind up ahead by $6,000— a 120% profit, after tax.

The projected tax savings alone are equivalent to a 7% annual after-tax return, considering the time value of the added cash flow. If investors get their money back at the end of the deal (probably 15 years after the investment), the effective return will be about 12%, after tax.

Clients who control a C corporation can invest corporate dollars and earn even higher returns by deducting passive losses that are not deductible for most individual investors.

For retirees, affordable housing credits mix well with Social Security benefits:

- The credits are not considered earned income so benefits are not reduced.

- The credits aren't considered *income* at all, so receiving them doesn't expose Social Security benefits to income tax. By contrast, investing in tax-exempt municipal bonds may expose those benefits to income tax.

Upper Limits

Low-income housing credits are so appealing that there are limits on the amount of credits investors can use. In most cases, clients can offset the tax on $25,000 worth of other income. If Jim Peters's last $25,000 of taxable income is in the 36% bracket, the tax on that income would be $9,000, so Jim can use up to $9,000 worth of credits. In a 39.6% bracket, he could use up to $9,900 in tax credits per year: $9,900 is 39.6% of $25,000.

Tax bracket	Maximum credits allowed
39.6%	$9,900
36	9,000
31	7,750
28	7,000

Affordable housing tax credits that clients can't use in a given year can be carried back 3 years or forward up to 15 years.

Suppose Jim Peters invests $75,000 in a low-income housing partnership and gets a $9,000 tax credit each year for 10 years (12% of

$75,000 is $9,000.) Each year, Jim can withdraw $25,000 from his IRA and incur a $9,000 tax obligation. The $9,000 tax credit offsets his tax obligation, leaving him with the $25,000 free and clear.

Over 10 years, he can withdraw $250,000 from his IRA and owe no tax. Under current law, there are no income limits—clients such as Jim Peters can use these credits to cut their tax bills no matter how much money they earn.

Go with a Pro

The most popular way to earn affordable housing credits is to participate in an investment partnership that buys apartments around the United States. The minimum investment usually is $5,000. In these partnerships, investors rely on the general partner to deal with all the various requirements such as verifying tenant eligibility, handling the paperwork, and providing investors with clear reports. Check on a sponsor carefully before advising clients to invest; you should ask to speak with other investors who have at least 5 years of positive experiences to relate. You also should ask the sponsor what help is provided to clients' accountants when it's time to prepare the necessary tax return schedules.

When clients invest in such a partnership, they're not involved in public housing. The properties are privately owned and managed, generally located in small towns and rural areas. For example, partnerships might own garden apartments in areas such as Aurora, Illinois, or Wayne, New Jersey. Tenants tend to be retirees or low-income workers, so the buildings usually don't get abused.

The partnerships rent their apartments to qualified tenants, who frequently pay below-market rents. A retiree living on Social Security might pay $350 a month to rent an apartment that otherwise would rent for $450 a month. Government subsidies such as 50-year federal loans with effective 1% rates help to keep the rents low. Therefore, clients are not likely to receive much cash flow from the venture: The rental income goes almost entirely to debt service, operating expenses, and property maintenance so not much is left over to distribute to investors.

On the positive side, the below-market rents probably will keep occupancy rates near 100%.

Before clients invest in an affordable housing partnership, you should help them to choose a sponsor with a long and successful track record. These partnerships anticipate long holding periods and there's no formal secondary market. Therefore, prepare your clients to buy and hold. However, if they need to cash out, the sponsor or the broker likely can find a buyer.

Under market conditions that permit a 12% annual tax credit, the maximum amount clients can effectively invest in such a partnership is:

Tax bracket	Maximum effective investment
39.6%	$82,500
36	75,000
31	64,500
28	58,000

Thus, a client in a 39.6% bracket could invest $82,500 and receive $9,900 per year in credits (12% of $82,500). Clients who have passive income from other sources, perhaps from rental properties that generate taxable income, probably can invest more in affordable housing than the limits just described and use more credits.

Additional tax credits can offset any tax clients owe on passive income, but not on investment income such as interest or dividends. Thus, if Jim Peters buys his parents' house and leases it back to them, generating taxable income from this activity, he can use excess tax credits to offset that tax.

However, if Jim deducts passive losses from actively managed property, that deduction directly reduces his $25,000 deduction equivalent. Suppose that Jim deducts $6,000 each year from a hands-on real estate investment. His deduction equivalent for these tax credits would be reduced to $19,000, so he can only use $6,840 in low-income housing tax credits (not $9,000), in a 36% tax bracket.

Original deduction equivalent	$25,000
(Minus) Investment property loss	(6,000)
Allowable deduction equivalent	19,000
Amount taxed at 36%	19,000
Credits allowed ($19,000 × 36%)	6,840

The math may be even more complicated because we assumed that Jim has a full $25,000 worth of income in the 36% bracket. Suppose, though, that he winds up the year with $10,000 in the 36% bracket and the other $15,000 in the 31% bracket. Now, he is entitled to only $8,250 worth of tax credits for the year, not $9,000.

Deduction equivalent	$25,000
Amount taxed at 36%	10,000
Credits allowed ($10,000 × 36%)	3,600
Balance taxed at 31% ($25,000 – $10,000)	15,000
Credits allowed ($15,000 × 31%)	4,650
Total credits allowed	8,250

If Jim has claimed a $6,000 loss from his investment property, his maximum use of low-income housing credits drops to $6,390.

Original deduction equivalent	$25,000
(Minus) Investment property loss	(6,000)
Allowable deduction equivalent	19,000
Amount taxed at 36%	10,000
Credits allowed ($10,000 × 36%)	3,600
Balance taxed at 31% ($19,000 – $10,000)	9,000
Credits allowed ($9,000 × 31%)	2,790
Total credits allowed	6,390

Therefore, it may be impossible to forecast exactly how many low-income housing credits a client will use over the next 10–12 years, but you should have a reasonable estimate. If you think a client will be able to use $7,000 worth of credits per year, for example, you might recommend an investment up to $58,000. With a 12% tax credit, your client will receive about $7,000 worth of credits per year. If he earns more credits than he can use immediately, the excess can be carried forward for 15 years. Nevertheless, it doesn't pay to overinvest and receive deferred credits.

Real Risks

In addition to the risk of investing too much and receiving suspended credits, what are the other hazards of low-income housing partnerships?

The tax credits can't be used to offset taxes below the alternative minimum tax (AMT) liability. Therefore, clients shouldn't invest until estimating their tentative minimum tax (TMT). If clients cut their regular tax too much using tax credits, they'll owe the AMT, which effectively limits the amount of the tax credits they can use. For example, if a client's regular tax obligation is $30,000 and his AMT obligation is $28,000, he can use only $2,000 worth of tax credits.

You may need to perform some complex calculations so that a client invests enough to maximize tax credits without plunging into the AMT, now or in the future. As a rule of thumb, anyone investing over $30,000 in a tax credit partnership should check closely the AMT exposure.

Participating in an affordable housing tax credit deal is a long-term, illiquid investment. If a client needs cash 5 years from now, she probably can sell her partnership shares but new investors will want a discount for bailing her out. Realistically, investors should plan on holding for at least 12 years.

Clients must invest with a proven sponsor. There are many technical requirements to comply with and many things that can go wrong; violation of the 15-year property occupancy requirements, for example, may lead to recapture of some tax credits previously taken. Other technical problems could wipe out all the tax credits taken, forcing your clients to pay back taxes, interest, and possibly penalties. An experienced general partner will know to avoid these pitfalls so be sure you do your "due diligence" so you can recommend a proven sponsor.

Building Blocks

If you and your clients proceed with care, affordable housing tax credits can enable them to withdraw money from a retirement plan without owing tax. Then the money can be transferred to a trust, for further wealth building.

For example, suppose that every time Jim Peters withdraws $25,000 from his IRA, he transfers the money to a trust he has established. His two children are the trust beneficiaries. Jim and his wife Lana elect to make joint gifts each year. Because they are allowed to give away up to $20,000 worth of assets per year to each of their children, they could make $40,000 worth of such gifts. Thus, the $25,000 they transfer to the trust each year falls within the annual gift tax exclusion and is not subject to tax.

When clients make gifts in trust, certain formalities have to be followed if they want to use the gift tax exclusion. The trustee must write to each beneficiary notifying them of the gift and giving them the right to withdraw the funds they've been given. This right lapses after a specific time period, often 30 days.

The beneficiaries' right to withdraw their money from a trust is called a *Crummey power*, after a landmark court case. The IRS is very strict about enforcing these rules. Even if one of Jim's children is the trustee as well as the beneficiary, that trustee should write a letter to himself or herself (trustee to beneficiary), giving Crummey power notification.

After the Crummey power lapses, the trustee can buy stocks, pay life insurance premiums, and so forth. If the money is invested wisely, it will grow over the years. Indeed, periodic investing becomes a form of dollar-cost averaging, enabling your clients to catch market lows as well as highs, lowering their average cost per share.

Thus, with prudent management, the $250,000 that a client can invest over 10 years may grow to $400,000, $500,000, or more. Those funds, held in an irrevocable trust, escape estate tax. If necessary, your clients' heirs can use this money to pay estate tax on other assets—such as a large IRA—and allow those assets to remain intact. If an IRA does not have to be tapped for estate tax payments, it can provide many decades of tax-deferred wealth building.

What's more, planners may be pleasantly surprised by clients' reactions to low-income housing tax credits. Each year, when they file their income tax returns, they'll see the results in actual tax savings—a welcome outcome for virtually every client.

Low-income housing investments can offer tax reduction, real estate participation, and something more—the opportunity to provide affordable housing for those of modest means. Some clients will appreciate the feeling of giving something back while they take out a significant return for themselves and their own families.

SUMMARY

- Clients may be able to offset the tax on retirement withdrawals by making an investment in affordable housing that generates tax credits.

- By investing $58,000–$75,000, clients may be able to offset the tax on $25,000 worth of retirement plan withdrawals each year for 10 years.

- Clients may get their original investment back, too, when the properties eventually are sold.

- The money withdrawn from a client's retirement plan, sheltered by tax credits, may be given to a trust set up for your client's children.

- Once the money is in the trust, the trustee can invest in life insurance or growth stocks for long-term appreciation.

- When the retirement plan passes to the next generation, the trust can provide money for taxes so the retirement plan remains intact and continues to grow, tax deferred.

Family Values

Retirement Plan Issues in Divorce and Remarriage

While "happily ever after" may be the ideal, not all married couples even manage the "ever after" part. As a financial advisor, chances are that some of your clients will wind up dissolving their marriage and you'll be called on to help with the financial settlement, including the disposition of a tax-deferred retirement plan. Therefore, you should know how these matters proceed. When clients are negotiating a divorce or marital separation, a division of marital assets is likely. Typically, each spouse winds up with some of the property accumulated during the marriage.

If you represent one spouse, advise that spouse to try to keep the tax-deferred retirement account, which probably will be an even more valuable asset in the future. Your client might offer the spouse other assets such as real estate or securities in return for leaving the retirement account intact.

However, your client may not be able to preserve the retirement account. If the account balance is a sizable portion of the couple's net worth, or if your client would prefer to keep other assets (shares in a closely held company, for example), your client may have to part with a portion of the retirement account. In that case, your client needs to proceed with caution. If he withdraws money from his tax-deferred plan in order to transfer funds to a spouse or ex-spouse, he'll owe income tax. Before age 59½, he'll also owe a 10% penalty.

Law and Order

How can divorcing spouses avoid this trap? The divorce negotiation can include a Qualified Domestic Relations Order (QDRO). In essence, a QDRO is an order to the plan administrator to transfer part of the owner's interest in the plan to a spouse or ex-spouse while maintaining the tax deferral.

A QDRO must be issued by a state court. It can be applied to any type of tax-deferred retirement account (profit-sharing plan, 401(k), Keogh, SEP, and so others). For a plan administrator to accept a QDRO, it must be valid. That is, it must include:

- The identities of both spouses.
- The amounts to be paid, the date payments will begin, and the type of payment.
- The name of the plan to which the QDRO applies.

Faulty preparation can cause a QDRO to be rejected and the tax benefits to be lost. For example, if annuity payments are to be made, the QDRO should state whether the payments will be made for a single life, the lives of both spouses, or some other method.

Therefore, you and your client should make sure the QDRO is drafted by an attorney who specializes in such matters, so that all relevant issues are covered in the document. A model QDRO form is available from the IRS.

For belt-and-suspenders safety, your client should show the QDRO to his plan administrator before signing any agreement, confirming that it's acceptable. This permits needed additions or revisions to be made before it's too late.

Splitting Pairs

For a plan administrator, the extra record keeping required by a QDRO can be a burden. Therefore, you and your clients should see that the QDRO is drafted to minimize any difficulties. What's more, if the agreement spells out all the details precisely, the chance of expensive disputes in the future is reduced.

Suppose, for example, that Lou Martin has $200,000 in his 401(k) account, all of which was accumulated during his marriage to Nancy. Their divorce settlement calls for 50% of that account balance ($100,000) to go to Nancy. Subsequent contributions are solely Lou's property.

What are the possible complications?

- If Lou continues to make all the allocation decisions, he'll be investing Nancy's money—probably not in the way she'd choose.

- As the account grows, it may be difficult to track what belongs to Lou and what belongs to Nancy.

If the plan administrator agrees, one possible solution is to carve out $100,000 worth of Lou's account and let Nancy invest this amount. Net of this carve-out, the balance will belong to Lou.

Alternatively, clients who effectively control their own plans (perhaps because they're business owners or professionals) may be able to avoid such confusion. They can terminate the plan, distribute the amounts in the plan to the participants as well as to the spouse or ex-spouse, then start over with a new plan. Tax deferral can be maintained via IRA rollovers, if that's desired.

About Time

When can retirement funds be distributed to a spouse or ex-spouse under a QDRO? Generally, when your client (the participating employee) becomes eligible for a distribution, according to the language of the plan. This might be:

- After the plan is terminated.
- After your client leaves the company to retire or take another job.
- After your client reaches the early retirement age specified in the plan.
- After your client reaches age 50.

At this point, your client's spouse or former spouse can roll over the funds from the tax-deferred retirement account into an IRA, maintaining the tax deferral. Money will only be taxed as it is withdrawn, for living expenses or other purposes. Moreover, the 10% penalty tax on withdrawals before age 59½ does not apply to payments made to a spouse or ex-spouse under a QDRO.

In general, when the money is withdrawn, the income tax will be paid by your client's spouse or ex-spouse, not by your client. However, if a QDRO calls for payments to be made to the children—a drafting error that occurs occasionally—your client will owe the income tax when such payments are made.

If a client is covered by a defined benefit plan (a traditional pension), a QDRO works a bit differently.

- Figuring out what portion of the pension will go to each spouse may be extremely complicated, requiring sophisticated actuarial analysis.
- Some form of annuity payment should be specified in the QDRO. Often, the plan administrator must write two checks, one to each spouse.
- Payments generally are taxed as they are received.

As an advisor, you should keep in mind that a nonworking spouse is entitled to mandatory survivor's benefits from the other spouse's pension and retirement plan, unless that right has been waived. Once couples are divorced, an ex-spouse is no longer entitled to those mandatory benefits.

Getting a divorce might benefit a client whose spouse is entitled to large retirement benefits. Through divorce negotiations, your client might wind up receiving some of those benefits.

Contingency Plans

From an estate planning point of view, money directed to a spouse or ex-spouse under a QDRO escapes gift and estate tax. Nevertheless, some provision in the QDRO should spell out what happens in the case of either party's death.

- If your client dies, should his interest in the retirement account go to his spouse or ex-spouse? If this is not what your client wants, the QDRO should state who'll inherit your client's interest.

- If your client's spouse or ex-spouse dies, will her interest go to the children or to some other party? The QDRO should cover contingencies for her dying before or (in the case of a pension) after beginning to receive benefits.

Remarriage Vows

Clients who divorce don't necessarily stay single. They may remarry; indeed, they may remarry others who are willing to take a second (or third) chance at marital bliss. Thus, you may be advising a blended family on financial matters, including the proper handling of a retirement plan.

Prenuptial agreements are generally a good idea—clients shouldn't remarry without one. A prenup can spell out which assets each spouse is bringing into a marriage and which ones they want to keep, free to pass on to other heirs. It can specify what the other spouse will receive, in the event of death or divorce.

Without a prenup, all of a client's assets might get sucked into a second marriage, to the dismay of other relatives. (Even with a prenup, clients should keep personal assets separate from those of a spouse, because commingled assets may be considered marital property, subject to division.)

The idea of a prenup may seem materialistic but a well-executed agreement removes a large area of uncertainty and puts everyone's mind at ease. As long as a prenup is structured fairly, a source of potential friction is removed.

For a prenup to work, it must be valid. Both parties must have their own counsel and there must be full disclosure of assets on either side.

Terms of a prenup will vary, according to the circumstances, but the basic structure is yours-mine-ours. That is, each spouse retains the assets he or she brings into the marriage while assets accumulated during the marriage are owned by both. In some states, a surviving spouse is automatically entitled to a certain share in the other spouse's estate but such an entitlement can be waived through a legitimate prenup.

When a couple is planning on remarrying, talking about a prenuptial agreement can be awkward, to say the least. As an advisor, you might downplay the possibility of divorce. Instead, ask both spouses what will happen when one of them dies. They'll want their own children to be protected, so they may be more receptive to the idea of a prenuptial agreement.

Of course, you can be the bad guy when it comes to a remarriage. A soon-to-be-married can tell a prospective spouse, "You know I love you, honey, but my financial advisor insists I sign a prenup."

Early Worms Get the Bird

Distributions from pension plans and some profit-sharing plans need to have a spouse's written consent, if the amount is more than $5,000.

Similarly, a spouse will be the plan's beneficiary unless this right is formally waived. Thus, marriage (or remarriage) gives the new spouse access to the other spouse's retirement plan, even to the amounts that were accumulated before the marriage. Whether this is an advantage or disadvantage depends on whether your primary client is the one who earned the money in the plan.

If you represent the spouse with the retirement plan, it's to your client's advantage to stay unmarried because marriage gives the spouse access to the retirement plan. The only way to get around this is to persuade the new spouse to waive those rights.

In such a case, don't advise your client to rely on a prenuptial agreement. Before the marriage, a future spouse can't sign away any rights to a spouse-to-be's retirement plan. Only a spouse can legally do that.

If it's possible, advise your client to terminate his retirement plan before the marriage and roll the balance into an IRA, where spousal rights don't apply. Your client may be able to start a new plan after the marriage, at which time the new spouse can waive his or her rights, if agreeable. Make sure such a waiver is included in the plan administration documents.

However, if you represent the party without the retirement fund, marriage may be very much in your client's best interest because rights to that plan are then acquired.

Sooner or Later

In one variety of prenup, the amount of net worth a client has accumulated before a second marriage might go to the children from the first marriage while assets accumulated subsequently might go to the second spouse and any children from that marriage. However, it may not be easy to draw such lines. If most of a client's net worth is in a retirement plan and a securities portfolio, how can they be split into pre- and post-nuptial segments?

One common technique in such situations is the use of a QTIP (Qualified Terminable Interest Property) trust. Assets left to such a trust are considered marital assets so no estate tax is due at the first spouse's death. All income from the trust goes to the surviving spouse. Sometimes, but not always, the survivor has access to the trust principal, too.

After the death of the surviving spouse, estate tax is due and the remaining trust assets go to heirs named by the trust creator. Thus, clients can direct the assets to the children of a first marriage, if that's their desire.

Although this plan sounds good on paper, it may be very difficult for the surviving spouse to understand that she has no control over the ultimate disposition of the trust assets. A certain amount of explaining usually is required.

Nevertheless, a QTIP can be a valuable tool. In fact, a QTIP-like trust may be named as retirement plan beneficiary. If the remarriage does not work, the beneficiary designation can be changed to the client's grown children, so there is some room to adapt to changing circumstances.

QTIPs pose additional planning challenges, though. They may put the trustee in an awkward position, having to decide between the interests of the surviving spouse and those of the ultimate beneficiaries. The surviving spouse may want everything in bonds, even risky high-yield bonds, to maximize her annual income. She might not care if the principal is stable or shrinks a bit. The children from the first marriage, however, are likely to urge the trustee to invest in growth stocks so their inheritance will appreciate, even if there is scant income for the surviving spouse.

A trustee may use a total return rather than a current income approach: Invest largely in stocks and sell some each year to provide adequate cash flow to the surviving spouse. However, this strategy forces the trustee to make continuing portfolio decisions (buy, sell, hold) and perhaps risk alienating one or more trust beneficiaries.

For that reason, it may be advisable to name an independent professional as trustee or cotrustee along with the surviving spouse or a child from the first marriage. In any case, serving as trustee of a QTIP trust can be demanding, especially if the trustee has discretion to distribute trust principal to the surviving spouse.

If you are advising a client who's setting up a trust, you probably should suggest including a provision that allows the beneficiary to replace an unsatisfactory trustee. Obviously, the beneficiary can't name just anyone but courts have approved trusts in which the beneficiary can replace an independent trustee with another unrelated, independent trustee.

Long Division

Yet another problem relates to the timing of QTIP distributions. Suppose your client dies at age 80, leaving a 60-year-old widow and children from a first marriage who are 55 and 50. By the time his widow dies and his children inherit, they could be well into their 70s, having spent the past 20 years waiting for their stepmother to die so they can inherit—if there is anything left to inherit.

Liquidity may be a concern, too, especially for clients who accumulate most of their wealth in a tax-deferred retirement plan. Such a plan, held in a QTIP-type trust, can pass from surviving spouse to the children of a first marriage. However, estate tax may be due then. If the estate tax needs to be paid from the IRA, withdrawals will trigger income tax as well, stripping out a great deal of the plan's value and sharply reducing the children's inheritance.

What techniques can be used to avoid such problems? Clients can make gifts to an irrevocable trust, which can use the money to buy life insurance. The insurance proceeds, payable when estate tax is due, can protect the retirement plan. (See Chapter 15 for more on providing estate liquidity.)

If a client feels that he has more than enough wealth to provide comfortably for himself and his spouse, he might give away some of that wealth to his children while he is still alive. Clients can give up to $10,000 worth of assets ($20,000 if the spouse consents) to any number of recipients each year, free of gift tax.

Starting in 1999, those limits were indexed to inflation in $1,000 increments, so by 2002 clients likely will be able to give away up to $11,000 or $22,000 per recipient per year. (In addition, clients can make direct payments of a grandchild's tuition expense without any gift tax consequences.)

Whether or not your clients make lifetime gifts, they can make outright bequests to their children at their death. For 1999, clients can leave up to $650,000 worth of assets to their children, free of federal estate tax, a number that will increase to $1 million by 2006. Thus, it's possible to leave some assets to children from a first marriage and some assets, outright or in trust, to a second spouse.

Clients who choose the latter strategy must decide which assets to leave to the children. One approach is for a client to divide an IRA into two or more IRAs. One IRA can have the spouse as beneficiary while the other IRA or IRAs can be left to each of the children. Your client can determine how much goes into each IRA. It's a relatively easy process and it provides each heir with control over an IRA.

Popular Policies

Another option is to keep the IRA intact, going to the surviving spouse, while appreciated securities or real estate is left to the children. Inherited assets get a step-up in basis, so the children can sell those assets without owing any tax on the appreciation during your client's lifetime.

Naming retirement plan beneficiaries may be difficult for a remarried client, especially if a sizable sum has built up over the years. For tax purposes, it makes the most sense to name a spouse as beneficiary—this permits the tax deferral to be extended, increasing the wealth buildup and delaying the income tax bill. However, if the surviving spouse inherits the retirement plan, the money in the plan may not ultimately go to the children of the original plan owner. Again, a sophisticated financial plan may call for making it up to the children with a bequest of other assets or with life insurance. It's possible to structure a QTIP-like arrangement for retirement plans so that the children are the ultimate beneficiaries, but it may take many years before they inherit whatever is left in the plan after the second spouse's death.

Sometimes, life insurance is a vital ingredient to resolving such an impasse. A client might plan on leaving the bulk of his estate to his spouse, particularly if there's a second set of children, and provide for the children from his first marriage with an insurance policy that pays off at his death. Alternatively, assets accumulated before the second marriage might go to the children of the first marriage while life insurance protects the second spouse and her children, if any.

Clients who have remarried soon learn that they can't leave everything to everybody, particularly if the new wife is much younger than your client. She might outlive him by many years, during which time other heirs (the children) may get relatively little, if your client has set up a QTIP trust for most of his assets.

Some of the shortfall may be offset by life insurance, held in an irrevocable trust so creditors don't have access to the cash value. That is, your client might take some of the money that would have been left in a QTIP and use it to insure his life, payable to his kids. The spouse will get less but there likely will be enough for her to live comfortably; the kids will get an inheritance at your client's death, thanks to the insurance proceeds, which may make it easier for them to manage until the surviving spouse dies and they inherit in full.

Something for Everyone

Suppose, for example, Bill Walker was remarried to Joy, who was not the mother of his children. He might decide to name a trust as IRA beneficiary, providing that Joy receive all the trust income (that is, the IRA income) during her lifetime while the remainder goes to Dick and Diane, his children. However, Joy might use up most or all of the IRA, leaving little or nothing for Bill's children.

One solution to this dilemma is to split the IRA into three parts so that, at Bill's death, each of his children as well as Joy can inherit an individual IRA. Careful planning will make the most of Bill's gift/estate tax exemption, scheduled to reach $1 million in 2007.

Another strategy is to leave the entire IRA to Joy, outright or in trust, and buy a single-life insurance policy on Bill, payable to his children. This purchase will provide them with an inheritance after his death and avoid a situation in which they're eagerly waiting for Joy to die so they can inherit whatever might be left of Bill's IRA. Premiums for this insurance policy might be funded by withdrawals from Bill's IRA.

If an insurance policy is held in an irrevocable trust and all the formalities are followed, the beneficiaries can receive the full insurance proceeds, uncut by income or estate taxes. Such a trust can become a *dynasty trust* (see Chapter 16), which will remain in place to protect future generations.

Cover Your Anatomy

Some clients don't want to buy insurance just to give their kids some extra spending money. That may be fine for a client who wants to keep a child from becoming too rich too fast, but there might be hazards in such a situation for financial advisors: In today's litigious society, the children might sue you, even though they weren't your clients. These children might charge that you failed to protect their interests. Therefore, if you are going to recommend that a client buy insurance to benefit his children, you should put that recommendation in writing. You may need the letter in your own defense some day.

Especially where there's substantial net worth in a remarriage, you might urge everyone to sign a *family integrity agreement*. By signing such an agreement, family members promise not to go to court in case of disputes over money. Instead, they agree to submit any arguments to binding arbitration.

Why is this a good idea? Often, some family member feels slighted over money matters. Perhaps funds have been distributed to some trust beneficiaries but not to others. By removing the threat of a lawsuit, you remove the unhappy person's trump card; he can't say, "I'll take you to court." So these agreements encourage the family members to work things out among themselves. Even if a dispute can't be resolved, binding arbitration tends to be faster and cheaper than litigation.

SUMMARY

- When you are advising clients in a divorce, it may be possible to keep a retirement plan intact and use other assets to balance a property settlement.

- If a retirement plan must be divided in a divorce settlement, a Qualified Domestic Relations Order (QDRO) allows part or all of the plan to be assigned to the other spouse without triggering an income tax.

- When a client remarries, the new spouse may automatically gain an interest in that client's retirement plan.

- Although prenuptial agreements are recommended in case of a remarriage, they don't cover retirement plans because a prospective spouse can't waive spousal rights.

- A remarried client may decide to leave a retirement plan or IRA to a surviving spouse and use life insurance to provide an offsetting inheritance for children from a prior marriage.

CHAPTER 15

The Waiting Game

Deferring Estate Tax on Retirement Plans

The income tax rules on tax-deferred retirement plans (including IRAs) are relatively simple. As long as the money stays in the plan, income taxes are deferred; when money comes out, taxes are due. Those rules are for *income* tax. An entirely different set of rules apply to *estate* tax. What's more, the estate tax can be much more punishing. Although federal income tax rates go from 15% to 39.6%, federal estate tax rates kick in at 37% and reach as high as 55%. State taxes might take another bite out of a client's estate.

Here's the picture. You advise a client to build wealth through a tax-deferred retirement plan. The client follows your advice and accumulates a huge plan, perhaps one that's worth several million dollars.

At your client's death, that retirement plan is included in his taxable estate, along with all of his other assets. Depending on your client's net worth, as much as 55% of that plan may be lost in estate tax.

Then or Never

Fortunately, with some astute planning you can help your clients avoid or defer the estate tax on their retirement plans. If the estate tax is deferred, tax-free wealth building can continue. Here are the major techniques for estate tax avoidance and deferral.

Charitable gifts and bequests.   It's possible to make deferred donations to charity yet still avoid the estate tax. For details, see Chapter 16.

Credit shelter planning.   Each taxpayer can give or bequeath a certain amount of assets, tax free, thanks to a unified credit that can be applied to gift or estate tax. This credit shelters $650,000 worth of assets in 1999, a number that will escalate until it reaches $1 million in 2006.

Clients can decide which assets to use for this credit shelter. Usually, it's better to fund this credit shelter with assets other than a retirement plan. However, some clients will have so much money in their IRA, and little elsewhere, that the credit shelter must be funded from the IRA. Therefore, a client with a large IRA can split off a $650,000 account and leave it to his children, tax free, in 1999. Each year, if the client is still alive, that IRA may be allowed to retain earnings and increase to the credit shelter limit, reaching $1 million in 2006.

Spousal planning.   Married clients can leave unlimited amounts of assets to a surviving spouse, tax free. Thus, a tax-deferred retirement plan of any magnitude can be left to the spouse, for estate tax deferral, with children named as contingent beneficiaries. (The spouse can disclaim what she does not need so the children can inherit the IRA and stretch out distributions over their longer life expectancy. Such a move will save estate tax at the spouse's death.) Alternatively, clients who have large plans might leave some to their children, sheltered by the unified credit, and some to the spouse, sheltered by the unlimited marital deduction from gift and estate tax.

Kid Stuff

Using an IRA or other tax-deferred retirement plan to take advantage of the unified credit may be a sound strategy. When your client dies, the IRA will pass to the children, free of estate tax. The children can take minimum distributions based on their life expectancies, stretching out the tax deferral.

There may be better solutions, though. For example, your client might hold significant amounts of appreciated securities or real estate. If so, your client may prefer to use up the credit shelter by bequeathing those assets to the children, who'll inherit with a step-up in basis. Thus, the children will be able to sell those assets, tax free.

In other situations, your client may hold shares of a family business that he wishes to pass to the children, who'll run the company. If so, it may make sense to leave the shares to the children, using the unified credit to shelter tax on that bequest.

If your client decides to leave the IRA to the children, sheltered by the unified credit, yet another decision must be made: Should the IRA be left outright to the children or should a trust be the beneficiary?

In many cases, it makes sense to leave the assets in trust for the following reasons:

- The IRA can be protected from squandering, assuming a capable trustee is in place.

- The trust can add an extra layer of creditor protection to the inherited IRA.

- The surviving spouse can be named a trust beneficiary so that she'll have access to the money in the IRA, if necessary. If the surviving spouse won't need the money, children or even grandchildren can be named as beneficiaries, increasing the tax deferral. In the case of children whose ages are far apart, creating separate trusts for each child benefits the younger children. Grandchildren can be named as trust beneficiaries for a super stretch-out, as long as care is taken to comply with the generation-skipping tax.

Survivor's Benefits

Perhaps the greatest drawback to leaving the IRA to the owner's children is that the surviving spouse may need the money for retirement income. If that's the case, then the IRA can be left to the surviving spouse; no estate tax is due on spousal bequests.

For some clients, then, estate tax deferral is fairly simple. The IRA owner names his spouse as beneficiary. If the owner dies before the required beginning date (RBD) for minimum distributions, the surviving spouse can wait until the year when the IRA owner would have reached 70½, then take minimum distributions. Those distributions can be stretched over the survivor's life expectancy.

A better option, in most cases, is for the surviving spouse to treat the inherited IRA as her own. This provides a fresh start and opens up more planning opportunities. Suppose, for example, that Jane Smith inherits her husband John's IRA after he died at age 69. Jane, now 60, can claim John's IRA as her own. She can defer taking distributions until she reaches 70½, if she wishes, and she can name someone else as her beneficiary for this IRA.

What if the IRA owner dies after the RBD? Again, the surviving spouse can claim the IRA as her own and name new beneficiaries. She can do so even if she's over 70½. This is a special exception for spouses; other beneficiaries can't name new beneficiaries after age 70½. In any case, no estate tax is due until the death of the surviving spouse, when the children inherit the IRA.

Complications Arise

However, other situations will arise where this simple solution won't work.

There are no other assets available to use the unified credit. Suppose, for example, that George Williams has an estate that's large enough to require tax planning but most of his assets are jointly held, so they can't go to the children. In that case, the IRA can be left to the children, up to the unified credit amount, so that this tax break isn't wasted.

One solution, as described previously, is to give the surviving spouse the ability to disclaim all or part of the IRA in favor of the children or a credit shelter trust.

The IRA is so large that the spouse won't need the entire amount. Suppose, at his death, Henry Baker has a $3 million IRA while his wife Katherine likely will be able to live on the income generated by a $2 million IRA. Assuming that Henry lives until 2006, when the unified credit will shelter $1 million, he can split his IRA into smaller units. For a $2 million IRA he can designate Katherine as beneficiary while their children are the beneficiaries of the other $1 million. At Henry's death, if the children inherit the $1 million IRA and no other assets, no estate tax will be due, thanks to the unified credit.

The surviving spouse is not likely to be able to handle a large IRA successfully. The spouse might be inexperienced with money or susceptible to requests from friends and family. In such circumstances, it probably is better to leave the IRA in trust and name the surviving spouse as a trust beneficiary.

The client is remarried, with children from a first marriage. In this situation, leaving the IRA to the surviving spouse defers estate tax but the client's children may never see any of it. That is, the surviving spouse may leave the inherited IRA to her children or to other relatives rather than to the IRA owner's children. Again, a trust may be the most likely IRA beneficiary; specifically, a trust that acts like a QTIP trust.

Hers and His

As explained in Chapter 10, a standard QTIP trust is one in which the surviving spouse gets all the income while the first spouse to die gets to name the ultimate beneficiary. There are technical problems with putting an IRA or a qualified plan in a standard QTIP trust but a special section of the tax code [2056(b)(8)] permits taxpayers to accomplish virtually the same thing with an IRA or qualified plan.

For example, Alan Carson's IRA can be left to a trust, with no estate tax due. After Alan dies, his executor can make a QTIP election for a marital trust. All payouts from this trust will go to his second wife Jan; in case of need, the trustee can distribute more funds to Jan. At Jan's death, whatever remains in the IRA will go to Alan's children from his first marriage.

In essence, Jan must be the only one entitled to trust income and principal. However, the ultimate beneficiaries of the QTIP trust assets (after Jan's death) are named by Alan. Thus, the QTIP election gives the first decedent the ability to direct assets as desired yet still defer estate tax until after the second spouse's death.

QTIP trusts are valuable estate planning tools but using them may present complications. What happens if the surviving spouse uses up most or all the IRA so there's little or nothing for the kids?

Again, one possible solution is to split the IRA so that the kids and the surviving spouse can each inherit. Another approach is to leave the entire IRA to the spouse and buy a life insurance policy on the owner, payable to the children. IRA withdrawals may pay the insurance premiums, if necessary. Indeed, once required minimum distributions begin, the IRA owner can pay the tax and use the after-tax proceeds for insurance premiums. This is an excellent technique for paying life insurance premiums.

Mortal Wounds

Another possible situation should be considered when you advise clients on the subject of estate tax. Generally, married couples should balance their estates so that they each can make full use of their unified credit. However, that may be more difficult when one spouse has a huge IRA and the other spouse has relatively few assets.

Suppose, for example, both Paul and Margie Jordan live past the year 2005, so the unified credit will shield $1 million of assets apiece. Paul has total assets of $1.3 million, Margie has $100,000 in wealth, and they jointly own a house worth $600,000.

If Paul dies first, estate tax won't be a problem. Paul can leave $1 million to their children, sheltered by the unified credit. The other

$300,000 of his estate can go to Margie, along with his half of their house. At Margie's death, she'll have a total of $1 million to pass to their children, free of estate tax. The bottom line: the couple passes $2 million to their kids, tax free.

Now look what happens if Margie dies first. She has only $100,000 to leave to their children. Paul becomes the sole owner of their house, boosting his estate to $1.9 million. At his death, about $400,000 will go to the IRS—a wholly unnecessary loss of $400,000.

No Exit

Some basic planning can remedy this situation. Paul can transfer $300,000 to Margie as well as his interest in the house. Such gifts between spouses are tax free. Then, no matter which spouse dies first, each will have a $1 million estate to pass to their children, tax free.

That strategy will work, assuming that Paul and Margie have a solid marriage. But what if Paul's $1.3 million consists of an IRA? He can't transfer money from his IRA to Margie unless he takes it out—and pays income tax on the withdrawal.

Does it make sense to pay income tax now to avoid estate tax later? Perhaps. However, you'll probably need to be persuasive to convince Paul that he should move $300,000 out of his IRA now and pay as much as $120,000 in income tax, so his heirs can save about $140,000 in estate tax, some time in the future.

Whether or not early withdrawals make sense, some steps can be taken. For instance, as much of the non-IRA assets as possible should be transferred to the spouse with the lesser net worth. In this example, Paul should transfer his share of the house to Margie and her will should call for the house to be left to their children. Then, if Margie dies first, Paul will have a $1.3 million estate, not a $1.9 million estate.

In truth, there may not be an efficient way to defer the estate tax on a large IRA, if the IRA owner is the first spouse to die. However, if you advise your clients to move other assets to the other spouse, you can make the tax bite a great deal less painful.

SUMMARY

- Large retirement plans accumulated by your clients are subject to estate tax, at rates up to 55%, when those plans pass to the next generation.

- Up to $650,000 (in 1999) worth of assets can be left to heirs, free of estate tax, and retirement plans can be included in such bequests.

- In most cases, retirement plans are left to the surviving spouse, a strategy that defers estate tax until the surviving spouse dies.

- Clients who have remarried may leave their plan to a trust for the surviving spouse but specify that the trust fund goes to their own children from a prior marriage after the survivor's death.

- In some cases, it makes sense to split an IRA into separate accounts for the children and for the surviving spouse.

- In marriages where one spouse has a large IRA, transferring non-IRA assets to the other spouse may help to reduce the family's estate tax obligation.

14

Super Stretch

Prolonging Tax Deferral for Descendants

For some clients, there are limits to the planning you can provide regarding their tax-deferred retirement accounts. While you can urge them to maximize contributions and help them with their investment strategies, ultimately clients who need IRAs to finance retirement lifestyles will take money out, as needed, and pay the required income taxes.

In other situations, though, planning can be incredibly complex. Many clients won't need to tap their IRAs to any meaningful extent because they have other sources of retirement income. Here, savvy financial planning can defer taxes as long as possible and extend the tax-free buildup. Good advice can provide years of cash flow to your clients, their children, and even their grandchildren while errors can lead to most of a client's IRA being taxed away when it passes from one generation to the next.

The key to successful planning lies in knowing how to manage the minimum required distribution rules. Tax deferral can't go on forever. By April 1 of the year after an IRA owner reaches age 70½, distributions must begin. If these distributions are below a required amount, any shortfall will be hit with a 50% penalty tax. Therefore, IRA distribution planning revolves around keeping these required distributions to the lowest possible level. The less that must be withdrawn, the more that can remain inside the IRA, growing tax free.

In order to minimize distributions, planning should begin with beneficiary designations. Clients generally should not name their estate or a charity as sole IRA beneficiary; neither should they name no beneficiary at all. With these beneficiary designations, if the client dies before the date when minimum required distributions begin, all of the IRA money must be distributed—and all the income tax must be paid—by the end of the fifth calendar year following the year the IRA owner dies.

Suppose, for example, that Bill Evans dies at age 69 in 2000 with a no-beneficiary IRA. By the end of 2005 (5 calendar years), all of Bill's IRA must be paid out. That's the end of the tax shelter.

In most situations, though, an IRA owner names a spouse as beneficiary. This provides a fresh start and more planning opportunities. Carol Evans can take the inherited IRA as her own and name someone else as her beneficiary—a child or children, in many cases.

Lovely Legacy

Although most IRA owners name spousal beneficiaries, some clients won't do so, perhaps because they're widowed or divorced. In these cases, other beneficiaries can be named, perhaps children or grandchildren. Then, if the owner dies before the RBD, the beneficiary is not bound by the 5-year rule. Instead, the beneficiary can use his or her own life expectancy and stretch out the required distributions.

Suppose that Bill Evans had named his son Ed as IRA beneficiary. At Bill's death at 69, in 2000, Ed is 35 years old. Ed must start taking distributions by the end of the next year—2001 in this example. Now, Ed is 36 with a 46.4-year life expectancy, so Ed can take distributions over 46.4 years. In 2001, for example, Ed is required to withdraw only

2.1552% of the IRA balance. Assuming the IRA earns more than 2.1552%, it will continue to grow.

Even if you assume a conservative 7% growth rate, the IRA will double in about 16 years. Ed will receive an increasing stream of cash each year. In this example, it will take about 33 years before the required distributions exceed the IRA's assumed 7% growth rate and the IRA stops growing.

Because of the power of compounding, the total wealth generation can be astounding. If Bill dies in 2000 with $642,000 in his IRA and 35-year-old Ed inherits, Ed can pull out more than $1 million by the time he's 61 and still have $1.8 million in the account. At that point, Ed's minimum distributions will be over $90,000 per year. (If the IRA earns over 7% per year, the results will be even more impressive.) (See Figure 14.1.)

Figure 14.1

Details of scenario in which Bill Evans dies in 2000 with a $642,000 IRA balance and names 35-year-old Ed as beneficiary.

Inputs for Alternative 1	
General Inputs	
First Year of Analysis	2000
Length of Analysis	60
12/31/1999 Pension Fund Balance	$642,000
12/31/1999 Roth IRA Balance	$0
12/31/1999 Other Assets Balance	$0
Inflation Rate	3.00%
Assumed Growth Rate	10%
Plan Owner's Birthdate	1/1/1931
Nonspousal Beneficiary's Birthdate	1/1/1965
Assume Plan Owner Dies in	*2000
Assume Nonspousal Beneficiary Survives the Analysis	
Minimum Distributions Options	
Recalculate Owner's Life Expectancy?	Yes
Recalculate Beneficiary's Life Expectancy?	No
Start Minimum Distributions (Client's 70½ Year)	2001

Figure 14.1 continues

Figure 14.1 (*Continued*)

				Minimum Distributions—Alternative 1		
Year	Owner L/E	Benef. L/E	Joint L/E	Pension Fund Begin Value	Life Exp	Minimum Distributions
*2000	16.8	47.3	47.6	$ 642,000	47.6	$ 0
2001	0.0	46.4	46.4	686,940	46.4	14,805
2002	0.0	45.4	45.4	719,184	45.4	15,841
2003	0.0	44.4	44.4	752,577	44.4	16,950
2004	0.0	43.4	43.4	787,121	43.4	18,136
2005	0.0	42.4	42.4	822,814	42.4	19,406
2006	0.0	41.4	41.4	859,647	41.4	20,764
2007	0.0	40.4	40.4	897,605	40.4	22,218
2008	0.0	39.4	39.4	936,664	39.4	23,773
2009	0.0	38.4	38.4	976,793	38.4	25,437
2010	0.0	37.4	37.4	1,017,951	37.4	27,218
2011	0.0	36.4	36.4	1,060,084	36.4	29,123
2012	0.0	35.4	35.4	1,103,128	35.4	31,162
2013	0.0	34.4	34.4	1,147,004	34.4	33,343
2014	0.0	33.4	33.4	1,191,617	33.4	35,677
2015	0.0	32.4	32.4	1,236,856	32.4	38,175
2016	0.0	31.4	31.4	1,282,589	31.4	40,847
2017	0.0	30.4	30.4	1,328,664	30.4	43,706
2018	0.0	29.4	29.4	1,374,905	29.4	46,765
2019	0.0	28.4	28.4	1,421,110	28.4	50,039
2020	0.0	27.4	27.4	1,467,046	27.4	53,542
2021	0.0	26.4	26.4	1,512,449	26.4	57,290
2022	0.0	25.4	25.4	1,557,020	25.4	61,300
2023	0.0	24.4	24.4	1,600,420	24.4	65,591
2024	0.0	23.4	23.4	1,642,267	23.4	70,182
2025	0.0	22.4	22.4	1,682,131	22.4	75,095
2026	0.0	21.4	21.4	1,719,529	21.4	80,352
2027	0.0	20.4	20.4	1,753,919	20.4	85,976
2028	0.0	19.4	19.4	1,784,699	19.4	91,995
2029	0.0	18.4	18.4	1,811,193	18.4	98,434

Figure 14.1 (*Continued*)

Minimum Distributions—Alternative 1						
Owner Year	Benef. L/E	Joint L/E	Pension Fund L/E	Life Begin Value	Minimum Exp	Distributions
2030	0.0	17.4	17.4	1,832,652	17.4	105,325
2031	0.0	16.4	16.4	1,848,240	16.4	112,698
2032	0.0	15.4	15.4	1,857,030	15.4	120,586
2033	0.0	14.4	14.4	1,857,995	14.4	129,027
2034	0.0	13.4	13.4	1,849,996	13.4	138,059
2035	0.0	12.4	12.4	1,831,773	12.4	147,724
2036	0.0	11.4	11.4	1,801,932	11.4	158,064
2037	0.0	10.4	10.4	1,758,939	10.4	169,129
2038	0.0	9.4	9.4	1,701,097	9.4	180,968
2039	0.0	8.4	8.4	1,626,538	8.4	193,635
2040	0.0	7.4	7.4	1,533,206	7.4	207,190
2041	0.0	6.4	6.4	1,418,837	6.4	221,693
2042	0.0	5.4	5.4	1,280,944	5.4	237,212
2043	0.0	4.4	4.4	1,116,793	4.4	253,817
2044	0.0	3.4	3.4	923,384	3.4	271,584
2045	0.0	2.4	2.4	697,426	2.4	290,594
2046	*0.0*	*1.4*	*1.4*	*435,310*	*1.4*	*310,936*
2047	0.0	0.4	0.4	133,080	0.4	133,080
2048	0.0	0.0	0.0	0	0.0	0
2049	0.0	0.0	0.0	0	0.0	0
2050	0.0	0.0	0.0	0	0.0	0
2051	0.0	0.0	0.0	0	0.0	0
2052	0.0	0.0	0.0	0	0.0	0
2053	0.0	0.0	0.0	0	0.0	0
2054	0.0	0.0	0.0	0	0.0	0
2055	0.0	0.0	0.0	0	0.0	0
2056	0.0	0.0	0.0	0	0.0	0
2057	0.0	0.0	0.0	0	0.0	0
2058	0.0	0.0	0.0	0	0.0	0
2059	0.0	0.0	0.0	0	0.0	0

Figure 14.1 continues

Figure 14.1 (*Continued*)

	Total Pension and IRA Distributions—Alternative 1			
Year	Pension Fund Distributions	Income Tax on Pension Distributions	Yearly After-Tax Distributions	Cumulative After-Tax Distributions
*2000	$ 0	$ 0	$ 0	$ 0
2001	14,805	4,145	10,660	10,660
2002	15,841	4,435	11,406	22,066
2003	16,950	4,746	12,204	34,270
2004	18,136	5,078	13,058	47,328
2005	19,406	5,434	13,972	61,300
2006	20,764	5,814	14,950	76,250
2007	22,218	6,221	15,997	92,247
2008	23,773	6,656	17,117	109,364
2009	25,437	7,122	18,315	127,679
2010	27,218	7,621	19,597	147,276
2011	29,123	8,154	20,969	168,245
2012	31,162	8,725	22,437	190,682
2013	33,343	9,336	24,007	214,689
2014	35,677	9,990	25,687	240,376
2015	38,175	10,689	27,486	267,862
2016	40,847	11,437	29,410	297,272
2017	43,706	12,238	31,468	328,740
2018	46,765	13,094	33,671	362,411
2019	50,039	14,011	36,028	398,439
2020	53,542	14,992	38,550	436,989
2021	57,290	16,041	41,249	478,238
2022	61,300	17,164	44,136	522,374
2023	65,591	18,365	47,226	569,600
2024	70,182	19,651	50,531	620,131
2025	75,095	21,027	54,068	674,199
2026	80,352	22,499	57,853	732,052
2027	85,976	24,073	61,903	793,955
2028	91,995	25,759	66,236	860,191

Figure 14.1 (*Continued*)

| | | Income Tax | Yearly | Cumulative |
| | **Pension Fund** | **on Pension** | **After-Tax** | **After-Tax** |
Year	Distributions	Distributions	Distributions	Distributions
		Total Pension and IRA Distributions—Alternative 1		
2029	98,434	27,562	70,872	931,063
2030	105,325	29,491	75,834	1,006,897
2031	112,698	31,555	81,143	1,088,040
2032	120,586	33,764	86,822	1,174,862
2033	129,027	36,128	92,899	1,267,761
2034	138,059	38,657	99,402	1,367,163
2035	147,724	41,363	106,361	1,473,524
2036	158,064	44,258	113,806	1,587,330
2037	169,129	47,356	121,773	1,709,103
2038	180,968	50,671	130,297	1,839,400
2039	193,635	54,218	139,417	1,978,817
2040	207,190	58,165	149,025	2,127,842
2041	221,693	62,479	159,214	2,287,056
2042	237,212	67,101	170,111	2,457,167
2043	253,817	72,058	181,759	2,638,926
2044	271,584	77,366	194,218	2,833,144
2045	290,594	83,053	207,541	3,040,685
2046	*310,936*	89,149	*221,787*	*3,262,472*
2047	133,080	37,262	95,818	3,358,290
2048	0	0	0	3,358,290
2049	0	0	0	3,358,290
2050	0	0	0	3,358,290
2051	0	0	0	3,358,290
2052	0	0	0	3,358,290
2053	0	0	0	3,358,290
2054	0	0	0	3,358,290
2055	0	0	0	3,358,290
2056	0	0	0	3,358,290
2057	0	0	0	3,358,290
2058	0	0	0	3,358,290
2059	0	0	0	3,358,290

Naming a younger beneficiary locks in a long-term payout, no matter what happens in subsequent years. In this example, Ed is taking distributions over a 46.4-year life expectancy. If he dies 35 years later, at age 71, Ed's heirs still have another 10.4 years to extend IRA distributions. As Ed takes distributions he receives an income tax credit for estate taxes paid at his father's death under IRC 691(c), thereby increasing his net income along the way.

Divide to Conquer

What if Bill has two children, Ed and Lynn, whom he names as beneficiaries, and Bill dies before the RBD? The distributions can be stretched out over the life expectancy of the oldest beneficiary.

A problem may arise, though, if one beneficiary wishes to draw cash from the inherited IRA at a faster rate than the other. In such situations, the IRA can be split into two or more IRAs so that each beneficiary controls the pace of distributions. Although an inherited IRA can be divided, it may be better if this division takes place while the owner is alive, into one IRA for each beneficiary. Then, after the owner's death, each beneficiary can use his or her own life expectancy for extending minimum distributions. A lifetime division is especially important if there's a large discrepancy between the beneficiaries' ages. Otherwise, the youngest beneficiary may have to withdraw IRA funds based on the oldest beneficiary's life expectancy.

This is a difficult concept to convey to clients but it's worth the effort because the amounts involved can be substantial. Especially if both the spouse and the children are intended beneficiaries, it is important to segregate IRAs.

Other situations may call for setting up multiple IRAs with different beneficiaries. If it's desirable to use the IRA owner's estate tax credit, an IRA containing $650,000 (in 1999) can be set up for a child or children. If a charitable bequest is desired, a separate IRA can be created with a charitable beneficiary. The remaining IRA money may be left to a spouse.

Takeout Order

As the IRA owner nears the RBD, additional financial planning decisions must be made. The IRA owner needs to make an irrevocable
choice between minimum distribution methods: One method is called
recalculation while the other is called by various names such as *term
certain*, *fixed number of years*, *reduce by one*, and other names. No matter what the name, the key feature is that life expectancy is not recalculated each year.

Regardless of which method a client chooses, the beneficiary designation is crucial. Suppose, for example, that Bill Evans is 71 when he
begins required minimum distributions. He names no beneficiary so he
uses a single life expectancy and he chooses the recalculation method
(see Figure 14.2).

Figure 14.2

Details of scenario in which Bill Evans uses single life expectancy and the
recalculation minimum distribution method.

Inputs for Alternative 1	
General Inputs	
First year of Analysis	2001
Length of Analysis	60
12/31/2000 Pension Fund Balance	$642,000
12/31/2000 Roth IRA Balance	$0
12/31/2000 Other Assets Balance	$0
Inflation Rate	3.00%
Assumed Growth Rate	10%
Plan Owner's Birthdate	1/1/1931
No Beneficiary Specified	
Assume Plan Owner Dies in	2030
Minimum Distributions Options	
Recalculate Owner's Life Expectancy?	Yes
Start Minimum Distributions (Client's 70½ Year)	2001

Figure 14.2 continues

Figure 14.2 (*Continued*)

		Minimum Distributions—Alternative 1		
Year	Owner L/E	Pension Fund Begin Value	Life Exp	Minimum Distributions
2001	16.0	$642,000	16.0	$40,125
2002	15.3	644,006	15.3	42,092
2003	14.6	644,048	14.6	44,113
2004	13.9	641,930	13.9	46,182
2005	13.2	637,450	13.2	48,292
2006	12.5	630,399	12.5	50,432
2007	11.9	620,565	11.9	52,148
2008	11.2	608,206	11.2	54,304
2009	10.6	592,675	10.6	55,913
2010	10.0	574,335	10.0	57,434
2011	9.5	553,084	9.5	58,219
2012	8.9	529,506	8.9	59,495
2013	8.4	502,912	8.4	59,870
2014	7.9	474,055	7.9	60,007
2015	7.4	443,031	7.4	59,869
2016	6.9	409,983	6.9	59,418
2017	6.5	375,105	6.5	57,708
2018	6.1	339,615	6.1	55,675
2019	5.7	303,816	5.7	53,301
2020	5.3	268,051	5.3	50,576
2021	5.0	232,698	5.0	46,540
2022	4.7	199,189	4.7	42,381
2023	4.4	167,785	4.4	38,133
2024	4.1	138,728	4.1	33,836
2025	3.9	112,234	3.9	28,778
2026	3.7	89,298	3.7	24,135
2027	3.4	69,724	3.4	20,507
2028	3.2	52,662	3.2	16,457
2029	3.0	38,739	3.0	12,913
2030	*2.8*	*27,634*	*2.8*	*9,869*

Figure 14.2 (*Continued*)

	Minimum Distributions—Alternative 1			
Year	Owner L/E	Pension Fund Begin Value	Life Exp	Minimum Distributions
2031	0.0	19,009	0.0	19,009
2032	0.0	0	0.0	0
2033	0.0	0	0.0	0
2034	0.0	0	0.0	0
2035	0.0	0	0.0	0
2036	0.0	0	0.0	0
2037	0.0	0	0.0	0
2038	0.0	0	0.0	0
2039	0.0	0	0.0	0
2040	0.0	0	0.0	0
2041	0.0	0	0.0	0
2042	0.0	0	0.0	0
2043	0.0	0	0.0	0
2044	0.0	0	0.0	0
2045	0.0	0	0.0	0
2046	0.0	0	0.0	0
2047	0.0	0	0.0	0
2048	0.0	0	0.0	0
2049	0.0	0	0.0	0
2050	0.0	0	0.0	0
2051	0.0	0	0.0	0
2052	0.0	0	0.0	0
2053	0.0	0	0.0	0
2054	0.0	0	0.0	0
2055	0.0	0	0.0	0
2056	0.0	0	0.0	0
2057	0.0	0	0.0	0
2058	0.0	0	0.0	0
2059	0.0	0	0.0	0
2060	0.0	0	0.0	0

Figure 14.2 continues

Figure 14.2 (*Continued*)

	Total Pension and IRA Distributions—Alternative 1			
Year	Pension Fund Distributions	Income Tax on Pension Distributions	Yearly After-Tax Distributions	Cumulative After-Tax Distributions
2001	$40,126	$11,122	$29,003	$ 29,003
2002	42,092	11,670	30,422	59,425
2003	44,113	12,235	31,878	91,303
2004	46,182	12,821	33,361	124,664
2005	48,292	13,402	34,890	159,554
2006	50,432	13,999	36,433	195,987
2007	52,148	14,473	37,675	233,662
2008	54,304	15,072	39,232	272,894
2009	55,913	15,526	40,387	313,281
2010	57,434	15,932	41,502	354,783
2011	58,219	16,146	42,073	396,856
2012	59,495	16,514	42,981	439,837
2013	59,870	16,605	43,265	483,102
2014	60,007	16,639	43,368	526,470
2015	59,869	16,584	43,285	569,755
2016	59,418	16,458	42,960	612,715
2017	57,708	15,982	41,726	654,441
2018	55,675	15,405	40,270	694,711
2019	53,301	14,728	38,573	733,284
2020	50,576	13,963	36,613	769,897
2021	46,540	12,827	33,713	803,610
2022	42,381	11,653	30,728	834,338
2023	38,133	10,463	27,670	862,008
2024	33,836	9,244	24,592	886,600
2025	28,778	7,827	20,951	907,551
2026	24,135	6,517	17,618	925,169
2027	20,507	5,501	15,006	940,175
2028	16,457	4,345	12,112	952,287
2029	12,913	3,347	9,566	961,853
2030	*9,869*	*2,486*	*7,383*	*969,236*

Figure 14.2 (*Continued*)

	Total Pension and IRA Distributions—Alternative 1			
Year	Pension Fund Distributions	Income Tax on Pension Distributions	Yearly After-Tax Distributions	Cumulative After-Tax Distributions
2031	19,009	2,694	16,315	985,551
2032	0	0	0	985,551
2033	0	0	0	985,551
2034	0	0	0	985,551
2035	0	0	0	985,551
2036	0	0	0	985,551
2037	0	0	0	985,551
2038	0	0	0	985,551
2039	0	0	0	985,551
2040	0	0	0	985,551
2041	0	0	0	985,551
2042	0	0	0	985,551
2043	0	0	0	985,551
2044	0	0	0	985,551
2045	0	0	0	985,551
2046	0	0	0	985,551
2047	0	0	0	985,551
2048	0	0	0	985,551
2049	0	0	0	985,551
2050	0	0	0	985,551
2051	0	0	0	985,551
2052	0	0	0	985,551
2053	0	0	0	985,551
2054	0	0	0	985,551
2055	0	0	0	985,551
2056	0	0	0	985,551
2057	0	0	0	985,551
2058	0	0	0	985,551
2059	0	0	0	985,551
2060	0	0	0	985,551

At age 71, his life expectancy is 16 years so he must withdraw at least $\frac{1}{16}$ of the amount in his IRA. The next year, at 72, his life expectancy will be 15.3 years, so he must withdraw at least $\frac{1}{15.3}$. At age 73, he must withdraw a least $\frac{1}{14.6}$ of his IRA balance. And so on. Each year he recalculates his life expectancy and withdraws a slightly larger percentage. However, Bill will never run out of life expectancy, no matter how long he lives. Even at age 95, he'll have a 3.7-year life expectancy and will have to withdraw at least $\frac{1}{3.7}$ of his IRA. That fraction represents 27% of his IRA, meaning he can retain 73% of his IRA money for further tax deferral.

Most clients, though, should never use a single life expectancy. As long as a person or a qualified trust is named as IRA beneficiary, a joint life expectancy can be used, extending the payout. (If a trust is named as beneficiary, the trust beneficiary's age is considered when computing joint life expectancies. In case of multiple beneficiaries, regardless of whether a trust is used, the oldest beneficiary's age is used.)

If the IRA owner's spouse is named as a beneficiary, which usually is the case, their joint life expectancy is used. Suppose Bill Evans's wife Carol is 68 when Bill is 71 and minimum distributions begin. Their joint life expectancy is 21.2 years the first year. Now, instead of taking out 6.25% of the IRA that year, with Bob's single life expectancy, they can take out as little as 4.72%, using a joint life expectancy (see Figure 14.3). If Carol is 58 when Bill is 71, their life expectancy is 27.5 years and the first-year withdrawal can be as little as 3.64% of Bill's IRA.

If they choose the recalculation method, they can recalculate their joint life expectancy each year, never running out. At ages 85 and 82, for example, their joint life expectancy would be 10.6 years and they could withdraw as little as 9.43% of Bill's IRA.

Things are different, though, when a nonspouse beneficiary is chosen. Again, a joint life expectancy can be used. However, for purposes of this calculation, the beneficiary may not be considered more than 10 years younger than the IRA owner: This is the minimum distribution incidental benefit (MDIB), or 10-year spread rule.

Bill, at age 71, can choose his daughter Lynn, age 42, or even his granddaughter Ashley, age 9, as beneficiary (see Figure 14.4). It makes no difference. In the first year, when Bill is 71, Lynn or Ashley will be considered to be 61 for the purposes of calculating joint life expectancy. The next year, when Bill is 72, Lynn or Ashley will be counted as 62 and their joint life expectancy will be recalculated. And so on. However, after Bill's death, the MDIB rules no longer apply. Lynn or Ashley can continue taking distributions over her true life expectancy, as shown in Figure 14.4.

Figure 14.3

Details of scenario in which Bill Evans names his wife, Carol, as beneficiary.
(Bill is 71 and Carol is 68.)

Inputs for Alternative 1	
General Inputs	
First Year of Analysis	2000
Length of Analysis	60
12/31/1999 Pension Fund Balance	$642,000
12/31/1999 Roth IRA Balance	$0
12/13/1999 Other Assets Balance	$0
Inflation Rate	3.00%
Assumed Growth Rate	10%
Plan Owner's Birthdate	1/1/1929
Spousal Beneficiary's Birthdate	1/1/1932
Assume Plan Owner Dies in	*2017
Assume Spouse Dies in	2020
Minimum Distributions Options	
Recalculate Owner's Life Expectancy?	Yes
Recalculate Beneficiary's Life Expectancy?	Yes
Start Minimum Distributions (Client's 70½ Year)	1999

Figure 14.3 continues

Figure 14.3 (*Continued*)

				Minimum Distributions—Alternative 1		
Year	Owner L/E	Spouse L/E	Joint L/E	Pension Fund Begin Value	Life Exp	Minimum Distributions
2000	15.3	17.6	21.2	$642,000	21.2	$ 30,283
2001	14.6	16.8	20.3	654,537	20.3	32,243
2002	13.9	16.0	19.4	665,855	19.4	34,322
2003	13.2	15.3	18.6	675,740	18.6	36,330
2004	12.5	14.6	17.8	684,169	17.8	38,436
2005	11.9	13.9	17.0	690,934	17.0	40,643
2006	11.2	13.2	16.2	695,811	16.2	42,951
2007	10.6	12.5	15.4	698,560	15.4	45,361
2008	10.0	11.9	14.7	698,923	14.7	47,546
2009	9.5	11.2	14.0	969,973	14.0	49,784
2010	8.9	10.6	13.2	692,492	13.2	52,462
2011	8.4	10.0	12.5	684,832	12.5	54,787
2012	7.9	9.5	11.9	674,148	11.9	56,651
2013	7.4	8.9	11.2	660,722	11.2	58,993
2014	6.9	8.4	10.6	643,850	10.6	60,741
2015	6.5	7.9	10.0	623,927	10.0	62,393
2016	6.1	7.4	9.4	600,841	9.4	63,919
*2017	5.7	6.9	8.9	574,507	8.9	64,551
2018	0.0	6.5	6.5	545,653	6.5	83,947
2019	0.0	6.1	6.1	494,025	6.1	80,988
2020	*0.0*	*5.7*	*5.7*	*441,950*	*5.7*	*77,535*
2021	0.0	0.0	0.0	389,924	0.0	389,924
2022	0.0	0.0	0.0	0	0.0	0
2023	0.0	0.0	0.0	0	0.0	0
2024	0.0	0.0	0.0	0	0.0	0
2025	0.0	0.0	0.0	0	0.0	0
2026	0.0	0.0	0.0	0	0.0	0
2027	0.0	0.0	0.0	0	0.0	0
2028	0.0	0.0	0.0	0	0.0	0
2029	0.0	0.0	0.0	0	0.0	0

Figure 14.3 (*Continued*)

				Minimum Distributions—Alternative 1		
Year	Owner L/E	Spouse L/E	Joint L/E	Pension Fund Begin Value	Life Exp	Minimum Distributions
2030	0.0	0.0	0.0	0	0.0	0
2031	0.0	0.0	0.0	0	0.0	0
2032	0.0	0.0	0.0	0	0.0	0
2033	0.0	0.0	0.0	0	0.0	0
2034	0.0	0.0	0.0	0	0.0	0
2035	0.0	0.0	0.0	0	0.0	0
2036	0.0	0.0	0.0	0	0.0	0
2037	0.0	0.0	0.0	0	0.0	0
2038	0.0	0.0	0.0	0	0.0	0
2039	0.0	0.0	0.0	0	0.0	0
2040	0.0	0.0	0.0	0	0.0	0
2041	0.0	0.0	0.0	0	0.0	0
2042	0.0	0.0	0.0	0	0.0	0
2043	0.0	0.0	0.0	0	0.0	0
2044	0.0	0.0	0.0	0	0.0	0
2045	0.0	0.0	0.0	0	0.0	0
2046	0.0	0.0	0.0	0	0.0	0
2047	0.0	0.0	0.0	0	0.0	0
2048	0.0	0.0	0.0	0	0.0	0
2049	0.0	0.0	0.0	0	0.0	0
2050	0.0	0.0	0.0	0	0.0	0
2051	0.0	0.0	0.0	0	0.0	0
2052	0.0	0.0	0.0	0	0.0	0
2053	0.0	0.0	0.0	0	0.0	0
2054	0.0	0.0	0.0	0	0.0	0
2055	0.0	0.0	0.0	0	0.0	0
2056	0.0	0.0	0.0	0	0.0	0
2057	0.0	0.0	0.0	0	0.0	0
2058	0.0	0.0	0.0	0	0.0	0
2059	0.0	0.0	0.0	0	0.0	0

Figure 14.3 continues

Figure 14.3 (*Continued*)

	Total Pension and IRA Distributions—Alternative 1			
Year	Pension Fund Distributions	Income Tax on Pension Distributions	Yearly After-Tax Distributions	Cumulative After-Tax Distributions
2000	$ 30,283	$ 8,479	$ 21,804	$ 21,804
2001	32,243	9,028	23,215	45,019
2002	34,322	9,610	24,712	69,731
2003	36,330	10,172	26,158	95,889
2004	38,436	10,762	27,674	123,563
2005	40,643	11,380	29,263	152,826
2006	42,951	12,026	30,925	183,751
2007	45,361	12,701	32,660	216,411
2008	47,546	13,313	34,233	250,644
2009	49,784	13,940	35,844	286,488
2010	52,462	14,689	37,773	324,261
2011	54,787	15,340	39,447	363,708
2012	56,651	15,862	40,789	404,497
2013	58,993	16,518	42,475	446,972
2014	60,741	17,007	43,734	490,706
2015	62,393	17,470	44,923	535,629
2016	63,919	17,897	46,022	581,651
*2017	64,551	19,385	45,166	626,817
2018	83,947	25,380	58,567	685,384
2019	80,988	24,442	56,546	741,930
2020	*77,535*	23,410	*54,125*	*796,055*
2021	389,924	134,048	255,876	1,051,931
2022	0	0	0	1,051,931
2023	0	0	0	1,051,931
2024	0	0	0	1,051,931
2025	0	0	0	1,051,931
2026	0	0	0	1,051,931
2027	0	0	0	1,051,931
2028	0	0	0	1,051,931
2029	0	0	0	1,051,931

Figure 14.3 (*Continued*)

	Total Pension and IRA Distributions—Alternative 1			
Year	**Pension Fund Distributions**	**Income Tax on Pension Distributions**	**Yearly After-Tax Distributions**	**Cumulative After-Tax Distributions**
2030	0	0	0	1,051,931
2031	0	0	0	1,051,931
2032	0	0	0	1,051,931
2033	0	0	0	1,051,931
2034	0	0	0	1,051,931
2035	0	0	0	1,051,931
2036	0	0	0	1,051,931
2037	0	0	0	1,051,931
2038	0	0	0	1,051,931
2039	0	0	0	1,051,931
2040	0	0	0	1,051,931
2041	0	0	0	1,051,931
2042	0	0	0	1,051,931
2043	0	0	0	1,051,931
2044	0	0	0	1,051,931
2045	0	0	0	1,051,931
2046	0	0	0	1,051,931
2047	0	0	0	1,051,931
2048	0	0	0	1,051,931
2049	0	0	0	1,051,931
2050	0	0	0	1,051,931
2051	0	0	0	1,051,931
2052	0	0	0	1,051,931
2053	0	0	0	1,051,931
2054	0	0	0	1,051,931
2055	0	0	0	1,051,931
2056	0	0	0	1,051,931
2057	0	0	0	1,051,931
2058	0	0	0	1,051,931
2059	0	0	0	1,051,931

Figure 14.4

Details of scenario in which Bill Evans names his daughter or granddaughter as beneficiary.

Inputs for Alternative 1	
General Inputs	
First year of Analysis	2000
Length of Analysis	60
12/31/1999 Pension Fund Balance	$2,000,000
12/31/1999 Roth IRA Balance	$0
12/31/1999 Other Assets Balance	$0
Inflation Rate	3.00%
Assumed Growth Rate	10%
Plan Owner's Birthdate	1/1/1930
Nonspousal Beneficiary's Birthdate	1/1/1958
Assume Plan Owner Dies in	*2015
Assume NonSpousal Beneficiary Dies in	2039
Minimum Distributions Options	
Recalculate Owner's Life Expectancy?	Yes
Recalculate Beneficiary's Life Expectancy?	No
Start Minimum Distributions (Client's 70½ Year)	2000

Life Expectancies—Alternative 1				
Year	Owner L/E	Benef. L/E	Actual Joint L/E	MDIB Life Exp.
2000	16.0	40.6	41.0	26.2
2001	15.3	39.6	40.1	25.3
2002	14.6	38.6	38.2	24.4
2003	13.9	37.6	37.2	23.5
2004	13.2	36.6	36.3	22.7
2005	12.5	35.6	35.3	21.8
2006	11.9	34.6	34.4	20.9
2007	11.2	33.6	33.5	20.1
2008	10.6	32.6	32.5	19.2
2009	10.0	31.6	31.6	18.4
2010	9.5	30.6	30.7	17.6

Figure 14.4 (*Continued*)

Life Expectancies—Alternative 1

Year	Owner L/E	Benef. L/E	Actual Joint L/E	MDIB Life Exp.
2011	8.9	29.6	29.8	16.8
2012	8.4	28.6	28.9	16.0
2013	7.9	27.6	27.1	15.3
2014	7.4	26.6	26.2	14.5
*2015	6.9	25.6	25.3	13.8
2016	0.0	24.6	24.6	24.6
2017	0.0	23.6	23.6	23.6
2018	0.0	22.6	22.6	22.6
2019	0.0	21.6	21.6	21.6
2020	0.0	20.6	20.6	20.6
2021	0.0	19.6	19.6	19.6
2022	0.0	18.6	18.6	18.6
2023	0.0	17.6	17.6	17.6
2024	0.0	16.6	16.6	16.6
2025	0.0	15.6	15.6	15.6
2026	0.0	14.6	14.6	14.6
2027	0.0	13.6	13.6	13.6
2028	0.0	12.6	12.6	12.6
2029	0.0	11.6	11.6	11.6
2030	0.0	10.6	10.6	10.6
2031	0.0	9.6	9.6	9.6
2032	0.0	8.6	8.6	8.6
2033	0.0	7.6	7.6	7.6
2034	0.0	6.6	6.6	6.6
2035	0.0	5.6	5.6	5.6
2036	0.0	4.6	4.6	4.6
2037	0.0	3.6	3.6	3.6
2038	0.0	2.6	2.6	2.6
2039	*0.0*	*1.6*	*1.6*	*1.6*
2040	0.0	0.6	0.6	0.6
2041	0.0	0.0	0.0	0.0
2042	0.0	0.0	0.0	0.0
2043	0.0	0.0	0.0	0.0
2044	0.0	0.0	0.0	0.0
2045	0.0	0.0	0.0	0.0

One Down

IRA owners may choose not to recalculate life expectancies each year. In that case, they begin with the same life expectancy but the life expectancy is automatically reduced by one year, each year. Bill Evans, who withdraws $\frac{1}{16}$ of his IRA the first year taking minimum withdrawals, would have to withdraw at least $\frac{1}{15}$ the second year, $\frac{1}{14}$ the third year, and so on, with this term certain method. If Bill and Carol, using a joint life expectancy, had to withdraw at least $\frac{1}{21.2}$ the first year, subsequent withdrawals would have to be $\frac{1}{20.2}$, $\frac{1}{19.2}$, $\frac{1}{18.2}$, and so on with term certain.

Which method works better? The recalculation method results in a smaller fraction and thus permits smaller withdrawals (greater tax deferral) each year. Ten years into the foregoing Bill-and-Carol example, when they're 81 and 78, they'd only have to take out $\frac{1}{13.2}$ (7.58%) of Bill's IRA with the recalculation method. With term certain, when Bill is 81 and Carol is 78 they'd have to withdraw at least $\frac{1}{11.2}$, or 8.93%. That is, their required minimum distribution would be 18% greater using term certain than it would be using the recalculation method.

What's more, with the recalculation method clients never run out of life expectancy so they'll never completely strip their IRA, no matter how long they live. With term certain, however, they will withdraw all of their IRA funds at some point: Bill at age 93, Carol at 90. If Carol had been only 58 when the countdown began, using the term certain method she would outlive her IRA at age 86.

Nevertheless, many knowledgeable professionals prefer the term certain method rather than recalculation. The math is simpler, for one reason. Even for advisors and clients who are math wizards, term certain may be a safer choice because it protects the IRA owner whose spouse dies first.

Expect the Unexpected

If an IRA owner or spousal beneficiary dies after minimum distributions begin, the consequences depend on the chosen distribution method.

Suppose the owner, who is older, dies first. The surviving spouse may continue to take distributions over her now-single life expectancy. In most cases, though, the surviving spouse will take a lump-sum withdrawal from the decedent's IRA and roll the excess (everything above the minimum) into her own IRA. Again, there's a fresh start, so the survivor can name a new beneficiary and a new distribution method.

However, consider what happens using the recalculation method if the IRA beneficiary should die first. The IRA owner is stuck with a single life expectancy IRA and is required to take distributions (and pay tax) at an accelerated rate. *At the IRA owner's death, the heirs will have to pay all the deferred income tax by the end of the following year.*

By contrast, once term certain is chosen, the term stays in place after one spouse's death and after both spouses die. Your clients can lock in a long-term distribution schedule and not worry about which spouse dies first.

Yet another option is to split distribution methods—use recalculation for the IRA owner but term certain for the beneficiary. With this so-called hybrid method, if the beneficiary dies first, minimum distributions won't be accelerated. Meanwhile, using the recalculation method for the IRA owner permits a longer stretch-out period and reduces minimum distributions, as long as the IRA owner is alive.

Business As Usual

If the term certain method is chosen and the IRA owner dies first, nothing is lost. Suppose the beneficiary is a spouse. She can roll the IRA into her own and name younger family members as beneficiaries. Again, the MDIB (10-year spread) rules apply to calculations of joint life expectancy after the rollover. However, once the surviving spouse dies, the MDIB rules no longer apply and younger beneficiaries can use their entire life expectancy.

Suppose, for example, Carol Evans inherits her husband Bill's IRA and names her daughter Lynn as beneficiary. When minimum distributions begin, Carol is 70 and Lynn is 44, with a life expectancy of 38.7 years.

As long as Carol is alive, she has to use a 10-year spread (for example, she's 70, Lynn is treated as 60) for calculating joint life expectancy. After Carol's death, though, Lynn can use her own life expectancy, minus the number of years Carol received minimum distributions.

Thus, Carol and Lynn start with a joint life expectancy of 26.2 years. Suppose Carol dies 5 years later, at age 75. In the sixth year, Lynn can take over the minimum distributions with a 32.7-year single life expectancy. (Her original 38.7 years minus 6 years of payouts to Carol.) Now Lynn can withdraw $\frac{1}{32.7}$ the first year, $\frac{1}{31.7}$ the second year, and so on, stretching the IRA payouts over more than 30 years (Figure 14.5).

This is, in effect, the same outcome that would have resulted if Carol's husband Bill had originally named Lynn as IRA beneficiary. During Bill's lifetime, the 10-year spread rules would have been in effect. After Bill's death, though, Lynn could have taken distributions over her own much longer life expectancy. Thus, careful planning can keep an IRA in play for decades to come, producing wealth that spans the generation gap.

Turning to Trusts

So far, we have been considering an idealized Mom-Pop-Kids family in which everyone is capable of managing his or her financial affairs. But what if an IRA owner's spouse is not experienced handling large sums of money? What if one child is incompetent or a spendthrift? In such cases, rather than name an individual as IRA beneficiary, good planning may call for a trust to be established so a reliable trustee can handle the distributions. However, when a trust is named as IRA beneficiary and the IRA owner dies before the RBD, distributions usually must be completed within 5 years. To avoid this trap, the trust must be constructed very carefully.

Such trusts must have individual beneficiaries and these beneficiaries must be identifiable from the trust instrument. Ideally, a letter should be sent to the IRA custodian and an acknowledgment should be received in return.

If a trust is named as IRA beneficiary, the trust beneficiary's age is considered when computing joint life expectancies. In case of multiple trust beneficiaries, the oldest beneficiary's age is used. (For more on the use of trusts as IRA beneficiaries, see Chapter 10.)

Insist on IRAs

Besides rollover IRAs, most people can have $2,000-per-year IRAs but contributions generally aren't deductible for clients of financial advisors. Some advisors urge clients to contribute to IRAs anyway, because

Figure 14.5

Details of scenario in which Carol inherits Bill's IRA and names
Lynn as beneficiary.

Inputs for Alternative 1	
General Inputs	
First Year of Analysis	2000
Length of Analysis	60
12/31/1999 Pension Fund Balance	$642,000
12/31/1999 Roth IRA Balance	$0
12/31/1999 Other Assets Balance	$0
Inflation Rate	3.00%
Assumed Growth Rate	10%
Plan Owner's Birthdate	1/1/1930
Nonspousal Beneficiary's Birthdate	1/1/1956
Assume Plan Owner Dies in	*2005
Assume Nonspousal Beneficiary Dies in	2020
Minimum Distributions Options	
Recalculate Owner's Life Expectancy?	Yes
Recalculate Beneficiary's Life Expectancy?	Yes
Start Minimum Distributions (Client's 70½ Year)	2000

Figure 14.5 continues

Figure 14.5 (*Continued*)

			Minimum Distributions—Alternative 1			
Year	Owner L/E	Benef. L/E	Joint L/E	Pension Fund Begin Value	Life Exp	Minimum Distributions
2000	16.0	38.7	39.2	$ 642,000	26.2	$ 24,504
2001	15.3	37.7	38.2	660,721	25.3	26,115
2002	14.6	36.7	36.4	679,028	24.4	27,829
2003	13.9	35.7	35.4	696,783	23.5	29,650
2004	13.2	34.7	34.5	713,832	22.7	31,446
*2005	12.5	33.7	33.6	730,153	21.8	33,493
2006	0.0	32.7	32.7	745,426	32.7	22,796
2007	0.0	31.7	31.7	773,215	31.7	24,392
2008	0.0	30.7	30.7	801,240	30.7	26,099
2009	0.0	29.7	29.7	928,401	29.7	27,926
2010	0.0	28.7	28.7	857,578	28.7	29,881
2011	0.0	27.7	27.7	885,636	27.7	31,972
2012	0.0	26.7	26.7	913,420	26.7	34,210
2013	0.0	25.7	25.7	940,755	25.7	36,605
2014	0.0	24.7	24.7	967,441	24.7	39,168
2015	0.0	23.7	23.7	993,252	23.7	41,909
2016	0.0	22.7	22.7	1,017,937	22.7	44,843
2017	0.0	21.7	21.7	1,041,211	21.7	47,982
2018	0.0	20.7	20.7	1,062,755	20.7	51,341
2019	0.0	19.7	19.7	1,082,213	19.7	54,935
2020	0.0	18.7	18.7	1,099,187	18.7	58,780
2021	0.0	17.7	17.7	1,113,235	17.7	62,895
2022	0.0	16.7	16.7	1,123,864	16.7	67,297
2023	0.0	15.7	15.7	1,130,527	15.7	72,008
2024	0.0	14.7	14.7	1,132,615	14.7	77,049
2025	0.0	13.7	13.7	1,129,456	13.7	82,442
2026	0.0	12.7	12.7	1,120,305	12.7	88,213
2027	0.0	11.7	11.7	1,104,338	11.7	94,388
2028	0.0	10.7	10.7	1,080,647	10.7	100,995
2029	0.0	9.7	9.7	1,048,228	9.7	108,065

Figure 14.5 (*Continued*)

				Minimum Distributions—Alternative 1		
Year	Owner L/E	Benef. L/E	Joint L/E	Pension Fund Begin Value	Life Exp	Minimum Distributions
2030	0.0	8.7	8.7	1,005,974	8.7	115,629
2031	0.0	7.7	7.7	952,669	7.7	123,723
2032	0.0	6.7	6.7	886,972	6.7	132,384
2033	0.0	5.7	5.7	807,409	5.7	141,651
2034	0.0	4.7	4.7	712,361	4.7	151,566
2035	0.0	3.7	3.7	600,051	3.7	162,176
2036	0.0	2.7	2.7	468,526	2.7	173,528
2037	*0.0*	*1.7*	*1.7*	*315,648*	*1.7*	*185,675*
2038	0.0	0.7	0.7	139,071	0.7	139,071
2039	0.0	0.0	0.0	0	0.0	0
2040	0.0	0.0	0.0	0	0.0	0
2041	0.0	0.0	0.0	0	0.0	0
2042	0.0	0.0	0.0	0	0.0	0
2043	0.0	0.0	0.0	0	0.0	0
2044	0.0	0.0	0.0	0	0.0	0
2045	0.0	0.0	0.0	0	0.0	0
2046	0.0	0.0	0.0	0	0.0	0
2047	0.0	0.0	0.0	0	0.0	0
2048	0.0	0.0	0.0	0	0.0	0
2049	0.0	0.0	0.0	0	0.0	0
2050	0.0	0.0	0.0	0	0.0	0
2051	0.0	0.0	0.0	0	0.0	0
2052	0.0	0.0	0.0	0	0.0	0
2053	0.0	0.0	0.0	0	0.0	0
2054	0.0	0.0	0.0	0	0.0	0
2055	0.0	0.0	0.0	0	0.0	0
2056	0.0	0.0	0.0	0	0.0	0
2057	0.0	0.0	0.0	0	0.0	0
2058	0.0	0.0	0.0	0	0.0	0
2059	0.0	0.0	0.0	0	0.0	0

Figure 14.5 continues

Figure 14.5 (*Continued*)

		Total Pension and IRA Distributions—Alternative 1		
Year	**Pension Fund Distributions**	**Income Tax on Pension Distributions**	**Yearly After-Tax Distributions**	**Cumulative After-Tax Distributions**
2000	$ 24,504	$ 6,861	$ 17,643	$ 17,643
2001	26,115	7,312	18,803	36,446
2002	27,829	7,792	20,037	56,483
2003	29,650	8,302	21,348	77,831
2004	31,446	8,805	22,641	100,472
*2005	33,493	9,378	24,115	124,587
2006	22,796	6,383	16,413	141,000
2007	24,392	6,830	17,562	158,562
2008	26,099	7,308	18,791	177,353
2009	27,926	7,819	20,107	197,460
2010	29,881	8,367	21,514	218,974
2011	31,972	8,952	23,020	241,994
2012	34,210	9,579	24,631	266,625
2013	36,605	10,249	26,356	292,981
2014	39,168	10,967	28,201	321,182
2015	41,909	11,735	30,174	351,356
2016	44,843	12,556	32,287	383,643
2017	47,982	13,435	34,547	418,190
2018	51,341	14,375	36,966	455,156
2019	54,935	15,382	39,553	494,709
2020	58,780	16,458	42,322	537,031
2021	62,895	17,611	45,284	582,315
2022	67,297	18,843	48,454	630,769
2023	72,008	20,162	51,846	682,615
2024	77,049	21,574	55,475	738,090
2025	82,442	23,084	59,358	797,448
2026	88,213	24,700	63,513	860,961
2027	94,388	26,429	·67,959	928,920
2028	100,995	28,279	72,716	1,001,636
2029	108,065	30,258	77,807	1,079,443

Figure 14.5 (*Continued*)

	Total Pension and IRA Distributions—Alternative 1			
Year	Pension Fund Distributions	Income Tax on Pension Distributions	Yearly After-Tax Distributions	Cumulative After-Tax Distributions
2030	115,629	32,376	83,253	1,162,696
2031	123,723	34,642	89,081	1,251,777
2032	132,384	37,068	95,316	1,347,093
2033	141,651	39,662	101,989	1,449,082
2034	151,566	42,438	109,128	1,558,210
2035	162,176	45,409	116,767	1,674,977
2036	173,528	48,588	124,940	1,799,917
2037	*185,675*	52,009	*133,666*	*1,933,583*
2038	139,071	38,940	100,131	2,033,714
2039	0	0	0	2,033,714
2040	0	0	0	2,033,714
2041	0	0	0	2,033,714
2042	0	0	0	2,033,714
2043	0	0	0	2,033,714
2044	0	0	0	2,033,714
2045	0	0	0	2,033,714
2046	0	0	0	2,033,714
2047	0	0	0	2,033,714
2048	0	0	0	2,033,714
2049	0	0	0	2,033,714
2050	0	0	0	2,033,714
2051	0	0	0	2,033,714
2052	0	0	0	2,033,714
2053	0	0	0	2,033,714
2054	0	0	0	2,033,714
2055	0	0	0	2,033,714
2056	0	0	0	2,033,714
2057	0	0	0	2,033,714
2058	0	0	0	2,033,714
2059	0	0	0	2,033,714

of the tax-deferred buildup, whereas others feel that the gain from tax deferral isn't worth the pain of long-term record keeping. (Clients who meet the income limits can contribute to nondeductible Roth IRAs rather than to nondeductible traditional IRAs.)

However, for clients who participate in qualified retirement plans, there may be a good reason to set up a traditional IRA, even if it's nondeductible and even if the amount in the account is modest. By setting up an IRA now, a client may provide extra flexibility for a spouse, in case the plan participant dies at a relatively young age. An IRS letter supports the possible tax advantages.

In the Private Letter Ruling (9608042), the husband named his wife as beneficiary of both his IRA and his qualified plan account. He died before beginning to take distributions from either account. The qualified plan permits lump-sum distributions so the wife instructed the trustee to transfer the balance to the husband's IRA. Although she was entitled to elect to treat her husband's IRA as her own, she did not do so—that is, she remains the beneficiary of her late husband's IRA.

The IRS letter ruling describes what a lot of financial professionals had been advising their clients to do, but this ruling raises the comfort level. There had been some question as to whether such a transfer would maintain the tax deferral. Would such a rollover be a transfer to the wife, which would be taxable? In this letter ruling, the IRS confirms that such a transfer is a tax-free rollover. What's more, if the transfer is trustee-to-trustee (from the qualified plan to the husband's IRA), the 20% mandatory withholding rule will be avoided.

Another question this ruling answered concerned excess IRA contributions. There is a 6% excise tax each year on contributions to an IRA beyond the amount allowable as deductions: the $2,000 and $4,000 ceilings for individual and spousal IRAs. However, rollovers aren't taken into account when calculating excess contributions. The IRS has stated that because such a transfer—from the husband's qualified plan to the husband's IRA—is a rollover, the excise tax won't be applied.

Out of the Penalty Box

Thus, the IRS has said that a rollover to the decedent's IRA will be taxed like any other rollover. What are the benefits of maintaining the decedent's IRA rather than treating the IRA as belonging to the surviving spouse? Your client may be able to avoid the 10% penalty tax on distributions before age 59½.

The tax code lists several exceptions to that penalty, but they generally involve some commitments to take out certain amounts of money on a regular basis. With this strategy, the surviving spouse can have access to the IRA funds before 59½ without having to pay the 10% penalty and without having to conform to a withdrawal schedule.

The key factor: The 10% penalty is specifically not applied to distributions paid to a beneficiary on or after the participating employee's death. Because the IRA remains in the name of the husband (the employee), and the widow remains the beneficiary but not the owner of the IRA, the 10% penalty does not apply to distributions taken before age 59½. She can take out money if and when needed so she has a great deal of adaptability in getting access to the IRA. This advantage may be particularly important to younger surviving spouses.

What if the surviving spouse taps the decedent's IRA modestly or not at all? In cases where the decedent's surviving spouse is the designated beneficiary, distributions from a qualified plan or an IRA need not begin until the date the employee would have reached age 70½.

In this letter ruling, the IRS concluded that the wife who remains the beneficiary of her husband's IRA can defer distributions until that date and then begin to make minimum withdrawals. Thus, this strategy may prove helpful if the surviving spouse was older than the decedent: Minimum distributions may be deferred until the date the decedent would have reached 70½.

This strategy presents a "postmortem planning opportunity": If one spouse dies before beginning to take distributions for a retirement plan, the surviving spouse may have more options. Of course, for this option to be open, the decedent must have had an IRA, naming the spouse as beneficiary. That's why participants in a qualified plan may want to have at least some money in an IRA at the time of death, with the spouse named as beneficiary.

Alternate Routes

What other options are open to the surviving spouse of a plan participant who has not started to take distributions? That depends on the plan. In some plans an annuity is the only option for a beneficiary while other plans require a lump-sum distribution. Often, though, several choices may be available to a surviving spouse.

In many cases, the survivor may take the money out all at once, but that's usually recommended only if the family has a pressing need for cash right away. The downside of taking out all the money is that it will be fully taxed, probably in a high bracket: The amount of the distribution is added to the spouse's other income. Forward averaging (page 70) may be available to reduce the tax burden, but that opportunity is attractive for relatively few clients.

Another option open to the surviving spouse is to roll over the qualified plan into her own IRA or to treat the decedent's IRA as her own—some people like the simplicity of having everything in one IRA. When a 401(k) plan participant dies and the surviving spouse is the beneficiary, the most common practice is to take a lump sum and roll it over directly to the survivor's IRA. Depending on the circumstances, the surviving spouse may name a child or children as beneficiaries of that IRA.

If the survivor owns the IRA, she can't take penalty-free distributions at will before age 59½, but that may not be a great problem. By taking substantially equal payments (SEPPs), clients can take money from an IRA before 59½ without owing a penalty tax. SEPPs must be based on life expectancy and must be continued for 5 years or until age 59½, whichever comes later, to avoid the penalty tax. Moreover, the SEPP rules may be finessed so that IRA owners can take out virtually any amount, penalty free. Still, manipulating the SEPP rules involves an effort; the surviving spouse has more flexibility and fewer hoops to jump through as the beneficiary of the decedent's IRA.

However, a surviving spouse who elects to treat the decedent's IRA as his or her own can take minimum distributions based on his or her age, rather than the decedent's age, which may be an advantage if the survivor is younger or the IRA is earmarked for wealth transfer. What's more, the surviving spouse can name one or more additional beneficiaries. Then, if tax deferral is the goal, withdrawals can be stretched over an extended life expectancy.

After the surviving spouse's death, the presumably younger beneficiary may be able to take minimum distributions for many years, even decades. It is extremely important, though, that the IRA owner or an advisor is aware of the distribution options. If the single life expectancy recalculation method is chosen, for example, after the owner's death the beneficiary must take out the balance by the end of the year following the year of the survivor's death and pay income tax.

Sure Thing

Surviving spouses may have yet another option after the death of a qualified plan participant—they can take annuity payments. Generally, this choice is not attractive. The recipient of an annuity gives up control because there is no access to the principal in the account. Also, the interest rates on which annuity payments are based tend to be low. When a client chooses the annuity option, none of the principal may be bequeathed to charity or to another person. Nevertheless, clients should investigate the annuity option before making any decision. Sometimes the rates are attractive; some surviving spouses prefer the security of a lifetime income, even if the yields are a bit skimpy.

Sometimes the surviving spouse has little or no experience making investment decisions. Such survivors may not feel comfortable with the responsibility of managing a substantial IRA, so they're willing to take the lifetime annuity. As long as they have enough to live on, they're relieved not to be responsible for money management.

In some states, the annuity option may have added appeal. Generally, money inside qualified plans is protected from creditors' claims, and that's still true if the plan is paying out an annuity. However, once the money is rolled into an IRA, state laws apply, and the asset protection may be reduced. Therefore, if creditor protection is an issue and your client lives in a state where IRAs are vulnerable, the annuity choice may be desirable.

Advisors can't forecast the date of a client's death or the circumstances the family will face then. However, opening avenues and keeping them clear for possible future use is always a good idea. Based on this IRS letter ruling, clients who participate in a qualified plan may want to have an IRA as well, to provide one more path surviving spouses can follow if that looks like the best route.

Rights and Wrongs

Stretching out an IRA may sound simple but it certainly isn't. As an advisor, you should keep clients from making the following errors.

Don't permit a widow or widower to accept an IRA from a deceased spouse who has named the surviving spouse as the beneficiary. If the survivor maintains the old IRA, distributions must be taken relatively rapidly based on her single life expectancy. Instead, the survivor should roll over the inherited IRA into her own name and select her children or grandchildren as new beneficiaries. When these beneficiaries inherit, they can stretch distributions over their own life expectancies.

Don't permit a nonspouse to change the name of an inherited IRA. If your client Betsy Blake inherits an IRA from her mother, for example, and retitles the account in the name of Betsy Blake, her inheritance will be converted into a distribution that's taxable immediately. Betsy should keep her mother's name on the IRA, add her own name and Social Security number, then note that the original owner is now deceased, providing the date of death. This will permit her to stretch distributions over her life expectancy.

Unfortunately, many IRA custodians (banks, brokers, mutual fund companies) would simply retitle the account to Betsy's name. In effect, this converts the IRA inheritance into a distribution and the whole amount is taxable in a single year. Indeed, the IRA custodian may send Betsy a Form 1099 information report, which also informs the IRS that taxable income has been distributed. Moreover, if the IRA is retitled "for the benefit of the IRA owner's estate," income tax is accelerated and the benefits of a stretch-out are lost.

Make sure your clients retain all IRA documents. After an IRA owner dies, the heirs may need acknowledged copies of beneficiary forms and other correspondence to resolve disputes. Without this evidence, IRA distributions may be accelerated and the benefit of tax deferral is reduced.

In the real world, you can't count on the IRA custodian to retain this paperwork. With all the mergers among financial institutions these days, records may be lost. You or some other professional advisor keep the acknowledged copies. Make sure the heirs know that you're preserving these vital documents.

Make sure that IRA beneficiaries take the first distribution by December 31 of the year following the IRA owner's death. Failure to meet this deadline may mean that all funds have to be paid out of the IRA within a relatively short period of time.

Find a first-rate IRA attorney to advise your clients. Many attorneys are not up to speed in this area; errors they make may be beyond redress.

Suppose, for example, Betsy Blake discovers that her late mother wasn't properly advised, so the benefits of an IRA stretch-out are lost. Can she sue her mother's attorney for malpractice? Not in some states, such as New York. Her mother's attorney didn't represent Betsy so she can't file a malpractice suit. That's why it's vital to get a knowledgeable, experienced lawyer the first time around.

SUMMARY

- Some clients will not need to take significant amounts from their IRAs, beyond required minimum distributions.

- Never let your client use a single life expectancy, even if he or she is single.

- Such clients probably will want to leave the maximum amounts to their children and perhaps their grandchildren.

- To maximize IRA payouts, either the IRA owner or a spouse who has inherited an IRA should name a younger family member as IRA beneficiary.

- A pool of liquidity, perhaps provided by life insurance, can be used to pay estate tax and keep the IRA intact for younger family members.

- After the IRA passes to the next generation, IRA distributions can be stretched out over the beneficiary's remaining life expectancy.

- If two or more descendants are to inherit an IRA, splitting the IRA into one account per beneficiary provides more flexibility and tax deferral.

- A nonspouse who inherits an IRA should keep the IRA in the decedent's name to permit continued tax deferral.

- It's vital to work with a cooperative IRA custodian when planning for multigenerational tax deferral.

Pocket Money

Providing Estate Liquidity

For many of your clients, the good news is that the stock market is up nearly 15-fold since 1982. Assuming that a good portion of their retirement funds has been invested in stocks, they likely have accumulated a substantial amount of wealth in their IRAs, 401(k)s, or other tax-deferred plans.

Will the stock market continue to grow at 18% per year? Probably not. But even if your clients' retirement funds grow at a mere 11% per year, which is the long-term record for stocks, they will double in less than 7 years. A client who has $1 million in a plan in 1999 will have more than $2 million by 2006, nearly $5 million by 2013, compounding free of income tax.

How could this be bad? At some point, the assets in these large plans will pass to a beneficiary other than a spouse and federal estate tax will be due, at rates up to 55%. Some states impose their own tax. What's more, withdrawals from tax-deferred plans generally are subject to income tax, which might take a 40–50% bite. There are some offsets but the bottom line is that your clients' loved ones might lose 60%, 70%, 80% or more of the retirement plan to the tax collectors!

Astute advice can help your clients avoid such a disaster. Instead of retaining 30 cents on the dollar, clients can leverage their retirement plans into a 5:1, 10:1, or 15:1 payoff for their loved ones. Nevertheless, you must counsel your clients to create a source of liquidity to keep retirement plans intact when they pass to the next generation.

One Tax Leads to Another

Suppose, for example, that Al and Bonnie Carter make the right beneficiary designations, choose a prudent withdrawal method, and invest IRA funds wisely, as described in previous chapters. If so, the $1 million that Al managed to save in his retirement plan by age 65 might grow to $2.5 million when he dies and leaves it to Bonnie, and that IRA might increase to $3 million when Bonnie dies and leaves the account to their children. Counting other assets, Bonnie's total estate might add up to $5 million.

Assuming that Bonnie dies after 2006 and no major changes in federal estate tax law are enacted by the time of her death, their children will owe approximately $2 million in federal estate tax. That payment will be due within 9 months, in cash. Where will the children get that money?

If Bonnie has a $2 million portfolio of bank accounts and marketable securities, in addition to her IRA, the children can liquidate everything but the IRA and use the money to pay the estate tax. That wouldn't be an ideal solution but at least the IRA can remain intact, for ongoing tax deferral.

More likely, Bonnie's $5 million estate will consist largely of the $3 million IRA plus some real estate (including her home) and possibly shares in the family business, inherited from Al. In that case, raising the $2 million for estate tax will be difficult. The children's only realistic option may be to withdraw $2 million from the IRA to pay the estate tax.

Withdrawing $2 million from a $3 million IRA is bad enough—only $1 million would be left. However, withdrawing $2 million from the IRA is going to trigger income tax, too. By the time all the taxes are paid, virtually the entire IRA will be gone and the children won't have the opportunity to withdraw additional millions from the IRA over their lifetimes.

Of course, other factors must be in place for an effective IRA stretch-out: The beneficiary designation must be appropriate (don't let clients name their estate as beneficiary!) and the proper withdrawal method must be selected. But even the best-conceived plan will fail if the IRA has to be stripped to find money for estate tax.

Side Pocket Planning

Appropriate planning can produce better results. If the Carters are well advised, they can set up a trust to act as a "friendly banker," providing the money to pay the estate tax bill when the IRA is passed to the next generation. This planning enables the IRA to stay intact and generate decades of cash flow to the children.

Suppose, at the suggestion of their advisor, Al and Bonnie meet with an attorney who's knowledgeable about estate planning and they create the Carter Family Irrevocable Trust. Their children are named co-trustees while the same children and their four children (Al and Bonnie's grandchildren) are named as beneficiaries.

As trustees, the children can apply for a $2 million "second-to-die" insurance policy covering the lives of Al and Bonnie, who are in good health for their ages, 70 and 69. That is, after the deaths of Al and Bonnie, the insurance policy will pay $2 million to the trust. Because the policy is held by the trust, no estate tax will be due. Life insurance proceeds generally are free of income tax so the $2 million can be received completely tax free.

Al's advisor might determine that such a policy can be purchased with a $65,000 annual premium, paid for 10 years. (The exact cost depends on the investment returns on the premiums paid.) Working with a skilled lawyer, Al and Bonnie can transfer the $65,000 for premiums into the trust each year without owing gift tax.

Where will that money come from? After reaching age 70½, Al will be required to withdraw about $100,000 from his IRA each year. After paying income tax, there will be just about the right amount to fund the life insurance policy.

Prior to age 70½, it's best to use non-IRA funds to pay life insurance premiums. Securities can be sold at a loss or to generate tax-favored capital gains while money inside the IRA enjoys tax-deferred compounding.

Happy Ending

In this scenario, at some point Bonnie will die and leave a $5 million estate, along with a $2 million estate tax bill. As mentioned, the Carter Family Irrevocable Trust will be holding $2 million in life insurance proceeds. The trustees can buy assets (real estate, shares in the family business) from Bonnie's estate or lend money to the estate, secured by the estate's assets.

Once the $2 million in cash has been moved into the estate, the executor can use those funds to pay the estate tax. Bonnie's $3 million IRA remains intact so the children can enjoy tax deferral over the rest of their life expectancy.

As trustees, it's up to the children to decide which type of life insurance to buy. Their financial advisor suggests that they choose variable life. With variable life, the premiums may be invested in subaccounts that resemble stock market mutual funds. If those funds perform well over the years that the policy is in force, the death benefit may grow to exceed $2 million or policy premiums may be reduced while maintaining the $2 million death benefit.

What will happen to the Carter Family Irrevocable Trust after it has provided money for estate tax? Assume that the money has been used to purchase real estate and shares in the family business. The trust can dissolve and distribute those assets to the trust beneficiaries: Al and Bonnie's children and grandchildren.

Another option is to keep the trust in place even after Bonnie's estate has been settled. The trust likely will hold assets (real estate, family business shares) worth around $2 million. At some point, those assets can be sold for cash, which can be reinvested. Again, the assets held in the trust are likely to appreciate; they also are protected from creditors and divorcing spouses. Indeed, this trust can become a *dynasty trust*, described in Chapter 16.

Two Is Cheaper Than One

In the foregoing scenario, Al and Bonnie are advised to buy a *survivorship, or second-to-die life insurance policy*. With such policies, the proceeds are not paid until both individuals die. These policies are commonly used in estate planning for married couples. Under current tax law, the first spouse to die can leave unlimited amounts to the survivor without triggering an estate tax. However, when the survivor dies and the bulk of the estate passes to the next generation, the estate tax bill may be staggering. That's when second-to-die insurance kicks in, to provide cash when it's most needed.

Because a couple has a longer joint expectancy than either of the individuals, the insurance company has less risk. Therefore, second-to-die policies are relatively inexpensive. It's cheaper to buy one policy insuring Al and Bonnie than to buy two separate single-life policies.

Moreover, when life insurance is purchased for estate liquidity, neither your client nor the spouse should own the policy. If the client or the spouse owns the policy, the proceeds will wind up in the owner's taxable estate and the family may lose more than half the proceeds to estate tax.

Your client's children could own such a policy but there are disadvantages to such a plan. A six- or seven-figure insurance policy is tempting to creditors and divorcing spouses. It's also tempting to the children, who might tap the cash value for personal purposes. Then the full proceeds won't be available when they're really needed.

That's why you should suggest that an irrevocable trust own the policy and be the designated beneficiary. Have the trust make the original application and pay all the premiums. Then, after both spouses die, neither will have any "incidents of ownership" in the insurance policy so the proceeds won't be included in their taxable estate.

Your clients can transfer money (up to $10,000 per trust beneficiary per year, or $20,000 from a married couple) into a trust to pay premiums without owing gift tax. To do so, the trustee should send the trust beneficiaries a Crummey notice, advising them of their right to withdraw the gift within a certain time period. If that right lapses without being exercised, the trustee can use the money for life insurance premiums. (See Chapter 11 for more on Crummey notices.)

Cost-Cutter

Avoiding gift tax may be the main challenge for clients who have ample amounts of cash to pay premiums. Such clients, for example, might use the money they have to withdraw from their IRA after age 70½, when minimum distributions begin. In the case of Al, just described, a $100,000 minimum distribution becomes $65,000, after tax, and that money is used to buy life insurance, using the Crummey strategy to avoid gift tax.

Other clients may have affordability concerns because buying large amounts of insurance can be expensive. To cut this cost, such clients may prefer another approach: paying the life insurance premiums with tax-deductible dollars.

How can they do this? Clients who run their own business or professional practice can use some of the money that's contributed to a retirement plan each year to buy insurance. Clients who are semiretired, earning extra income as a consultant or an expert witness, may be able to set up a retirement plan for that occupation and divert tax-deductible contributions into life insurance premiums.

But what if clients don't have such an opportunity? One innovative strategy is to create a family limited partnership (FLP) to hold assets such as real estate and shares in a family business. Typically, a corporation or limited liability company would be the general partner, controlled (through a management contract) by your client or by both spouses. If the client does not own a majority interest, ownership won't be imputed. Limited partnership interests would be transferred to the children.

Because they control the general partner, your clients would manage the FLP assets and could be paid a management fee—say, $20,000 (2%) per year for managing $1 million worth of FLP assets. That $20,000 would be considered earned income so the clients could set up a profit-sharing plan. (An existing profit-sharing plan also can be used.)

Once a profit-sharing plan is in place, clients can roll an IRA into it. (A client with a large IRA could divide the account and roll one IRA into the profit-sharing plan.) Once ample amounts of money are in this plan, the funds can be used to buy life insurance, using pretax rather than after-tax dollars.

A truly sophisticated strategy might include creating an irrevocable trust as well. After a client has been paying for a life insurance policy with pretax dollars for several years, the trust can buy the policy, removing it from the client's taxable estate. Once the policy is in the trust, the proceeds can be used to pay estate tax while the IRA or pension plan remains intact, extending the tax-deferred buildup.

As an advisor, you should be certain that the transfer of the insurance policy is carefully structured. No aspect should be abusive; for example, the insurance policy should not have a *springing cash value* that becomes much larger after the transfer. Your client likely will have to pay income tax each year on the imputed economic value that's received. If the policy is transferred to a trust, you need to work with a life insurance professional to avoid the *transfer-for-value* rules and the resulting tax obligation.

Strategic Subtrusts

Another method of handling life insurance that's purchased inside a tax-deferred plan is to set up a separate trust-within-a-trust (a subtrust) specifically to own the life insurance policy.

Again, when your clients pay premiums through this subtrust arrangement, they're using pretax dollars—money on which they have not paid income tax. In other situations, life insurance is bought with after-tax dollars. To pay a $10,000 premium, a client might have to earn $20,000.

There is one drawback to this strategy: Subtrusts can't be set up within IRAs. Thus, they have to be used within an employer plan. Your client's plan might provide for the use of subtrusts; or, if your client is an important decision maker in a closely held company, he might be able to use his influence to help establish a subtrust, separate and distinct from the regular trust holding plan assets.

If your client is able to use a subtrust, the trustee of this subtrust cannot be your client (the plan participant) or your client's spouse. The trustee uses money credited to your client's retirement plan account to buy an insurance policy; the policy is owned solely by the subtrust, with all ownership rights exercised by the trust.

Then, your client can create yet another irrevocable trust, naming family members as beneficiaries. The subtrust's trustee, in turn, names this outside irrevocable trust as the insurance policy's beneficiary. This beneficiary designation must be irrevocable; that is, the insurance proceeds must go to the outside trust. Moreover, under no circumstances is your client allowed any access to the cash value of the policy.

Some other tax rules apply. To make the best use of a subtrust, your client must have been in the plan for at least 5 years. Alternately, premiums can be paid out of money that has been in the plan for at least 2 years. Because the policy's cash value can't be used to fund your client's retirement, there must be other funds in the plan for your client to use, at least enough to make the required minimum distributions.

While using the subtrust may avoid estate tax, there will be gift tax consequences. Your client will be considered to make a gift to the outside irrevocable trust (the policy beneficiary) each year. The gift tax generally is modest, though, in relation to the size of the policy (perhaps $5,000 or $6,000 per year for a $2 million insurance policy).

Despite these other concerns, using a subtrust may be an attractive strategy. For example, suppose your client Joe Martin is 65 and his wife Sally is 62. Joe has $2 million in a profit-sharing plan. Judging by past performance and anticipated tax rates, Joe expects to leave about

$850,000 to his family (from the plan and from money withdrawn from the plan) if they both die in 15 years. If the second death comes after 25 years, the total is expected to be over $1.5 million.

Instead, Joe uses about $600,000 of his plan money to set up a sub-trust and buy an insurance policy on both lives, with an original face value of $2 million. After 15 years, using similar projections, the net amount to the family is expected to be $2.1 million, not $850,000. After 25 years, the subtrust strategy is expected to net the family $2.3 million, versus $1.5 million without the subtrust.

Projections are necessarily imprecise but it's likely that a subtrust strategy, put together under your direction, can deliver more to a client's family and less to the tax collectors.

SUMMARY

- When assets pass from one generation to the next, estate tax is due.

- If those estate taxes must be paid from a tax-deferred plan, income taxes are triggered as well and most of the plan may be used, eliminating the possibility of extended tax deferral.

- To avoid paying estate tax from a tax-deferred plan, some provision should be made to pay the tax from other sources.

- A life insurance policy, held in an irrevocable trust, may be the best and least expensive way to provide the required liquidity.

- One technique for buying such life insurance is to have clients take minimum distributions, pay the income tax, and transfer the after-tax proceeds to the trust.

- Another more complex approach is to buy the life insurance inside a plan, with pretax dollars, and eventually transfer the policy outside of the client's estate.

A Strategy You Can Trust

Wealth Building with the Wealth Trust

hapter 15 explained the need for a source of liquidity to pay estate tax when assets move from one generation to the next. If taxes have to be paid from a tax-deferred retirement plan, the plan will be depleted. However, if there's an outside pool of funds to pay the tax, the retirement plan can remain intact and beneficiaries can withdraw enormous amounts of money over several decades. The money to pay the estate tax should be held in trust, to avoid inclusion in a decedent's estate. Moreover, some clients will want to have this trust remain in effect, acting as a *dynasty trust* to benefit future generations.

One particular type of dynasty trust, the Wealth Trust, should be considered in such situations. The Wealth Trust is a unique vehicle designed to provide great flexibility and security for your clients and their families for most if not all of the 21st century.

Let's start by describing the Wealth Trust:

- The Wealth Trust is an *inter vivos* trust, meaning that it is created while your client (the trust "grantor") is alive rather than at the client's death.

- The Wealth Trust is an irrevocable trust, so that it can't be canceled or materially altered. Thus, it is extremely important that each step be taken properly. Although "irrevocable" is a formidable word, don't let that stop your clients from adopting a Wealth Trust. Trusts don't become irrevocable until after the documents are signed. Before that, the trust creator sets the terms and conditions of the trust, so a Wealth Trust is a reflection of each client's goals and plans.

- The Wealth Trust is an asset protection trust. Clients can't transfer assets to cheat known creditors but they can transfer assets out of the reach of future creditors, claimants, divorcing in-laws, and so on.

- The Wealth Trust is an effective tool for reducing estate taxes. Once assets are beyond the reach of creditors, they're considered to be outside of the taxable estate as well.

- The Wealth Trust can be a dynasty trust. These trusts can cover a client's lifetime as well as those of children and grandchildren. If desired, the trust won't terminate until the last grandchild dies, and then the assets are distributed to great-grandchildren. Of course, it's possible to structure a Wealth Trust that will end sooner, if that's the client's wish.

- The Wealth Trust is a growth trust. Assets transferred into the trust can be invested and may accumulate into much larger amounts over the long term.

- The Wealth Trust can be a taxpayer. In some circumstances, income may be taxed to the trust at lower rates than would be paid by your client or by family members.

- The Wealth Trust can serve as an emergency retirement plan. Normally, the money in the trust should be the last money your clients ever use. However, if unforeseen events arise, trust assets may be distributed to close family members during the grantor's lifetime or even, in some circumstances, to the trust grantor.

- The Wealth Trust can serve as a landlord. If properly established, the trust can own one or more real estate properties, for use by the trust beneficiaries at little or no cost.

- The Wealth Trust can serve as a banker. The trustee can be given the power to lend money to the beneficiaries for certain purposes, such as starting a business.

- The Wealth Trust can alleviate family concerns. If one of the family members has special needs, the trustee can see to that beneficiary's well-being. The trust can also protect vulnerable family members from predators—and even from their own weaknesses.

- The Wealth Trust avoids probate. Assets owned by the trust won't go through probate at the death of your client or spouse.

- The Wealth Trust provides privacy. Although a will must be open to the public, provisions in trust documents are not exposed to prying eyes.

- The Wealth Trust provides seamless continuity in case of incapacity. Unfortunately, many clients will reach a point where they no longer can manage their own affairs. Assets held in trust are managed by a trustee or a successor no matter what your client's mental or physical state.

As you might expect from this list of benefits, creating a Wealth Trust is a complex task so clients will need an estate planning attorney, perhaps a tax advisor, and an insurance expert to get everything done correctly. Be sure that your clients are working with top-notch professionals.

Twenty Questions

Even though your client must work with an experienced attorney in order to create the Wealth Trust, you can add value by helping your client make key decisions in advance. Therefore, before your client makes an appointment to meet with an attorney, you should ask the client these questions:

1. Do you prefer a joint donor Wealth Trust or the Personal Access Version?

A joint donor Wealth Trust—the type that's usually created—is funded with gifts from a married couple. In 1999, a married couple can give away up to $1.3 million without owing gift tax. That number will gradually increase to $2 million by the year 2006.

Clients also can fund a Wealth Trust by using the annual gift tax exclusion, which does not count against the gift tax limits just mentioned. A married couple can give as much as $20,000 per year per trust beneficiary and maintain a gift tax exclusion. In one court case, gift tax exclusions were upheld for a trust with 18 beneficiaries! (This $20,000 annual gift tax exclusion is indexed to keep up with inflation.)

A Personal Access Version Wealth Trust is funded by gifts from one spouse. Indeed, each spouse can have his or her own Wealth Trust. If one spouse creates the trust (becomes the grantor), the initial tax-free funding can be only half as much. However, the other spouse may serve as trustee and make distributions to the trust beneficiaries, including himself.

Suppose, for example, that Ken Thomas, a successful business owner, transferred some of his wealth to his wife Nora, who used $650,000 to fund a Personal Access Version of the Wealth Trust, naming Ken as trustee. Their children and grandchildren are named as beneficiaries, along with Ken.

Ken, as trustee, can distribute trust assets to any of the beneficiaries, including himself. If such distributions are required by the trust documents to be for "health, education, maintenance and support," the trust assets will not be included in Ken's taxable estate. In practice, virtually any important need can be covered by those four words so Ken can distribute funds to himself if they're needed.

2. Who will be the trustee of your Wealth Trust? Will you name cotrustees?

In any trust, the trustee is responsible for managing the assets. Generally, the grantor should not be the trustee, too, because the IRS and creditors may assert that trust assets really belong to the grantor. (However, one spouse can be the trustee of the other spouse's Personal Access Version Wealth Trust.)

In many cases, your client will name a child as trustee or children as cotrustees. Grandchildren can be designated as successor trustees, after the children no longer are able to serve.

Another approach is to name a close family friend, a personal advisor, or a relative (a cousin, perhaps) as trustee. Such trustees need to be paid but they may be able to arbitrate family disputes. Your client's first concern should be to name a friendly trustee who is sympathetic to the needs of the trust beneficiaries.

3. What powers will you give the trustee?

Normally, the trustee should be able to distribute trust income (and principal, in some circumstances) to the trust beneficiaries, at the trustee's discretion. In addition, to make a regular irrevocable trust into a Wealth Trust, two powers should be added. First, there should be a provision enabling the trustee to buy and hold residential real estate. The trustee should be given the discretionary power—but not the obligation—to let the beneficiaries use the trust property or properties. Second, there should be a provision enabling the trustee, with the consent of the beneficiaries, to make distributions to pay the premiums for life insurance covering grandchildren, which might come in handy if the grandchildren leave taxable estates. Assuming the grandchildren are very young when the policies are purchased, such insurance will be relatively inexpensive.

4. If you name an outsider as trustee, who will have removal powers?

Circumstances change, and a trustee who performs well in 1999 may not be doing an outstanding job in 2009 or 2019. Alternatively, the second or third trustee of a Wealth Trust may not be up to par. Foreseeing such circumstances, a Wealth Trust should include a provision for trustee replacement. Often, this power is given to the trust beneficiaries, who can act by majority vote.

However, your client probably won't want the beneficiaries to put a puppet in there: This action may have adverse tax consequences and might override the purpose of establishing a trust. Therefore, the replacement trustee should have to meet certain criteria. The trust documents might state that a replacement outside trustee must be unrelated to any of the beneficiaries by blood or marriage, for example, or be a professional with an excellent reputation.

5. Who will be the beneficiaries?

In most cases, your client's children and grandchildren will be the beneficiaries. Working with a savvy attorney, they can get yet-unborn descendants added to the list.

Can your clients be beneficiaries of a Wealth Trust they create? Historically, the answer has been no: If there's a chance the grantor will get trust assets back, the assets in the trust will be subject to creditors and included in the grantor's taxable estate. However, Alaska and Delaware have enacted trust laws permitting a trust grantor to remain a discretionary beneficiary and still keep transferred assets from creditors and the IRS. Other states likely will follow.

There are some conditions to meet—Alaska requires an Alaskan trustee, for example. Clients who are interested in being a beneficiary of their own Wealth Trust should talk to an experienced estate planning attorney about these laws.

6. What will be the term of the trust?

If your client's main goal is simply to keep an estate intact, the Wealth Trust can terminate after your client and spouse die. Alternatively, it can remain intact until their grandchildren die.

Some states even permit perpetual trusts—they can go on forever. Again, clients who are interested should consult with a lawyer.

7. How will the trust be funded?

Normally, a Wealth Trust is funded with cash. However, other assets (securities, real estate, business interests) may be transferred into the trust. For estate planning purposes, your client should give away assets likely to appreciate because all appreciation after the date of transfer will be out of the taxable estate.

If clients give away assets that are difficult to value, such as real estate and interests in a closely held business, an unrelated party should perform an appraisal at the time of transfer.

Another noncash asset that may be hard to value is a cash value life insurance policy. If your client wants to transfer such a policy to a Wealth Trust, ask the company or your client's insurance agent for a valuation. Such a policy must be transferred at least 3 years before death in order to be excluded from the client's estate.

8. Will the annual gift tax exclusion be used to fund the trust?

Normally, gifts made to an irrevocable trust such as the Wealth Trust eat into the *unified credit*, which is a gift and estate tax shelter. Each individual can give away up to $650,000 worth of assets (in 1999) before any tax is due. That limit will gradually scale up to $1 million in 2006.

In some circumstances, though, clients can make gifts to a trust without reducing their unified credit. That's because each person can give away up to $10,000 per year to any number of recipients under an annual gift tax exclusion. (This $10,000 exclusion will increase with inflation.)

Unfortunately, there are many hoops to jump through in order to get this tax break for gifts to trusts:

- Your client (or your client and spouse) give assets to a Wealth Trust.
- The trustee notifies each beneficiary, in writing, of their right to withdraw their portion of such a gift during a given time period, perhaps 30 days.
- The beneficiaries take no action, allowing their withdrawal right to lapse.
- Then the trustee can use the assets as desired.

Suppose, for example, that Marie Lane makes a $150,000 gift to a Wealth Trust she has created. She has named 15 beneficiaries of this trust: her two children, their spouses, six grandchildren, three of their spouses, and two great-grandchildren.

After the gift, the trustee (her niece) sends notices to all 15 trust beneficiaries, informing them they each can withdraw up to $10,000 within 30 days. The time passes with no exercise of these withdrawal rights and Linda's niece uses the $150,000 to buy a life insurance policy on Linda's life. No gift tax is incurred because Linda used 15 annual gift tax exclusions.

9. How will trust funds be invested?

If the Wealth Trust is funded with cash, the trustee must invest the funds. You and your client can discuss the use of trust funds with the trustee but you cannot compel obedience.

Often, life insurance is held inside the Wealth Trust. Such policies might cover your client's life, the lives of your client and spouse, or their descendants. With life insurance, your client knows that a substantial amount will be paid to the trust when someone dies. Money invested in cash value life insurance won't be taxed as it compounds. In fact, the trustee may be able to borrow against the policy, tax free, and distribute cash to beneficiaries.

When the insured individual or individuals die, the trust collects the proceeds, tax free. What's more, when a Wealth Trust is fully invested in life insurance, there is no need to report income to the IRS each year. (Your client may have to file a gift tax return, though, if the generation-skipping tax (GST) is involved. See the answer to question 18 for more on the GST.)

Other investment alternatives may exist, especially if your client is in poor health so the trust would have to pay outsized sums to insure his life. The trustee might invest in municipal bonds for tax-exempt interest, growth stocks that are lightly taxed because they pay low dividends, or a combination of stocks, bonds, and life insurance.

10. If the trust will buy life insurance, which type of insurance will be chosen?

Insurance held in a Wealth Trust should be cash value insurance, generically known as *permanent* insurance because such policies endure until death, as long as the required premiums are paid. For estate planning purposes, life insurance that stays in force indefinitely is necessary.

Some insurance policies are investment-oriented: A minimum amount goes to buying insurance protection while most of the premiums are channeled to the cash value. This can lead to more buildup over the years. Other policies provide a relatively high death benefit for your premiums.

Recently, variable life insurance has become popular. Such policies offer the long-term growth potential of stock funds along with the tax advantages of permanent life insurance. If clients are reluctant to take stock market risks with their life insurance, universal life provides a steady return that fluctuates with interest rates. Whichever type of insurance policy that's used for a Wealth Trust, be wary of policy "illustrations" showing future growth. Pay special attention to the guaranteed policy values, not just to the projections showing current growth rates.

Some of these issues can be discussed with the prospective trustee before the Wealth Trust is formed. For best tax results, the trustee should be the one who applies for the policies and makes the appropriate premium payments.

11. If the Wealth Trust will hold an insurance policy, whom will it cover?

Generally, when a Wealth Trust is funded by a married couple, the life insurance that works best is survivorship or second-to-die life insurance. Such policies cover two lives, generally a husband and wife. The proceeds aren't paid until both individuals die.

Under current tax law, the first spouse to die can leave unlimited amounts to the survivor without triggering an estate tax. However, when the survivor dies and the bulk of the estate passes to the next generation, the estate tax bill may be staggering. That's when second-to-die insurance kicks in, to provide cash when it's most needed.

Because a couple has a longer joint life expectancy than either of the individuals, the insurance company has less risk. Therefore, second-to-die policies are relatively inexpensive. A couple, both aged 65, might be able to purchase a $1 million second-to-die insurance policy for 10 annual premium payments of $30,000 apiece. At current interest rates, no further premiums need be paid. In this example, that couple could obtain $1 million worth of funding for their Wealth Trust for $300,000, or 30 cents on the dollar. (These amounts are approximate, based on projected investment results. The actual premiums on a $1 million second-to-die policy might be higher or lower.)

12. Are the individuals to be insured in good health?

Very few people are absolutely uninsurable. However, those who have severe health conditions must pay steep premiums. Often, those individuals must undergo a preliminary medical exam before applying for insurance, to ascertain their current physical condition. A savvy insurance agent may help find a company to issue a policy at a reasonable cost. However, if insurability is a major issue, your client may want to plan for a Wealth Trust with less emphasis on life insurance and more on other investment vehicles.

13. Is professional asset management necessary?

If a Wealth Trust includes sizable amounts to be invested in stocks, bonds, and mutual funds, professional money management may be necessary. It's up to the trustee to hire the manager and review performance. However, as the client's advisor you can discuss money management with the trustee before contributions are made to the trust. You might want to manage the trust funds or have some say in the selection of the manager. You also should help to develop guidelines regarding money management—perhaps an investment policy statement—in the trust documents, to serve future trustees.

14. What role is envisioned for the Wealth Trust when estate taxes come due?

In a typical scenario, estate taxes are payable after the death of husband and wife. At that point, the Wealth Trust likely will have a great deal of cash, either from a life insurance policy or from other investments. Then the Wealth Trust can act as a "friendly banker." The trustee can lend the desired amount to the estate; alternatively, the trustee can use cash to buy assets from the estate.

Either way, your client's family can use the money to pay the tax bills and the estate assets can be preserved. This strategy is especially valuable if a large retirement plan is left to the next generation, because the plan can be left intact. If the retirement plan needs to be tapped for cash to pay estate tax, income tax is triggered and the plan will shrink.

Again, your client can indicate some of these options to the chosen trustee but there's no way of knowing what the circumstances will dictate when it's time for the Wealth Trust to provide estate liquidity.

Suppose, for example, that Charlie King died and left his IRA to his wife Diane, who lived on other assets while continuing to take minimum distributions from the IRA. When Diane died, she left her children an IRA worth $1 million, $500,000 worth of real estate, and $500,000 worth of interests in the family business. The estate tax bill and final expenses came to about $500,000; if the children needed to tap the IRA to pay those expenses, they would have had to withdraw about $850,000 to cover the income tax and estate tax obligations, leaving only $150,000 in the $1 million IRA.

Fortunately, Charlie and Diane had established a Wealth Trust, funding it with a life insurance policy. At Diane's death, the policy paid $1 million, tax free. The trustees of the Wealth Trust (their children) bought real estate and shares in the family business from the estate for $500,000, enabling the executors (also the children) to pay the tax bill without disturbing the IRA. Now, the $1 million IRA is intact. Although minimum distributions must continue, the remainder can grow, tax deferred. In addition, there are $1 million worth of assets in the Wealth Trust in insurance proceeds, real estate, and business interests, which can grow over the decades to come.

As another example, consider Dave and Grace Harris, who own a vineyard valued at $5 million, along with other assets. They estimate that their children will owe $2 million in estate taxes and other expenses after both parents die. Without planning, this family business would have to be sold to pay all the costs. Instead, Dave and Grace have established a Wealth Trust, which owns a $2 million second-to-die policy on their lives. After they die, the trustee will use the $2 million insurance proceeds to loan money to the estate. That money will pay estate tax and other expenses, enabling the vineyard to remain intact. In future years, their estate (essentially their children, who will inherit the business) will repay the loan by making payments to the Wealth Trust. Inside the trust, those payments will accumulate and grow, to the benefit of future generations.

15. Will you use your IRA distributions to fund your Wealth Trust?

In most cases, clients must begin taking minimum withdrawals from tax-deferred retirement plans after reaching age 70½. Even if they don't need IRA money for retirement expenses, they'll have to withdraw perhaps 4%, 5%, or 6% of their IRA balance each year, depending upon their age and that of their spouse. Inadequate withdrawals are subject to a 50% penalty. Thus, a client who has a $1 million IRA by age 71 might have to withdraw around $50,000 per year. If he owes $20,000 in tax (40%) and doesn't need the other $30,000 to live on, he can give that money to a Wealth Trust.

As explained previously, as long as your client has at least three trust beneficiaries and the proper procedures are followed, the client can transfer $30,000 to a Wealth Trust without owing any gift tax. In subsequent years, the required IRA withdrawals can be made, income tax paid, and unneeded funds transferred into the Wealth Trust.

16. What do you intend for your Wealth Trust after you and your spouse die?

In some circumstances a Wealth Trust will have cash after estate tax is paid. Moreover, if the trust has loaned money to the estate, it will hold notes; if it has purchased assets, it will hold those assets.

One approach would be for the trust to terminate then and distribute its assets to the trust beneficiaries. But that would mean giving up the long-term advantages of the Wealth Trust. Instead, a Wealth Trust might be divided into separate subtrusts, perhaps one for each of the children. Each of these new trusts can be created by your client, with suitable trustees and beneficiaries named in advance.

Still more trusts can be created—after the children die, trusts can be established for individual grandchildren. For any or all of these trusts, the trustee can be granted a *special power of appointment*, the ability to spread distributions among beneficiaries according to their various needs.

17. Why do you want your Wealth Trust split into subtrusts?

If a Wealth Trust is divided into a subtrust for each of the children, they will have access to the assets in that subtrust, independent of the subtrusts for the other children. The trustee can manage the trust in the best interest of one child, and probably his or her descendants, rather than considering the entire family. In fact, each child can be the trustee of his or her subtrust, as long as an "ascertainable standard" is included in the trust documents. That is, distributions of trust assets must be for "health, education, maintenance and support."

Dividing the Wealth Trust into subtrusts may be especially effective if the trusts are to provide liquidity for an IRA stretch-out (Figure 16.1). As mentioned, it may be desirable to have the IRA be split into separate accounts, one for each child. This extends tax deferral and gives each child more control over his or her IRA. With split IRAs, a subtrust approach can be used to match assets more precisely. Each child's subtrust can be used to provide liquidity for that child's share of the IRA, providing convenience and flexibility.

In addition, creating subtrusts may get money into the hands of the grandchildren faster. The terms of the subtrusts might say that whenever one of the children dies, one of the subtrusts terminates and the assets

Figure 16.1

Wealth Trust divided into subtrusts for IRA stretch-out.

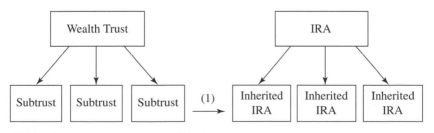

(1) Liquidity to pay estate tax at second death.

are distributed. Thus, some money is distributed then, while the remainder stays in trust.

The subtrust strategy is by no means the only one to use. If your client prefers to keep the assets in trust for as long as possible, the original trust could stay in place, with distributions delayed until all of the children have died.

As yet another alternative, distributions can be delayed until 21 years after the death of all the grandchildren who are alive when the trust is established. With this approach, clients can provide for great-grandchildren.

18. If your Wealth Trust is to be a dynasty trust, is it structured with the GST in mind?

At the top 55% estate tax rate, one dollar shrinks to around 20 cents after two generations and 10 cents after three generations. Therefore, clients might be tempted to leave money directly to children or grandchildren in order to avoid repeated rounds of estate tax.

However, the federal tax code includes a GST that penalizes such "skips" with a 55% tax bite. The GST applies to asset transfers for the benefit of a person or persons at least two generations younger than the property owner: grandchildren or great-grandchildren. Without proper planning, assets left directly to grandchildren might incur a 55% estate tax and a 55% generation-skipping tax, leaving only 20 cents on the dollar after both taxes are levied.

19. Does your Wealth Trust take full advantage of the GST exemption?

Fortunately, everybody is entitled to a $1 million exemption from the GST. Each client can transfer up to $1 million to a Wealth Trust without incurring the GST; married couples can donate up to $2 million. Remember, it's the amount of the contribution that counts. Even if the trust fund grows much larger, by the time of death, no GST will be due. If a client doesn't contribute the full amount while alive, the difference can be bequeathed at death.

Suppose, for example, one of your clients transfers $1 million to a Wealth Trust, using the GST exemption in full. That $1 million is used to buy life insurance and make various investments. By the time of death, that $1 million may have grown to $10 million, including life insurance proceeds. It makes no difference: No GST will be owed on all the interim growth.

If clients plant the seed wisely, their loved ones will reap a bountiful harvest.

20. What are your primary goals in creating a Wealth Trust?

We recommend that you tell clients to think of the money in a Wealth Trust as the last money they'll want to use—the family will prefer to maximize the tax-favored growth. However, in case of an emergency, the trustee can distribute funds to the trust beneficiaries, who are also family members.

Wealth Trust assets might be used to pay for a college education, to provide a down payment on a house, to fund a new business startup, or to cover a large medical expense. No other strategy is nearly as powerful when it comes to providing long-term security for loved ones.

Once you have gone over these 20 questions with your clients and they understand the issues involved, they'll be ready to see a lawyer to create a Wealth Trust.

Figure 16.2 gives you an idea of how a Wealth Trust can work. During their lifetimes, your clients and their spouses can transfer assets into these trusts. They can make substantial transfers without owing any gift tax. After both spouses die, the Wealth Trust can be subdivided into two subtrusts of equal size (if there are two children), three subtrusts (for three children), and so on. Each of the children may be the trustee of his or her own subtrust; this gives each of the children considerable control over a share of family wealth yet does not sacrifice tax or asset protection advantages.

At the deaths of the children, the subtrusts may be terminated and the assets distributed to the grandchildren. Or, subtrusts can be created for the next generation, for further tax savings and asset protection.

Figure 16.2

The Wealth Trust (joint donor trust).

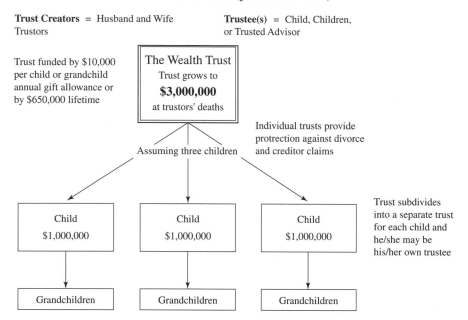

Trust Creators = Husband and Wife
Trustors

Trustee(s) = Child, Children,
or Trusted Advisor

Trust funded by $10,000
per child or grandchild
annual gift allowance or
by $650,000 lifetime

The Wealth Trust
Trust grows to
$3,000,000
at trustors' deaths

Individual trusts provide
protrection against divorce
and creditor claims

Assuming three children

| Child | Child | Child |
| $1,000,000 | $1,000,000 | $1,000,000 |

Trust subdivides
into a separate trust
for each child and
he/she may be
his/her own trustee

| Grandchildren | Grandchildren | Grandchildren |

Children can pass on to grandchildren what they do not spend, also estate
tax free and asset protected.

SUMMARY

- A trust can provide the funds needed to pay estate tax, leaving a tax-deferred retirement plan intact for the benefit of the next generation.

- Some clients will prefer to keep this trust in place, as a dynasty trust to benefit future generations.

- A dynasty trust can hold assets for the family, out of the reach of estate taxes, creditors, and divorcing spouses.

- One type of dynasty trust, the Wealth Trust, offers extraordinary advantages, such as being able to hold homes that trust beneficiaries can use and to buy low-cost life insurance on very young beneficiaries.

- One type of Wealth Trust, the Personal Access version, can allow trust funds to be paid to your client in case of an emergency.

- Sophisticated use of subtrusts set forth in the original trust document may keep a Wealth Trust from becoming unwieldy, to better serve each member of future generations.

Just Cause

Using Retirement Plans
for Charitable Giving

As an advisor, you probably tell your clients to give away appreciated assets instead of cash when making charitable contributions. By doing so, those clients will receive tax deductions based on the full value of the donated assets while the accrued capital gains tax obligation disappears. At the same time, it's likely that you advise clients to hold on to IRAs and other tax-deferred retirement plans as long as possible. The longer income tax can be deferred, the greater the wealth that builds inside the plan and the larger the ultimate payout.

These rules work fine—as long as clients are alive. However, when it comes to bequests, your clients probably will be better off shifting into reverse. That is, if clients plan to make charitable contributions when they die, they should give away their IRAs or qualified plans. At the same time, they're better off holding on to appreciated assets so they can leave them to their heirs.

Suppose, for example, an unmarried client (widowed or divorced) has a total estate of $1 million. Half of that is in an IRA and the other half is in highly appreciated securities and real estate. The client wants to leave $500,000 to children and $500,000 to a charity. Making a $500,000 charitable gift brings the estate below the $650,000 threshold (in 1999) so no estate tax is due.

Income taxes, though, are another story. If the appreciated assets are left to charity while the IRA goes to relatives, the heirs eventually have to pay income tax on all the money as it comes out of the IRA. Assuming a 40% tax rate, the heirs will actually inherit $300,000, not $500,000. State and local income taxes might further reduce their inheritance.

Instead, suppose your client leaves the IRA to charity and bequeaths the appreciated assets to the children. Again, there is no estate tax but his children inherit the appreciated assets with a step-up in basis. If they decide to sell those assets, they won't owe any capital gains tax on appreciation during your client's lifetime. They'll inherit a full $500,000. Therefore, this approach—IRA to charity and appreciated assets to loved ones—can pass on such an estate completely tax free and save hundreds of thousands of dollars in taxes.

Changing Course

Larger estates may owe estate tax, of course. To see how this might work, suppose that Carl Peters desired to leave $500,000 to his alma mater. At first, he wanted to make the bequest with appreciated securities. However, his financial advisor suggested that he use his IRA to make the bequest instead.

This $500,000 charitable bequest comes out of his taxable estate, saving $275,000 in taxes, in his 55% estate tax bracket. There is also an income tax savings because the deferred income tax that ordinarily would have to be paid on IRA withdrawals is avoided. After running all the numbers, Carl discovered that the net cost of making the $500,000 contribution was less than $150,000.

What's more, the appreciated securities that would have gone to his alma mater can be retained, to be passed to his heirs eventually. At that point, there will be a step-up in basis to market value. That is, Carl's heirs will owe estate tax on the value of the shares, but they won't have to pay any capital gains tax on all the prior appreciation.

Four-Play

In essence, there are four ways for Carl to make bequests from an IRA:

1. Leave the IRA directly to charity.
2. Leave the IRA to his wife Kate, who can leave it to charity at her death.
3. Leave the IRA to a QTIP trust that will provide income for Kate during her lifetime and then direct the remaining trust principal to charity.
4. Leave the IRA to a charitable remainder trust (CRT) that pays a lifetime interest to Kate based on a predetermined formula, after which the charity receives the remainder interest.

How do these techniques compare? As a practical matter, outright bequests work best if the donor is not married or if the bequest is relatively small in relation to the entire estate. Otherwise, the surviving spouse won't want to give up the IRA; in some states (including community property states) spousal consent is necessary in order to name the charity as beneficiary.

The suitability of the other methods depend on the IRA owner's wishes and family situation. If Carl is comfortable that Kate will always be able to handle the IRA wisely and make the appropriate charitable bequest at her death, his IRA can be left to her. However, assuming some sort of control or protection is desired, a trust may be preferred.

Distress Signals

What about QTIP trusts? In a standard QTIP trust, the surviving spouse gets all the income while the first spouse to die gets to name the ultimate beneficiary. However, naming a QTIP trust as an IRA beneficiary can be dangerous. QTIP trusts must follow extremely demanding rules; failure to follow those rules can result in acceleration of estate tax.

What's more, there may be a conflict between the QTIP rules, which state that all income be paid to the surviving spouse, and the IRA-required minimum distribution rules. In some QTIP trusts that have been named as IRA beneficiaries, the spouse is to get the greater of the trust income or the required minimum distribution. That's fine for the surviving spouse but, if she lives to her life expectancy, the IRA will be paid out and there will be nothing for the charity.

One solution to this problem is to pay only the trust income to the surviving spouse. That leaves something for the charity but might be expensive: The difference between the required minimum distributions from the IRA and the income paid to the spouse will be taxed at the trust's high income tax rate each year.

Therefore, it may be better to do without a QTIP trust and split the IRA, leaving some to the spouse and some to the charity. Another approach is to leave the entire IRA to the spouse and provide the charity with a contribution by buying life insurance on the IRA owner. Alternatively, if Carl wants to limit Kate's income from the IRA to provide more to charity, a CRT may be appropriate.

Contingency Plan

One innovative planning strategy is to name a CRT as backup IRA beneficiary. If a client names his spouse as primary IRA beneficiary and the client dies first, his spouse can claim the IRA as her own and name new beneficiaries (probably their children), so the IRA payouts can be stretched out for decades. But if the spouse dies first, the opportunity for such a long-term stretch-out won't be available.

Naming a CRT as backup beneficiary effectively provides an alternate stretch-out. If the spouse dies first, followed by the IRA owner, the IRA will be distributed to the CRT. Charitable trusts don't owe income tax so the amount in the IRA at that point can remain intact.

Subsequently, the normal CRT rules can take effect. Money is distributed periodically to the income beneficiaries your clients choose, perhaps for their lifetime. That income can be a fixed amount (annuity trust) or a fixed percentage (unitrust) of trust assets. At the end of the payout period, whatever remains in the trust will go to a charity or charities. Assuming the clients' children are the CRT income beneficiaries, the IRA income tax can be spread over the children's lifetimes even if the spouse-beneficiary dies first.

There may be a catch, though. If clients' children are young (say, under 40) at the time the money passes to the CRT, the trust might be disqualified because too little will go to charity. Therefore, clients might want to wait until their children are at least age 40 to name a CRT as backup IRA beneficiary and they should specify a 5% payout. The CRT likely will earn more than 5% per year so the children will get an increasing income stream as the trust assets grow.

As your clients (and their children) grow older, they can change their wills, if desired, raising the payout rate. Such trusts won't go into effect until clients die, so they can change the terms while they're alive.

Spreading the Wealth

A CRT also may come in useful for clients who are employees of publicly owned companies with company stock in their tax-deferred retirement plans. As explained in Chapter 7, when such employees leave the company and roll their plan balance into an IRA, the company stock can be withdrawn from the plan prior to the rollover. Eventually, the *net unrealized appreciation* (NUA) can qualify for capital gains treatment.

However, clients in this situation face a dilemma. If they continue to hold on to the NUA stock, they may have a large portion of their net worth tied to the fate of one company. If they sell some or all of the shares to reinvest in other securities, they'll owe tax on the deferred gains.

A 1999 IRS Letter Ruling (9919039) opens up a possible solution:

1. Your client could withdraw the NUA stock from the retirement plan.

2. The stock can then be contributed to a CRT.

3. The CRT's trustee can sell the stock and reinvest in a diversified portfolio.

4. Your client (and perhaps a spouse) can be income beneficiaries of the CRT, receiving lifetime payouts based on the full value of the securities.

5. After the deaths of the income beneficiaries, the remainder of the trust fund is distributed to charity.

In its ruling, the IRS held that NUA stock can be contributed to a CRT without triggering income tax. A subsequent sale of those shares won't create an immediate tax obligation, either. What's more, the income paid out by the CRT is taxed in the normal manner, so a sizable portion of the distributions to the income beneficiaries is taxed at capital gains rates, with proper planning.

Going Concerns

Another concern that needs to be addressed is the beneficiary designation. As explained previously, if a person is the IRA beneficiary, a joint life expectancy may be used, stretching out minimum distributions and extending the tax-free buildup. However, a charity has no life expectancy so naming one as the beneficiary means using a single life expectancy (the donor's) and speeding withdrawals. The same is true if a CRT is named as beneficiary. However, with a QTIP trust, both spouses' joint life expectancy can be used.

What's more, if the IRA owner dies before the RBD, all of the IRA money must be distributed—and all the income tax must be paid—by the end of the fifth calendar year following the year of death. Suppose, for example, that Carl Peters died at age 70 in 1999 with a no-beneficiary IRA. By the end of 2004 (5 calendar years), all of Carl's IRA must be paid out and that will be the end of the tax shelter.

Generous to a Fault

Finally, there's the question of magnitude. Suppose Carl has over $2 million in his IRA and wants to leave $500,000 to his alma mater, or $100,000, or $50,000. If he specifies a $500,000 bequest, for example, the IRS will treat that as a $500,000 withdrawal from the IRA and assess income tax on the withdrawal.

One way to avoid this trap is to name cobeneficiaries, perhaps saying that 25% of the IRA goes to Carl's alma mater while 75% goes to Kate. There is a risk, though, that naming a charity as cobeneficiary might endanger the ability to take withdrawals over a joint life expectancy. A single life expectancy might have to be used, accelerating income taxes after minimum distributions begin.

Another strategy might be for Carl to name Kate as primary IRA beneficiary and his alma mater as secondary beneficiary, which would permit distributions to be spread over a joint life expectancy. At Carl's death, Kate can disclaim a certain amount on the school's behalf. Then Carl's alma mater will inherit and no income tax will be due. This method gives Kate the chance to inherit the IRA, if access to the money is needed. However, there are no guarantees that Carl's alma mater actually will receive what Carl would like to donate.

A simpler, surer strategy is to split the IRA. If Carl has $2 million in his IRA he can rollover $500,000 to a new IRA, tax free. His alma mater could be named as beneficiary for the new $500,000 IRA while Kate remains the beneficiary for the old $1.5 million IRA. Now, Carl has to manage his IRAs. At a modest 7% growth rate, a $500,000 IRA created at age 70 becomes a $1 million IRA at 80, a $2 million IRA at 90. Carl may want to bequeath $500,000 to his alma mater but not $2 million. In such cases, further IRA splitting may be necessary.

Fortunately, if Carl keeps a close watch on his IRAs he may accomplish several goals by artful juggling. Suppose he divides his $2 million IRA into a $1 million IRA with Kate as beneficiary, two $250,000 IRAs for each of his children, and a $500,000 IRA with his alma mater as beneficiary. Assume that, according to the various life expectancies, Carl must withdraw at least 6% of the amount in the charitable IRA ($30,000), 5% of the spousal IRA ($50,000), and 4% of the parent-child IRAs ($20,000) this year, in order to avoid a 50% penalty.

These amounts need not be withdrawn pro rata from each IRA: If a total of $100,000 is withdrawn, no penalty is due. Assuming the charitable IRA earns $35,000, Carl might withdraw that $35,000 to keep the balance at $500,000. The other $65,000 might be drawn from the spousal IRA while the parent-child IRAs remain intact.

The same strategy can be pursued each year, as long as Carl lives. The charitable IRA will remain at a fixed amount while the rest of the withdrawals come out of the spousal IRA, providing retirement income or money for insurance premiums. The parent-child IRAs continue to grow.

When Carl dies, his alma mater will get its $500,000 bequest, Kate can inherit what's left of the spousal IRA (along with other assets), while the children inherit what may have become two $500,000 IRAs. The unified gift/estate tax credit will shelter the bequests to the children, each of whom can stretch withdrawals over his or her life expectancy, deferring income tax payments for decades.

Lasting Impression

There's yet one more strategy Carl might want to consider if he's thinking of leaving at least $1 million to charity: He can set up a private foundation. At his death, $1 million or more of his IRA can go to create the Carl Peters Foundation. Alternatively, that $1 million+ can be left to a CRT, which will provide lifetime income to Kate. After her death, the reminder will go to the Peters Foundation.

When Carl creates a private foundation, he can name his children as trustees or executive directors, providing them with control. They'll decide which causes merit contributions each year. If Carl's alma mater adopts some bizarre policies, they can switch contributions to charities that care for needy children or research dreaded diseases.

Besides control, there are other advantages to establishing a private foundation. Recognition, for example. With a private foundation and the power to distribute the proceeds in any direction, each year, Carl's children will get plenty of attention from the local movers and shakers.

Moreover, Carl will be providing meaningful employment—and substantial compensation—to his children, grandchildren, and more distant descendants. He can name them as replacement trustees or directors, to succeed his children.

A private foundation must distribute at least 5% of its assets each year. Suppose Carl leaves $2 million to a private foundation and that the foundation earns 9% per year, or $180,000. Of that $180,000, $100,000 (5% of $2 million) must go to recognized charities. The other $80,000 can go to legitimate expenses, including salaries and travel costs for Carl's children.

Such savvy IRA planning can provide for charity, for a surviving spouse, and for future generations, leaving as little as possible for the IRS.

SUMMARY

- Testamentary charitable bequests should be made from IRAs or other retirement plans in order to avoid the deferred income tax.

- If the bequest is small or the client is unmarried, such bequests can be made directly at the client's death, perhaps by splitting off an IRA for the charity to inherit.

- Married clients may want to defer substantial bequests until after both spouses have died.

- Deferred bequests can be left to the surviving spouse's discretion or to a trust.

- Naming QTIP trusts as IRA beneficiaries may pose problems, but charitable remainder trusts can provide for both a charity and a surviving spouse.

- Charitable remainder trusts also should be considered as backup IRA beneficiaries, providing an effective stretch-out if the IRA owner's spouse dies first.

A Friend in Need

Finding a Cooperative Retirement Plan Custodian

Thanks to the bull market that dominated the 1980s and 1990s, many clients have seen their IRAs or other tax-deferred retirement accounts move past six figures into seven-figure territory. Savvy planning, as described in previous chapters, can stretch a $1 million IRA into a $4 million or $5 million bonanza for the client, the surviving spouse, and the next generation. That is, a bountiful stretch-out is possible with the right support. However, many IRA custodians (including banks, brokers, mutual fund companies, and insurers) are unwilling or unable to provide the necessary service.

Going forward, when IRA owners and IRA beneficiaries die, sizable amounts of money may be at stake. In the absence of guidance from the IRS, decisions are often left up to IRA custodians, and policies vary enormously among custodians. When an ambitious financial plan meets a balky IRA custodian, the client loses. IRA withdrawals are accelerated, depriving beneficiaries of years of tax-deferred compounding. In some situations the shortfall may add up to hundreds of thousands—even millions—of dollars.

In order to deal with inflexible custodians, you should keep in mind how an IRA stretch-out works in an ideal scenario. Such planning generally is done on behalf of clients who have extremely large IRAs (generally from a rollover) or clients who need not rely heavily on their IRAs for retirement income. Such clients probably will be advised to take minimum IRA distributions, beginning after age 70½, based on the IRA owner's life expectancy and that of a named beneficiary.

After the IRA owner's death, the surviving spouse can roll over the inherited IRA to her own, name new beneficiaries (such as the children), and begin a new schedule of minimum distributions. When the survivor dies, the children can continue the minimum distributions over their life expectancies, which might be 30 years or longer. If the children die before reaching the end of the payout period, the distributions can continue until the end of that period has been reached, payable to beneficiaries they have designated.

This plan, of course, assumes the IRA owner has a spouse to be named as IRA beneficiary. If not, the IRA owner can leave the account directly to children or even grandchildren and have them enjoy the stretch-out benefits.

Textbook Example

To see how an IRA stretch-out is supposed to work, consider the example of Bert Roberts, who died at age 69 with $1.3 million in his IRA. He had named his 35-year-old son Edward as beneficiary. Assuming the IRA earns a modest 7% per year, Edward can pull out more than $2 million over the next 25 years and still have more than $3.5 million in the account.

That's how an IRA stretch-out works in the textbooks, or at least in estate planning seminars. In the real world, though, the custodian may not go along.

A Surfeit of Snags

What could happen?

Some IRS custodians won't let IRA beneficiaries name their own beneficiaries. At the first beneficiary's death, the IRA terminates. All the remaining funds in the IRA assets are distributed and income taxes are due.

For example, suppose Bert Roberts dies and his IRA passes to his son Edward, who has a 35-year life expectancy at that point. Edward dies 25 years later. Some IRA custodians will let Edward's beneficiary, his son Frank, spread out distributions over 10 years, but some won't allow the last 10 years of the stretch-out.

Conversely, some IRA custodians will give IRA beneficiaries the full rights of an IRA owner. Therefore, they can name their own beneficiaries, change investments, even move the account. The IRS has indicated that such actions are permissible. However, not every IRA agreement offers the same benefits; some companies say that beneficiary rights are covered by state law, which can be very complex.

Some custodians automatically pay the balance of an inherited IRA to the deceased beneficiary's estate. Again, this triggers all the deferred income tax. Some large mutual fund companies followed this practice but the trend is gradually moving toward more flexibility for IRA beneficiaries.

Some custodians require that an IRA balance be distributed at the owner's death if a marital trust is named as the beneficiary. What's more, in some trusts that payout may not be distributed to the beneficiary right away. Thus, the income may be trapped in the trust, taxable at high trust income tax rates.

Some custodians don't offer much flexibility to beneficiaries. For example, a custodian might permit beneficiaries only two options: a lump-sum distribution, which would generate a large income tax bill upfront, or annuitization, which locks in a payment stream and eliminates access to the principal.

The tax code permits a beneficiary to take minimum withdrawals over his or her life expectancy but custodians aren't required to offer this option. Some custodians, though, permit more flexibility than others. You might advise clients in this situation to choose another custodian, one that will permit a stretch-out, and execute a tax-free rollover to the other custodian.

Some custodians do not permit an IRA beneficiary to create separate IRAs. A surviving spouse, for example, might want to create a separate IRA for each successor beneficiary (her children), providing more flexibility and slowing the pace of taxable withdrawals. Some major mutual fund companies have refused to split IRAs, at least at first. Advisors report that it's possible to keep after these companies, going higher in the organization, until reaching an agreement. Therefore, advisors need to be persistent. It also helps if the amounts involved are large enough that the fund company wants to keep the money—there might be less cooperation with small IRAs.

Many problems with stretch-out IRAs result from limited beneficiary designation forms. Often, IRA providers' forms don't offer investors the opportunity to name multiple beneficiaries or successor beneficiaries. Still other IRA providers have lost the account's beneficiary forms altogether—the latter problem is especially likely to occur when financial institutions have been merged, which happens frequently.

Without a beneficiary designation, the IRA probably will be distributed to the IRA owner's estate. Then, the IRA must be paid within 5 years, if the owner had not begun minimum distributions. If minimum distributions had begun, the IRA may have to be paid out by December 31 of the year after the death (if the recalculation method of determining minimum distributions had been chosen).

A Proactive Posture

How can you increase your clients' chances of enjoying a full IRA stretch-out? When advising a client who's setting up a sizable IRA, you should recommend he or she not deal with the person sitting behind the customer service desk or with a person who's just a voice on the phone. That person may have little or no training on complex IRA issues.

Instead, you or your client should insist on speaking with someone who's truly knowledgeable. Most financial institutions have higher-level people in the retirement department who keep up with such matters. Be persistent until you're working with them. Before clients place money with an IRA custodian, they should find out if the desired IRA stretch-out is permitted.

What's more, don't assume that a client's tax preparer or family attorney knows all about IRAs and other tax-deferred retirement plans. This subject is complicated and keeping abreast is difficult. You and your client should question such professionals to determine their levels of expertise.

A Matter of Form

In addition, you might advise that clients not rely on the beneficiary form provided by the IRA custodian. Regular beneficiary forms usually don't have enough room, so investors have to squeeze in the information; they often wind up scribbling so their entries might not be legible, especially if they're designating a trust or multiple beneficiaries.

As an alternative, some accountants and attorneys have customized beneficiary forms that can be submitted. You might advise clients to attach two copies of such custom forms to their beneficiary forms. One copy of this rider, which spells out the desired arrangements, is to be signed, dated, and returned. The person who signs should be asked to include a title, too, because that person may not be around when the form is needed.

Some IRA custodians accept customized beneficiary forms but not everyone does. These forms must conform to the custodian's IRA agreement, so someone has to screen them, which is beyond the scope of a data entry person at a large financial institution.

A custom beneficiary form tends to be extremely comprehensive, involving trusts and powers of attorney and disclaimer rights. Moreover, they need to be stored for future reference, which might be years in the future, which is another reason some custodians are reluctant to accept them. Again, a little persistence may result in the acceptance of a custom beneficiary form.

Clients who already have one or more IRAs should make sure that a form is on file with the custodian—that is, they should check to make sure it hasn't been lost. All of the information on the beneficiary form should be checked for accuracy because errors such as an incorrect birth date can have serious consequences.

To prevent future misunderstandings, tell your clients to keep copies of all their IRA beneficiary forms. As an added precaution, have them reiterate their instructions as they approach age 70½. They should send a letter to the custodian, with their instructions relating to beneficiary designations and distribution methods. The custodian should be asked to return a signed copy, confirming that these instructions are on file.

Basic Training

Other basics should be in place in order to plan for a stretch-out IRA. Clients shouldn't name their estate as beneficiary or contingent beneficiary because this may result in a quick payout after the client's death. Instead, one or more individuals or a qualified trust should be named. In addition, minors should not be named as IRA beneficiaries: Minors are not allowed to be IRA beneficiaries so the issue may get tied up in court.

Clients should specify a distribution method—recalculation, term certain, or hybrid—by age 70½. If no choice is made, the IRA custodian may use the recalculation method, even if that's not the best choice, and name the estate as beneficiary. Some IRA custodians only permit the recalculation method; if another method is desired a change of custodians may be necessary.

Once minimum distributions begin, you should check closely on the calculations. According to press reports, more than one-third of IRA providers make mistakes with these calculations; mistakes, if not corrected, may be extremely costly over the long term.

Following Up

Over that long term, you're likely to find yourself representing IRA beneficiaries as well as IRA owners. When representing a beneficiary, your first step should be to check that the beneficiary forms and related paperwork are in place. Ascertain whether a long term stretch out is permitted. If not, switching to a more cooperative custodian may be appropriate.

Accepting a check that terminates an inherited IRA may also terminate the tax-deferred compounding, so you must caution your clients not to deposit such checks. Nonspouses should insist that the IRA custodian keep the IRA in the deceased owner's name. If the IRA is retitled in the name of a nonspouse, distributions will be accelerated. In addition, the new owner's taxpayer identification number should be added to the account, to help the IRS match income properly and prevent audit notices. Some custodians now create special *beneficiary distribution accounts* to aid tax deferral and compliance with the tax law.

Even the best-advised clients may run into problems in this area. Clients with acknowledged letters from the IRA custodian, agreeing to a stretch-out, have discovered that the custodian still refused to go along. In such situations the beneficiaries can sue, just as they can if an IRA provider has lost or destroyed beneficiary designation forms. That may not be the most desirable approach but there may be no choice, considering the amounts of money that can be at stake in a successful IRA stretch-out.

SUMMARY

- An IRA or other retirement plan that's passed on to the second generation can result in a rich stream of tax-deferred cash flow but an uncooperative custodian may interfere.

- Perhaps most important, some custodians won't let IRA beneficiaries name new beneficiaries.

- If a full stretch-out is not permitted, IRA funds are distributed earlier than necessary and tax deferral is curtailed.

- To prevent such a shortfall, you and your clients should question IRA custodians before committing funds.

- Be sure all the proper paperwork is in place, acknowledged by the custodian, and that a copy is available in case of a dispute.

Appendix A: IRA Stretch-Out

Assumptions: Initial plan balance $1,000,000
10% growth
40% tax bracket

Owner	Age 65	(Death assumed age 83)
Spouse	Age 63	(Death assumed age 87)
Child #1	Age 38	
Child #2	Age 37	
Grandchild #1	Age 5	
Grandchild #2	Age 2	

Total Net After-Tax Income

Owner and spouse	(24 years' distribution)	$ 1,834,906*
Child #1	(20 years' distribution)	1,097,797
Child #2	(21 years' distribution)	1,161,854
Subtotal		**$ 2,259,651**
Grandchild #1	(51 years' distribution)	9,884,694
Grandchild #2	(54 years' distribution)	12,369,429
Subtotal		**$22,254,123**
Total IRA potential income		**$26,348,680**

*These figures are based on minimum distributions. Distributions may be increased at any time during your client's lifetime.

Mr. and Mrs. Client
Initial plan balance $1,000,000
Current ages 65 and 63

1. Minimum distributions based on husband's and wife's joint life expectancies.

2. Assume upon husband's death at age 83 in year 2016,* wife takes a spousal rollover. She also names the children and/or grandchildren as her joint beneficiaries and takes minimum distributions during her lifetime based on their joint life expectancies. (Regardless of age, children and grandchildren are deemed to be 10 years younger than the wife.)

3. Assume wife dies at age 87 in year 2022,* the IRA balance splits into inherited IRAs for each of the children and/or grandchildren. Children and/or grandchildren will then take minimum distributions based on their own individual life expectancies.

Minimum Distributions—Alternative #1

Year	Client L/E	Spouse L/E	Joint L/E	2nd Benef. L/E	2nd Joint L/E	Pension Fund Begin Value	Life Exp.	Minimum Distributions
1998	20.0	21.6	26.0	44.4	45.1	$1,000,000	26.0	$ 0
1999	19.2	20.8	25.1	43.5	44.1	1,100,000	25.1	0
2000	18.4	20.0	24.2	42.5	43.1	1,210,000	24.2	0
2001	17.6	19.2	23.3	41.5	42.2	1,331,000	23.3	0
2002	16.8	18.4	22.4	40.6	41.2	1,464,100	22.4	0
2003	16.0	17.6	21.5	39.6	40.2	1,610,510	21.5	74,907
2004	15.3	16.6	20.2	38.7	39.3	1,689,163	20.2	83,622
2005	14.6	15.6	19.4	37.7	38.3	1,766,095	19.4	91,036
2006	13.9	14.6	18.5	36.8	37.3	1,842,565	18.5	99,598
2007	13.2	13.6	17.3	35.9	36.4	1,917,264	17.3	110,825
2008	12.5	12.6	16.5	34.9	35.4	1,987,083	16.5	120,429
2009	11.9	11.6	15.4	34.0	34.5	2,053,319	15.4	133,332
2010	11.2	10.6	14.6	33.1	33.6	2,111,986	14.6	144,657
2011	10.6	9.6	13.5	32.2	32.6	2,164,062	13.5	160,301
2012	10.0	8.6	12.5	31.3	31.7	2,204,137	12.5	176,331
2013	9.5	7.6	11.6	30.4	30.8	2,230,587	11.6	192,292
2014	8.9	6.6	10.8	29.5	29.9	2,242,125	10.8	207,604
2015	8.4	5.6	9.8	28.6	29.0	2,237,973	9.8	228,365
*2016	7.9	4.6	8.9	27.7	28.1	2,210,569	8.9	248,379
2017	0.0	8.4	3.6	26.8	27.2	2,158,409	16.0	134,901

Minimum Distributions—Alternative #1 *(Continued)*

Year	Client L/E	Spouse L/E	Joint L/E	2nd Benef. L/E	2nd Joint L/E	Pension Fund Begin Value	Life Exp.	Minimum Distributions
2018	0.0	7.9	2.6	25.8	25.4	2,225,859	15.3	145,481
2019	0.0	7.4	1.6	24.8	24.5	2,288,416	14.5	157,822
2020	0.0	6.9	0.6	23.8	23.7	2,343,653	13.8	169,830
2021	0.0	6.5	0.0	22.8	22.8	2,391,205	13.1	182,535
*2022	0.0	6.1	0.0	21.8	21.9	2,429,537	12.4	195,930
2023	0.0	0.0	0.0	20.8	20.8	2,456,968	20.8	118,123
2024	0.0	0.0	0.0	19.8	19.8	2,572,730	19.8	129,936
2025	0.0	0.0	0.0	18.8	18.8	2,687,073	18.8	142,929
2026	0.0	0.0	0.0	17.8	17.8	2,798,558	17.8	157,222
2027	0.0	0.0	0.0	16.8	16.8	2,905,470	16.8	172,945
2028	0.0	0.0	0.0	15.8	15.8	3,005,778	15.8	190,239
2029	0.0	0.0	0.0	14.8	14.8	3,097,093	14.8	209,263
2030	0.0	0.0	0.0	13.8	13.8	3,176,613	13.8	230,189
2031	0.0	0.0	0.0	12.8	12.8	3,241,066	12.8	253,208
2032	0.0	0.0	0.0	11.8	11.8	3,286,644	11.8	278,529
2033	0.0	0.0	0.0	10.8	10.8	3,308,927	10.8	306,382
2034	0.0	0.0	0.0	9.8	9.8	3,302,800	9.8	337,020

Child #1
Born 5/6/60
Inherited IRA $607,384

(Assuming upon wife's death at age 87 in year 2022, the balance of $2,429,537 splits into four inherited IRAs of $607,384 for each child and grandchild.)

Minimum Distributions—Alternative #1

Year	2nd Benef. L/E	2nd Joint L/E	Pension Fund Begin Value	Life Exp.	Minimum Distributions
2023	20.8	20.8	$607,384	20.8	$ 29,201
2024	19.8	19.8	636,001	19.8	32,121
2025	18.8	18.8	664,268	18.8	35,333
2026	17.8	17.8	691,829	17.8	38.867
2027	16.8	16.8	718,258	16.8	42,753
2028	15.8	15.8	743,056	15.8	47,029
2029	14.8	14.8	765,630	14.8	51,732

(continues)

Minimum Distributions—Alternative #1 (*Continued*)

Year	2nd Benef. L/E	2nd Joint L/E	Pension Fund Begin Value	Life Exp.	Minimum Distributions
2030	13.8	13.8	785,288	13.8	56,905
2031	12.8	12.8	801,221	12.8	62,595
2032	11.8	11.8	812,489	11.8	68,855
2033	10.8	10.8	817,997	10.8	75,740
2034	9.8	9.8	816,483	9.8	83,315
2035	8.8	8.8	806,485	8.8	91,646
2036	7.8	7.8	786,323	7.8	100,811
2037	6.8	6.8	754,063	6.8	110,892
2038	5.8	5.8	707,488	5.8	121,981
2039	4.8	4.8	644,058	4.8	134,179
2040	3.8	3.8	560,867	3.8	147,597
2041	2.8	2.8	454,597	2.8	162,356
2042	1.8	1.8	321,465	1.8	178,592
2043	0.8	0.8	157,160	0.8	157,160
2044	0.0	0.0	0	0.0	0
2045	0.0	0.0	0	0.0	0
2046	0.0	0.0	0	0.0	0
2047	0.0	0.0	0	0.0	0
2048	0.0	0.0	0	0.0	0
2049	0.0	0.0	0	0.0	0
2050	0.0	0.0	0	0.0	0
2051	0.0	0.0	0	0.0	0
2052	0.0	0.0	0	0.0	0
2053	0.0	0.0	0	0.0	0
2054	0.0	0.0	0	0.0	0
2055	0.0	0.0	0	0.0	0
2056	0.0	0.0	0	0.0	0
2057	0.0	0.0	0	0.0	0
2058	0.0	0.0	0	0.0	0
2059	0.0	0.0	0	0.0	0
2060	0.0	0.0	0	0.0	0
2061	0.0	0.0	0	0.0	0
2062	0.0	0.0	0	0.0	0
2063	0.0	0.0	0	0.0	0
2064	0.0	0.0	0	0.0	0
2065	0.0	0.0	0	0.0	0
2066	0.0	0.0	0	0.0	0
2067	0.0	0.0	0	0.0	0
2068	0.0	0.0	0	0.0	0
2069	0.0	0.0	0	0.0	0

Child #1
Born 5/6/60
Inherited IRA $607,384

(Assuming upon wife's death at age 87 in year 2022, the balance of $2,429,537 splits into four inherited IRAs of $607,384 for each child and grandchild.)

Total Distributions—Alternative #1

Year	Pension Fund Distributions	Income Tax on Distributions	Yearly After-Tax Distributions	Cumulative After-Tax Distributions
2023	$ 29,201	$11,680	$ 17,521	$ 17,321
2024	32,121	12,848	19,273	36,794
2025	35,333	14,133	21,200	57,994
2026	38,867	15,547	23,320	81,314
2027	42,753	17,101	25,652	106,966
2028	47,029	18,812	28,217	135,183
2029	51,732	20,693	31,039	166,222
2030	56,905	22,762	34,143	200,365
2031	62,595	25,038	37,557	237,922
2032	68,855	27,542	41,313	279,235
2033	75,740	30,296	45,444	324,679
2034	83,315	33,326	49,989	374,668
2035	91,646	36,658	54,988	429,656
2036	100,811	40,324	60,487	490,143
2037	110,892	44,357	66,535	556,678
2038	121,981	48,792	73,189	629,867
2039	134,179	53,672	80,507	710,374
2040	147,597	59,039	88,558	798,932
2041	162,356	64,942	97,414	896,346
2042	178,592	71,437	107,155	1,003,501
2043	157,160	62,864	94,296	1,097,797
2044	0	0	0	1,097,797
2045	0	0	0	1,097,797
2046	0	0	0	1,097,797
2047	0	0	0	1,097,797
2048	0	0	0	1,097,797
2049	0	0	0	1,097,797
2050	0	0	0	1,097,797
2051	0	0	0	1,097,797

(*continues*)

Total Distributions—Alternative #1 (*Continued*)

Year	Pension Fund Distributions	Income Tax on Distributions	Yearly After-Tax Distributions	Cumulative After-Tax Distributions
2052	0	0	0	1,097,797
2053	0	0	0	1,097,797
2054	0	0	0	1,097,797
2055	0	0	0	1,097,797
2056	0	0	0	1,097,797
2057	0	0	0	1,097,797
2058	0	0	0	1,097,797
2059	0	0	0	1,097,797
2060	0	0	0	1,097,797
2061	0	0	0	1,097,797
2062	0	0	0	1,097,797
2063	0	0	0	1,097,797
2064	0	0	0	1,097,797
2065	0	0	0	1,097,797
2066	0	0	0	1,097,797
2067	0	0	0	1,097,797

Child #2
Born 12/29/61
Inherited IRA $607,384

(Assuming upon wife's death at age 87 in year 2022, the balance of $2,429,537 splits into four inherited IRAs of $607,384 for each child and grandchild.)

Minimum Distributions—Alternative #1

Year	2nd Benef. L/E	2nd Joint L/E	Pension Fund Begin Value	Life Exp.	Minimum Distributions
2023	21.7	21.7	$607,384	21.7	$ 27,990
2024	20.7	20.7	637,333	20.7	30,789
2025	19.7	19.7	667,198	19.7	33,868
2026	18.7	18.7	696,663	18.7	37,255
2027	17.7	17.7	725,349	17.7	40,980

Minimum Distributions—Alternative #1 *(Continued)*

Year	2nd Benef. L/E	2nd Joint L/E	Pension Fund Begin Value	Life Exp.	Minimum Distributions
2028	16.7	16.7	752,806	16.7	45,078
2029	15.7	15.7	778,501	15.7	49,586
2030	14.7	14.7	801,807	14.7	54,545
2031	13.7	13.7	821,988	13.7	59,999
2032	12.7	12.7	838,188	12.7	65,999
2033	11.7	11.7	849,408	11.7	72,599
2034	10.7	10.7	854,490	10.7	79,859
2035	9.7	9.7	852,094	9.7	87,845
2036	8.7	8.7	840,674	8.7	96,629
2037	7.7	7.7	818,450	7.7	106,292
2038	6.7	6.7	783,374	6.7	116,921
2039	5.7	5.7	733,098	5.7	128,614
2040	4.7	4.7	664,932	4.7	141,475
2041	3.7	3.7	575,803	3.7	155,622
2042	2.7	2.7	462,199	2.7	171,185
2043	1.7	1.7	320,115	1.7	188,303
2044	0.7	0.7	144,993	0.7	144,993
2045	0.0	0.0	0	0.0	0
2046	0.0	0.0	0	0.0	0
2047	0.0	0.0	0	0.0	0
2048	0.0	0.0	0	0.0	0
2049	0.0	0.0	0	0.0	0
2050	0.0	0.0	0	0.0	0
2051	0.0	0.0	0	0.0	0
2052	0.0	0.0	0	0.0	0
2053	0.0	0.0	0	0.0	0
2054	0.0	0.0	0	0.0	0
2055	0.0	0.0	0	0.0	0
2056	0.0	0.0	0	0.0	0
2057	0.0	0.0	0	0.0	0
2058	0.0	0.0	0	0.0	0
2059	0.0	0.0	0	0.0	0
2060	0.0	0.0	0	0.0	0
2061	0.0	0.0	0	0.0	0
2062	0.0	0.0	0	0.0	0
2063	0.0	0.0	0	0.0	0
2064	0.0	0.0	0	0.0	0
2065	0.0	0.0	0	0.0	0
2066	0.0	0.0	0	0.0	0
2067	0.0	0.0	0	0.0	0
2068	0.0	0.0	0	0.0	0
2069	0.0	0.0	0	0.0	0

Child #2
Born 12/29/61
Inherited IRA $607,384

(Assuming upon wife's death at age 87 in year 2022, the balance of $2,429,537 splits into four inherited IRAs of $607,384 for each child and grandchild.)

Total Distributions—Alternative #1

Year	Pension Fund Distributions	Income Tax on Distributions	Yearly After-Tax Distributions	Cumulative After-Tax Distributions
2023	$ 27,990	$11,196	$ 16,794	$ 16,794
2024	30,789	12,316	18,473	35,267
2025	33,868	13,547	20,321	55,588
2026	37,255	14,902	22,353	77,941
2027	40,980	16,392	24,588	102,529
2028	45,078	18,031	27,047	129,576
2029	49,586	19,834	29,752	159,328
2030	54,545	21,818	32,727	192,055
2031	59,999	24,000	35,999	228,054
2032	65,999	26,400	39,599	267,653
2033	72,599	29,040	43,559	311,212
2034	79,859	31,944	47,915	359,127
2035	87,845	35,138	52,707	411,834
2036	96,629	38,652	57,977	469,811
2037	106,292	42,517	63,775	533,586
2038	116,921	46,768	70,153	603,739
2039	128,614	51,446	77,168	680,907
2040	141,475	56,590	84,885	765,792
2041	155,622	62,249	93,373	859,165
2042	171,185	68,474	102,711	961,876
2043	188,303	75,321	112,982	1,074,858
2044	144,993	57,997	86,996	1,161,854
2045	0	0	0	1,161,854
2046	0	0	0	1,161,854
2047	0	0	0	1,161,854
2048	0	0	0	1,161,854
2049	0	0	0	1,161,854
2050	0	0	0	1,161,854
2051	0	0	0	1,161,854
2052	0	0	0	1,161,854

Total Distributions—Alternative #1 *(Continued)*

Year	Pension Fund Distributions	Income Tax on Distributions	Yearly After-Tax Distributions	Cumulative After-Tax Distributions
2053	0	0	0	1,161,854
2054	0	0	0	1,161,854
2055	0	0	0	1,161,854
2056	0	0	0	1,161,854
2057	0	0	0	1,161,854
2058	0	0	0	1,161,854
2059	0	0	0	1,161,854
2060	0	0	0	1,161,854
2061	0	0	0	1,161,854
2062	0	0	0	1,161,854
2063	0	0	0	1,161,854
2064	0	0	0	1,161,854
2065	0	0	0	1,161,854
2066	0	0	0	1,161,854
2067	0	0	0	1,161,854

Grandchild #1
Born 10/18/93
Inherited IRA $607,384

(Assuming upon wife's death at age 87 in year 2022, the balance of $2,429,537 splits into four inherited IRAs of $607,384 for each child and grandchild.)

Minimum Distributions—Alternative #1

Year	2nd Benef. L/E	2nd Joint L/E	Pension Fund Begin Value	Life Exp.	Minimum Distributions
2023	52.0	52.0	$ 607,384	52.0	$ 11,680
2024	51.0	51.0	655,274	51.0	12,849
2025	50.0	50.0	706,668	50.0	14,133
2026	49.0	49.0	761,789	49.0	15,547
2027	48.0	48.0	820,866	48.0	17,101
2028	47.0	47.0	884,142	47.0	18,812
2029	46.0	46.0	951,863	46.0	20,693

(continues)

Minimum Distributions—Alternative #1 (*Continued*)

Year	2nd Benef. L/E	2nd Joint L/E	Pension Fund Begin Value	Life Exp.	Minimum Distributions
2030	45.0	45.0	1,024,287	45.0	22,762
2031	44.0	44.0	1,101,678	44.0	25,038
2032	43.0	43.0	1,184,304	43.0	27,542
2033	42.0	42.0	1,272,438	42.0	30,296
2034	41.0	41.0	1,366,356	41.0	33,326
2035	40.0	40.0	1,466,333	40.0	36,658
2036	39.0	39.0	1,572,643	39.0	40,324
2037	38.0	38.0	1,685,551	38.0	44,357
2038	37.0	37.0	1,805,313	37.0	48,792
2039	36.0	36.0	1,932,173	36.0	53,671
2040	35.0	35.0	2,066,352	35.0	59.039
2041	34.0	34.0	2,208,044	34.0	64,942
2042	33.0	33.0	2,357,412	33.0	71,437
2043	32.0	32.0	2,514,573	32.0	78,580
2044	31.0	31.0	2,679,592	31.0	86,438
2045	30.0	30.0	2,852,469	30.0	95,082
2046	29.0	29.0	3,033,126	29.0	104,591
2047	28.0	28.0	3,221,389	28.0	115,050
2048	27.0	27.0	3,416,973	27.0	126,555
2049	26.0	26.0	3,619,460	26.0	139,210
2050	25.0	25.0	3,828,275	25.0	153,131
2051	24.0	24.0	4,042,658	24.0	168,444
2052	23.0	23.0	4,261,635	23.0	185,288
2053	22.0	22.0	4,483,982	22.0	203,817
2054	21.0	21.0	4,708,182	21.0	224,199
2055	20.0	20.0	4,932,381	20.0	246,619
2056	19.0	19.0	5,154,338	19.0	271,281
2057	18.0	18.0	5,371,363	18.0	298,409
2058	17.0	17.0	5,580,249	17.0	328,250
2059	16.0	16.0	5,777,199	16.0	361,075
2060	15.0	15.0	5,957,736	15.0	397,182
2061	14.0	14.0	6,116,609	14.0	436,901
2062	13.0	13.0	6,247,679	13.0	480,591
2063	12.0	12.0	6,343,797	12.0	528,650
2064	11.0	11.0	6,396,662	11.0	581,515
2065	10.0	10.0	6,396,662	10.0	639,666
2066	9.0	9.0	6,332,696	9.0	703,633
2067	8.0	8.0	6,191,969	8.0	773,996
2068	7.0	7.0	5,959,770	7.0	851,396
2069	6.0	6.0	5,619,211	6.0	936,535

Grandchild #1
Born 10/18/93
Inherited IRA $607,384

(Assuming upon wife's death at age 87 in year 2022, the balance of $2,429,537 splits into four inherited IRAs of $607,384 for each child and grandchild.)

Minimum Distributions—Alternative #1

Year	2nd Benef. L/E	2nd Joint L/E	Pension Fund Begin Value	Life Exp.	Minimum Distributions
2070	5.0	5.0	$5,150,944	5.0	$1,030,189
2071	4.0	4.0	4,532,831	4.0	1,133,208
2072	3.0	3.0	3,739,585	3.0	1,246,528
2073	2.0	2.0	2,742,363	2.0	1,371,182
2074	1.0	1.0	1,508,299	1.0	1,508,299
2075	0.0	0.0	0	0.0	0
2076	0.0	0.0	0	0.0	0
2077	0.0	0.0	0	0.0	0
2078	0.0	0.0	0	0.0	0
2079	0.0	0.0	0	0.0	0
2080	0.0	0.0	0	0.0	0
2081	0.0	0.0	0	0.0	0
2082	0.0	0.0	0	0.0	0

Grandchild #1
Born 10/18/93
Inherited IRA $607,384

(Assuming upon wife's death at age 87 in year 2022, the balance of $2,429,537 splits into four inherited IRAs of $607,384 for each child and grandchild.)

Total Distributions—Alternative #1

Year	Pension Fund Distributions	Income Tax on Distributions	Yearly After-Tax Distributions	Cumulative After-Tax Distributions
2023	$ 11,680	$ 4,672	$ 7,008	$ 7,008
2024	12,849	5,140	7,709	14,717
2025	14,133	5,653	8,480	23,197
2026	15,547	6,219	9,328	32,525

(*continues*)

Total Distributions—Alternative #1 (*Continued*)

Year	Pension Fund Distributions	Income Tax on Distributions	Yearly After-Tax Distributions	Cumulative After-Tax Distributions
2027	17,101	6,840	10,261	42,786
2028	18,812	7,525	11,287	54,073
2029	20,693	8,277	12,416	66,489
2030	22,762	9,105	13,657	80,146
2031	25,038	10,015	15,023	95,169
2032	27,542	11,017	16,525	111,694
2033	30,296	12,118	18,178	129,872
2034	33,326	13,330	19,996	149,868
2035	36,658	14,663	21,995	171,863
2036	40,324	16,130	24,194	196,057
2037	44,357	17,743	26,614	222,671
2038	48,792	19,517	29,275	251,946
2039	53,671	21,468	32,203	284,149
2040	59,039	23,616	35,423	319,572
2041	64,942	25,977	38,965	358,537
2042	71,437	28,575	42,862	401,399
2043	78,580	31,432	47,148	448,547
2044	86,438	34,575	51,863	500,410
2045	95,082	38,033	57,049	557,459
2046	104,591	41,836	62,755	620,214
2047	115,050	46,020	69,030	689,244
2048	126,555	50,622	75,933	765,177
2049	139,210	55,684	83,526	848,703
2050	153,131	61,252	91,879	940,582
2051	168,444	67,378	101,066	1,041,648
2052	185,288	74,115	111,173	1,152,821
2053	203,817	81,527	122,290	1,275,111
2054	224,199	89,680	134,519	1,409,630
2055	246,619	98,648	147,971	1,557,601
2056	271,281	108,512	162,769	1,720,370
2057	298,409	119,364	179,045	1,899,415
2058	328,250	131,300	196,950	2,096,365
2059	361,075	144,430	216,645	2,313,010
2060	397,182	158,873	238,309	2,551,319
2061	436,901	174,760	262,141	2,813,460
2062	480,591	192,236	288,355	3,101,815
2063	528,650	211,460	317,190	3,419,005
2064	581,515	232,606	348,909	3,767,914
2065	639,666	255,866	383,800	4,151,714
2066	703,633	281,453	422,180	4,573,894
2067	773,996	309,598	464,398	5,038,292

Grandchild #1
Born 10/18/93
Inherited IRA $607,384

(Assuming upon wife's death at age 87 in year 2022, the balance of $2,429,537 splits into four inherited IRAs of $607,384 for each child and grandchild.)

Total Distributions—Alternative #1

Year	Pension Fund Distributions	Income Tax on Distributions	Yearly After-Tax Distributions	Cumulative After-Tax Distributions
2068	$ 851,396	$340,558	$510,838	$5,549,130
2069	936,535	374,614	561,921	6,111,051
2070	1,030,189	412,076	618,113	6,729,164
2071	1,113,208	453,283	679,925	7,409,089
2072	1,246,528	498,611	747,917	8,157,006
2073	1,371,182	548,473	822,709	8,979,715
2074	1,508,299	603,320	904,979	9,884,694
2075	0	0	0	9,884,694
2076	0	0	0	9,884,694
2077	0	0	0	9,884,694
2078	0	0	0	9,884,694
2079	0	0	0	9,884,694
2080	0	0	0	9,884,694
2081	0	0	0	9,884,694
2082	0	0	0	9,884,694

Grandchild #2
Born 3/15/96
Inherited IRA $607,384

(Assuming upon wife's death at age 87 in year 2022, the balance of $2,429,537 splits into four inherited IRAs of $607,384 for each child and grandchild.)

Minimum Distributions—Alternative #1

Year	2nd Benef. L/E	2nd Joint L/E	Pension Fund Begin Value	Life Exp.	Minimum Distributions
2023	54.9	54.9	$ 607,384	54.9	$ 11,063
2024	53.9	53.9	655,953	53.9	12,170
2025	52.9	52.9	708,161	52.9	13,387
2026	51.9	51.9	764,251	51.9	14,725
2027	50.9	50.9	824,479	50.9	16,198
2028	49.9	49.9	889,109	49.9	17,818
2029	48.9	48.9	958,420	48.9	19,600
2030	47.9	47.9	1,032,702	47.9	21,560
2031	46.9	46.9	1,112,256	46.9	23,715
2032	45.9	45.9	1,197,395	45.9	26,087
2033	44.9	44.9	1,288,439	44.9	28,696
2034	43.9	43.9	1,385,717	43.9	31,565
2035	42.9	42.9	1,489,567	42.9	34,722
2036	41.9	41.9	1,600,330	41.9	38,194
2037	40.9	40.9	1,718,350	40.9	42,013
2038	39.9	39.9	1,843,971	39.9	46,215
2039	38.9	38.9	1,977,532	38.9	50,836
2040	37.9	37.9	2,119,366	37.9	55,920
2041	36.9	36.9	2,269,791	36.9	61,512
2042	35.9	35.9	2,429,107	35.9	67,663
2043	34.9	34.9	2,597,588	34.9	74,429
2044	33.9	33.9	2,775,475	33.9	81,872
2045	32.9	32.9	2,962,963	32.9	90,060
2046	31.9	31.9	3,160,193	31.9	99,066
2047	30.9	30.9	3,367,240	30.9	108,972
2048	29.9	29.9	3,584,095	29.9	119,869
2049	28.9	28.9	3,810,649	28.9	131,856
2050	27.9	27.9	4,046,672	27.9	145,042
2051	26.9	26.9	4,291,793	26.9	159,546
2052	25.9	25.9	4,545,472	25.9	175,501
2053	24.9	24.9	4,806,968	24.9	193,051
2054	23.9	23.9	5,075,309	23.9	212,356
2055	22.9	22.9	5,349,248	22.9	233,592

Minimum Distributions—Alternative #1 *(Continued)*

Year	2nd Benef. L/E	2nd Joint L/E	Pension Fund Begin Value	Life Exp.	Minimum Distributions
2056	21.9	21.9	5,627,222	21.9	256,951
2057	20.9	20.9	5,907,298	20.9	282,646
2058	19.9	19.9	6,187,117	19.9	310,910
2059	18.9	18.9	6,463,828	18.9	342,001
2060	17.9	17.9	6,734,010	17.9	376,202
2061	16.9	16.9	6,993,589	16.9	413,822
2062	15.9	15.9	7,237,744	15.9	455,204
2063	14.9	14.9	7,460,794	14.9	500,724
2064	13.9	13.9	7,656,077	13.9	550,797
2065	12.9	12.9	7,815,808	12.9	605,877
2066	11.9	11.9	7,930,924	11.9	666,464
2067	10.9	10.9	7,990,906	10.9	733,111
2068	9.9	9.9	7,983,575	9.9	806,422
2069	8.9	8.9	7,894,868	8.9	887,064

Grandchild #2
Born 3/15/96
Inherited IRA $607,384

(Assuming upon wife's death at age 87 in year 2022, the balance of $2,429,537 splits into four inherited IRAs of $607,384 for each child and grandchild.)

Minimum Distributions—Alternative #1

Year	2nd Benef. L/E	2nd Joint L/E	Pension Fund Begin Value	Life Exp.	Minimum Distributions
2070	7.9	7.9	$7,708,584	7.9	$ 975,770
2071	6.9	6.9	7,406,095	6.9	1,073,347
2072	5.9	5.9	6,966,023	5.9	1,180,682
2073	4.9	4.9	6,363,875	4.9	1,298,750
2074	3.9	3.9	5,571,638	3.9	1,428,625
2075	2.9	2.9	4,557,314	2.9	1,571,488
2076	1.9	1.9	3,284,409	1.9	1,728,636
2077	0.9	0.9	1,711,350	0.9	1,711,350
2078	0.0	0.0	0	0.0	0
2079	0.0	0.0	0	0.0	0
2080	0.0	0.0	0	0.0	0
2081	0.0	0.0	0	0.0	0
2082	0.0	0.0	0	0.0	0

Grandchild #2
Born 3/15/96
Inherited IRA $607,384

(Assuming upon wife's death at age 87 in year 2022, the balance of $2,429,537 splits into four inherited IRAs of $607,384 for each child and grandchild.)

Total Distributions—Alternative #1

Year	Pension Fund Distributions	Income Tax on Distributions	Yearly After-Tax Distributions	Cumulative After-Tax Distributions
2023	$ 11,063	$ 4,425	$ 6,638	$ 6,638
2024	12,170	4,868	7,302	13,940
2025	13,387	5,355	8,032	21,972
2026	14,725	5,890	8,835	30,807
2027	16,198	6,479	9,719	40,526
2028	17,818	7,127	10,691	51,217
2029	19,600	7,840	11,760	62,977
2030	21,560	8,624	12,936	75,913
2031	23,715	9,486	14,229	90,142
2032	26,087	10,435	15,652	105,794
2033	28,696	11,478	17,218	123,012
2034	31,565	12,626	18,939	141,951
2035	34,722	13,889	20,833	162,784
2036	38,194	15,278	22,916	185,700
2037	42,013	16,805	25,208	210,908
2038	46,215	18,486	27,729	238,637
2039	50,836	20,334	30,502	269,139
2040	55,920	22,368	33,552	302,691
2041	61,512	24,605	36,907	339,598
2042	67,663	27,065	40,598	380,196
2043	74,429	29,772	44,657	424,853
2044	81,872	32,749	49,123	473,976
2045	90,060	36,024	54,036	528,012
2046	99,066	39,626	59,440	587,452
2047	108,972	43,589	65,383	652,835
2048	119,869	47,948	71,921	724,756
2049	131,856	52,742	79,114	803,870
2050	145,042	58,017	87,025	890,895
2051	159,546	63,818	95,728	986,623
2052	175,501	70,200	105,301	1,091,924
2053	193,051	77,220	115,831	1,207,755
2054	212,356	84,942	127,414	1,335,169
2055	233,592	93,437	140,155	1,475,324

Total Distributions—Alternative #1 *(Continued)*

Year	Pension Fund Distributions	Income Tax on Distributions	Yearly After-Tax Distributions	Cumulative After-Tax Distributions
2056	256,951	102,790	154,171	1,629,495
2057	282,646	113,058	169,588	1,799,083
2058	310,910	124,364	186,546	1,985,629
2059	342,001	136,800	205,201	2,190,830
2060	376,202	150,481	225,721	2,416,551
2061	413,822	165,529	248,293	2,664,844
2062	455,204	182,082	273,122	2,937,966
2063	500,724	200,290	300,434	3,238,400
2064	550,797	220,319	330,478	3,568,878
2065	605,877	242,351	363,526	3,932,404
2066	666,464	266,586	399,878	4,332,282
2067	733,111	293,244	439,867	4,772,149

Grandchild #2
Born 3/15/96
Inherited IRA $607,384

(Assuming upon wife's death at age 87 in year 2022, the balance of $2,429,537 splits into four inherited IRAs of $607,384 for each child and grandchild.)

Total Distributions—Alternative #1

Year	Pension Fund Distributions	Income Tax on Distributions	Yearly After-Tax Distributions	Cumulative After-Tax Distributions
2068	$ 806,422	$322,569	$ 483,853	$ 5,256,002
2069	887,064	354,826	532,238	5,788,240
2070	975,770	390,308	585,462	6,373,702
2071	1,073,347	429,339	644,008	7,017,710
2072	1,180,682	472,273	708,409	7,726,119
2073	1,298,750	519,500	779,250	8,505,369
2074	1,428,625	571,450	857,175	9,362,544
2075	1,571,488	628,595	942,893	10,305,437
2076	1,728,636	691,454	1,037,182	11,342,619
2077	1,711,350	684,540	1,026,810	12,369,429
2078	0	0	0	12,369,429
2079	0	0	0	12,369,429
2080	0	0	0	12,369,429
2081	0	0	0	12,369,429
2082	0	0	0	12,369,429

How to Stretch Out an IRA

Maximize the total income stream over the lifetimes of your client and spouse and their children.

1. Elect the most beneficial payout method. We recommend a joint life expectancy recalculating life expectancy on the owner and term-certain on the wife. Minimum distributions are based on their joint life expectancies.

2. On the IRA owner's death, the wife will take a spousal rollover. At this point, there is no estate tax or income tax due.

3. The wife will take over the IRA. At this time she may elect a new beneficiary designation and payout method. The wife should name the children and/or grandchildren as her own beneficiaries and elect a joint life expectancy payout. Each beneficiary would be the beneficiary of a separate IRA. The children would be deemed 10 years younger than the wife, and the minimum distribution will be based on their joint life expectancies, thus stretching out the payout period. With this plan, your client and spouse may increase withdrawals at any time during their lifetimes if more income is needed.

4. Upon the wife's death, the IRA balance would split into individual inherited IRAs for each beneficiary. The payouts would now be based on their individual term-certain life expectancy. At this point, the estate taxes are due on the IRA balance going to the children. Monies from the IRA should not be withdrawn, because this would diminish the IRA balance after taxes are paid.

   We recommend utilizing assets other than the IRA to pay the estate tax. By preserving and allowing the IRA to grow, it could stretch out and slow down the distributions over the lifetimes of the children.

Appendix B: Estimated Cost Basis Calculation for In-Kind Distribution

Cost Basis

	Buys	Sells
Contribution 01	$130,389.68	0.00
Contribution 02	89,457.76	0.00
Contribution 03	0.00	0.00
Contribution 04	118,785.68	0.00
Contribution 06	0.00	0.00
Contribution 07	1,360.46	0.00
	$339,993.58	$0.00

$3,265,634.99	Market Value (MV) of Company Stock
67,6250	Current Share Price
48,290.3511	Equivalent Shares
339,993.58	Total Cost Basis (Incl. Fractional Shares)
$ 7.04	**Cost/Share**
3,296,745.69	Total Account Balance
3,265,611.25	(less MV of Whole Shares)
$ 31,134.44	**Value of Cash**
17,369.66	Limited Contribution
0.00	(less Limited Withdrawal)
$ 17,369.66	**After-Tax Contributions**

Estimate Only

$ 48,290	Equivalent Whole Shares
7.04	Cost/Share
$ 339,961.60	**Cost Basis of Whole Shares**
3,265,611.25	MV of Whole Shares
339,961.60	(less Cost Basis of Whole Shares)
$2,925,649.65	**Net Unrealized Appreciation (NUA)**
17,369.66	After-Tax Contributions
2,925,649.65	NUA
$2,943,019.31	**Total Nontaxable***
3,296,745.69	Current Total MV
2,943,019.31	(less Total Nontaxable)
$ 353,726.38	**Total Taxable[†]**
31,134.44	Value of Cash
70,745.28	20% Federal Taxes of Taxable Amount
$ 0.00	**Net Check**

---

*This amount is converted to long-term capital gains and is payable at the time securities are ultimately sold.

[†] This amount is immediately recognized by the participant as ordinary income at the time of the in-kind distribution.

Index